Al-Anbar Awakening
Volume II
Iraqi Perspectives
From Insurgency to Counterinsurgency in Iraq, 2004-2009

Edited by
Colonel Gary W. Montgomery
Chief Warrant Officer-4 Timothy S. McWilliams

U.S. Marine Corps Reserve

Marine Corps University
United States Marine Corps
Quantico, Virginia
2009

Al-Anbar Awakening

Volume II
Iraqi Perspectives

From Insurgency to Counterinsurgency in Iraq 2004-2009

*Edited by Colonel Gary W. Montgomery and
Chief Warrant Officer-4 Timothy S. McWilliams*

Foreword

by Lieutenant General John F. Kelly

Words like "won" or "victory" really do not apply when speaking of counterinsurgency operations. Insurgencies grow from problems and discontent within a given society. Solve the problems, and the insurgency goes away, as opposed to being defeated. The difficulty is that a government is not always willing to address the root causes of the insurgency because it is often the government itself that the insurgents want to eliminate.

In Iraq to a very large degree, we—the U.S. military and civilians—were the source of the insurgency. Honest men and women can argue the whys, what-ifs, and what might-have-beens, but ultimately, it was mostly about unfulfilled promises and the heavy-handed military approach taken by some over the summer of 2003 that caused events to spiral out of control. No doubt the insurgency radicalized over time with al-Qaeda and Shi'a extremists playing a key role, but the insurgents did not initiate the war and only took advantage of the discontent.

If you asked Anbaris during my third tour in Iraq in 2008 why the insurgency began, most would look away and try to find a way not to answer. They would tell you that "we are friends now, and the causes are unimportant. It's all water under the bridge now." If pressed, they would talk about mutual misunderstandings and a lack of cultural awareness on both sides. They would say that expectations were too high on the part of the Iraqis about what America could do for them and how fast, but they seldom if ever blamed us directly. Press them further and they would mention the 29 April 2003 "massacre" in Fallujah, but more about the lack of an apology than the 70-plus unarmed citizens allegedly shot that day.

Another factor they would bring up was the shock and humiliation of having their army disbanded. The army was the one institution in Iraq everyone was proud of—Shi'a and Sunni alike—especially for what it had accomplished in protecting the nation against the Iranians in the 1980s. They perceived the disbanding as intentional contempt directed toward Iraq as a nation and as a people. They also saw it as the disarming of the nation. In the minds of many, this is when our status as liberators ended and that of occupier began.

Press the Anbaris one more time, and they would look you in the eye—but only if you are considered a friend—and they would state that after Baghdad fell and throughout the summer of 2003, the Americans overreacted to small acts of resistance or violence and fought in a way that was cowardly and without honor. Here they would talk about the senseless use of firepower and midnight raids on innocent men. They said that by our escalation, we proved true the rhetoric of the nationalist firebrands about why we had invaded, and our actions played directly into the hands of organizations like Zarqawi's al-Qaeda in Iraq and Sadr's militia.

Ask the same Anbari citizens why sometime in 2006 they began to turn against the by-then al-Qaeda-led insurgency, and the answer would be more direct. To them, their alliance with the radicals was a marriage of convenience to fight the U.S. occupation. Al-Qaeda brought dedication, organization, funding, and a willingness to die. Over time, however, it overplayed its hand and wore out its welcome by forcing an extreme Islamic agenda on a generally secular and very tribal culture. Al-Qaeda's campaign evolved from assistance, to persuasion, to intimidation, to murder in the most horrific ways, all designed to intimidate Anbari society—tribes and sheikhs alike—to adopt the most extreme form of Islam. At a certain point, al-Qaeda's agenda became too much for the average Anbari to bear. It was increasingly directed at the sheikhs themselves, and just as importantly, it began to have an impact on the business interests of tribal leaders.

The 17 paramount-dignified sheikhs of the major Anbari tribes and tribal federation turned away from al-Qaeda for survival purposes and toward U.S. forces for the same reason. They will tell you that Iraqis were being hunted down and killed by both the terrorists and the Coalition forces in Anbar. They knew the unbending terrorists would never meet them halfway, but they were confident that the Americans would—and they were right. Many of these men were once as much a part of the insurgency as Zarqawi was, albeit for different reasons. Over time, it became glaringly obvious to them that it was in their personal interests, and the interests of their tribes, to put a stop to the war.

When I returned to Iraq in February 2008 as commander of I Marine Expeditionary Force and Multi National Force-West (MNF-W), I was amazed at what I found. Violent incidents, once over 400 a week in al-Anbar Province, were down to 50 and had been in steady decline for months. Where Iraqis once avoided us, as any interaction jeopardized their lives and those of their families at the hands of al-Qaeda terrorists or nationalist insurgents, they were now aggressive in wanting to engage with us. Things had turned. The obvious questions were why had the change occurred, and was it sustainable, or was it simply due to an operational pause in the insurgent's effort? For months, Major General Walt Gaskin and his superb II Marine Expeditionary Force team, our immediate predecessors as MNF-W, had been wrestling with the answers. Their conclusions were ours to verify.

For MNF-W's part, since March 2004 we had extended the hand of friendship and cooperation, even as we were forced into a brutal fight that knew no quarter on the part of the Iraqi insurgents and foreign fighters. It was the major theme of our campaign plan, and it never changed. The command philosophy, a philosophy programmed into every Marine and U.S. Army unit that served in al-Anbar since we took the province, was that we had come to Iraq not to conquer, but to free, that we would always endeavor to "first, do not harm." This was often difficult, and sometimes you simply had to do a Fallujah II, even if Fallujah I had been ill-advised and totally counterproductive to what you were trying to do in the first place.

No single personality was the key in Anbar, no shiny new field manual the reason why, and no "surge" or single unit made it happen. It was a combination of many factors, not the least of which—perhaps the most important—was the consistent command philosophy that drove operations in Anbar from March 2004 forward. Each MNF-W commander and the troops under him continued to build upon the work of all those who came before. They took what their predecessors had done and ran with it, calling audibles as opportunities presented themselves. Consistency counts, and persistent presence on your feet puts you in more danger, no doubt, but also stacks the deck in your favor as you see more, hear more, know more, and engage more. It is these Americans—Marines, soldiers, sailors, and airmen, as well as civilians—who deserve the individual and collective credit for our part in the miracle that took place in al-Anbar Province. They slogged it out for more than six years to help the Anbaris create a miracle that spread to other regions of the country in late 2007, throughout 2008, and now into 2009.

I urge a note of caution to those who might have an overly inflated opinion of the role they played in the Awakening, or to the "experts" who write today as if they, with complete clairvoyance, predicted the change in loyalties in al-Anbar. The sheikhs, politicians, Iraqi security force officials, and even the former Ba'athist members of the military who reside in Anbar have a different opinion. They will tell you it was the sense of hopelessness the war had brought to the citizenry. The only hope for the future they could see was to be found in what members of MNF-W had done and were doing on their behalf despite the heat, the criticism from home, and the killing and casualties. They began to see us as a force that was sharing in their agony. Once they tried reaching out to some soldier or Marine's outstretched hand in friendship, it was over.

The interviews collected in the two volumes of this anthology do what no previous work has done—they attempt to tell the story of the al-Anbar Awakening from both sides, American and Iraqi. Not all the voices could be included, but there are many pertinent ones. The story they tell is a complex but important one, and it should be read with interest by all who want to truly understand what happened in Iraq between 2004 and 2009.

John F. Kelly
Lieutenant General, U.S. Marine Corps

Preface

This two-volume anthology of interviews tells the story of the al-Anbar Awakening and the emergence of al-Anbar Province from the throes of insurgency. It presents the perspectives of both Iraqis (volume two) and Americans (volume one) who ultimately came to work together, in an unlikely alliance of former adversaries, for the stabilization and redevelopment of the province. The collection begins in the 2003-2004 time frame with the rise of the insurgency and concludes with observations from the vantage point of early-to-mid 2009.

The anthology demonstrates that there is not one history of the Awakening, but several histories intertwined. It is not a complete collection, but one that provides a broad spectrum of candid, unvarnished perspectives from some of the leading players.

The American volume focuses on the roles and views of U.S. Marines, who were the primary Coalition force in al-Anbar from spring 2004 onward. At the time of their arrival, many military experts considered the province irredeemable. This collection chronicles the efforts of the Marines, and the soldiers, sailors, airmen, and civilians who worked with them, to consistently employ counterinsurgency tactics and to continue to reach out to the Iraqis during even the darkest days of the insurgency.

The Iraqi volume collects from many of the key Awakening players their views on how and why Anbaris came to turn against the insurgency that many had initially supported and seek the aid—both military and economic—of the Americans. Those interviewed include former Ba'ath Party military officers, senior officers in Iraq's new military, tribal sheikhs, Sunni imams, governmental representatives, and civilians.

This anthology is drawn from oral history interviews collected by field historians of the U.S. Marine Corps History Division, based at Marine Corps University in Quantico, Virginia. Field historians assigned to the History Division have collected hundreds of interviews since the beginning of Operation Iraqi Freedom I to serve as primary resources for future scholarship. In support of this anthology project,

Colonel Gary W. Montgomery and Chief Warrant Office-4 Timothy S. McWilliams deployed to Iraq in February and March of 2009 to interview Iraqis and additional American military and civilian personnel. Lieutenant Colonel Kurtis P. Wheeler had conducted more than 400 interviews in earlier deployments.

Like courtroom testimonies, oral histories are told from one person's perspective and may include discrepancies with, or even contradictions of, another witness's views. They are not a complete history, but they provide the outlines for one, to be fleshed out with documents and other sources not often collected or declassified this soon after events.

The interviews in this collection are edited excerpts drawn from longer interviews. They have been transcribed and edited according to scholarly standards to maintain the integrity of the interviews. Only interjections, false starts, and profanity have been silently omitted. Details added for clarity and accuracy are indicated by brackets. Omissions are noted by three-dot ellipses for partial sentences and four-dot ellipses for full sentences or more. With the Iraqi interviews, the interchange with interpreters has been omitted except in a few cases where the interpreter is attempting to clarify a point. Much of what has been left out of the American interviews is material that is duplicated in other interviews in the anthology. The full interviews and complete transcripts are part of the oral history collection of the Marine Corps History Division.

Ranks of officers, particularly American officers, reflect the rank at the time of the deployment under discussion. We have not tried to insert "then" in front of the ranks of all officers who have since been promoted.

We have attempted to verify the Iraqi person, place, and tribe names as best as possible, but undoubtedly there are several discrepancies, particularly in the Iraqi volume, where language barriers, dialects, the use of interpreters, and the mentions of many minor actors and areas made accurate transcription and identification challenging. There are also many variations in the transliteration of Iraqi names and terms.

✻   ✻   ✻

The editors of this anthology acknowledge and thank a wide array of people for their support on this project. First and foremost, we thank the people whose stories are included for their time and candor. We particularly acknowledge Lieutenant General John F. Kelly, who wrote the foreword and who expedited the 2009 deployment of Colonel Montgomery and Chief Warrant Officer-4 McWilliams. In addition to the editors, those who conducted interviews included in the anthology are Colonel Jeffrey Acosta, Colonel Stephen E. Motsco, Colonel Michael D. Visconage, Lieutenant Colonel Craig H. Covert, Lieutenant Colonel John P. Piedmont, Lieutenant Colonel John R. Way, Staff Sergeant Bradford A. Wineman, Dr. David B. Crist, and Dr. Charles P. Neimeyer.

Dr. Neimeyer, director of the History Division; Mr. Charles D. Melson, chief historian; and Dr. Nathan S. Lowery, Field History branch head, provided guidance for the project. Mr. Kenneth H. Williams, senior editor for both the History Division and Marine Corps University Press, oversaw the editing and publication, assisted in the editing by Ms. Wanda J. Renfrow. Mr. Vincent J. Martinez provided layout and design for both volumes. Mr. Anthony R. Taglianetti, the History Division's oral historian, coordinated the timely transcription of the interviews. Lieutenant Colonel David A. Benhoff and Gunnery Sergeant Michael C. Coachman provided logistical support. Dr. Nicholas J. Schlosser, History Division historian, and Mr. Colin M. Colbourn, History Division intern, helped verify information.

Beyond the History Division, we are especially grateful to the interpreters. Those currently working in Iraq shall remain anonymous because of the inherent vulnerabilities peculiar to their vocation. Sometimes underappreciated and often overworked, their knowledge and perseverance was absolutely essential to our effort.

Many others labored to bring this project to fruition. Those who work outside of the normal publishing process are listed below. If we omitted anyone, it was inadvertent and not from lack of gratitude.

I Marine Expeditionary Force (Multi National Forces-West):
Lieutenant Colonel Bradley E. Weisz (G-3 Air Officer); Lieutenant Colonel Todd W. Lyons (G-9 Foreign Affairs Officer/Marine Corps Intelligence Activity); Major Adam T. Strickland (Engagement Officer); 1st Lieutenant Timothy J.

Malham (Economic and Political Intelligence Center); Sergeant Luke O. Vancleave (Economic and Political Intelligence Center); Corporal Travis L. Helm (Economic and Political Intelligence Center); Corporal Lamont J. Lum (Economic and Political Intelligence Center); Lance Corporal Cassidy C. Niblett (Economic and Political Intelligence Center); Lance Corporal Orell D. Fisher (Economic and Political Intelligence Center).

II Marine Expeditionary Force: Colonel Robert W. Lanham (G-9 Assistant Chief of Staff); Lieutenant Colonel Bowen Richwine (G-9 Engagements OIC); Major Steven K. Barriger (G-9 Governance); 2d Lieutenant Anthony M. Bramante (Economic and Political Intelligence Center); Staff Sergeant William J. Rickards (G-9 Support); Sergeant Robert A. Pittenridge (G-9 Governance); Lance Corporal Thomas P. Wiltshire (Combat Camera); "Jack" Mahmood S. Al-Jumaily (Interpreter); Mythm Hassin (Interpreter).

Center for Advanced Operational Culture Learning, Quantico: Mr. Richard C. McPherson; Ms. Basema Maki (Interpreter); Mr. Hamid Lellou (Interpreter).

Marine Corps Intelligence Activity, Quantico: Colonel Philip D. Gentile (Commanding Officer); Mr. Dan J. Darling (Threat Analyst).

U.S. Marine Corps MARCENT LNO Cell, Kuwait: Gunnery Sergeant John M. Neatherton.

Marine Air-Ground Combat Training Center, Twentynine Palms, California: Staff Sergeant Michael A. Blaha (Combat Camera); Lance Corporal Ricky J. Holt (Combat Camera).

Marine Corps Base, Camp Pendleton, California: Captain Scott M. Clendaniel (Aide to General Kelly); Sergeant Eric L. Alabiso II (Combat Camera).

Iraqi Perspectives

Introduction

I cannot describe the horror we lived in. Those were very bitter days. Those days we lived in hell. We looked like ghosts out of a cemetery. We were very tired. We had a lot of complaints to take to the Coalition forces, but we were afraid. Some days we wished to be dead just to be rested. But I have seven children. I was very tired.

Miriam, wife of a police officer,
describing life under al-Qaeda rule[1]

In an insurgency, the populace is the battlefield, and victory for the insurgent or the counterinsurgent tends toward the side better able to understand, influence, exploit, and satisfy the interests of the populace. Consequently, Miriam and hundreds of thousands of largely anonymous Anbaris were the final arbiters of the great issues of this period. So to understand the development of the insurgency, the rise of al-Qaeda in Iraq, and the al-Anbar Awakening, one must first understand the Anbaris.[2]

---

[1] All block quotations in the introduction are from interviews in this volume. "Miriam" is a pseudonym for the first interviewee in the book.
[2] This introduction is significantly informed by a massive report compiled by Marine Corps Intelligence Activity, "Study of the Insurgency in Anbar Province, Iraq," dated 13 June 2007.

The Anbaris

We are a country that is transforming from Bedouin to civilization. We depend on the elite and the notable. And these elite people are the link between us and you, the Americans. Where are the elite people? Where are the notable people? The civilization gap between us, I can say it reaches up to 200 years. Who is responsible for closing this gap between us? So you are the people who came from the future, and the elite people we're talking about understand you and understand Iraqi society.

General Ra'ad al-Hamdani
Former Republican Guard Corps Commander

General Ra'ad was referring to Iraq as a whole, but his comments are especially applicable to al-Anbar Province. Nearly all Anbaris are Sunni Arabs, and Sunni Arab elites have governed the Mesopotamian region for almost 500 years, first as surrogates under the Ottoman and British empires, and then outright in an independent Iraq. They had greater access to education, more opportunities for employment, and dominated the higher levels of government and the military. Over time, many developed a sense of entitlement and superiority relative to other Iraqis, and perhaps even a belief that they are the only ones capable of governing Iraq. If one's objective is a unified Iraq, then the latter opinion is also logical: the Kurds, though Sunnis, have strong separatist tendencies; and the Shi'a, though Arabs, are coreligionists with Iran, which is Iraq's arch enemy.

While al-Anbar's elites may be world-class in quality, they are relatively few in quantity. Their importance in society is probably reflected in the design of the first post-Ba'athist provincial council (roughly equivalent to a state legislature). The Anbaris chose to apportion representation according to vocational classification, not geographic precinct. Of the 49 seats comprising the council, 39 were designated for various professionals, such as doctors, engineers, and educators. The remaining 10 were reserved for tribal sheikhs.[3]

---

[3] Interview with Mr. Kamis Ahmad Abban al-Alwani, deputy chairman of the provincial council, interview 11 in this volume.

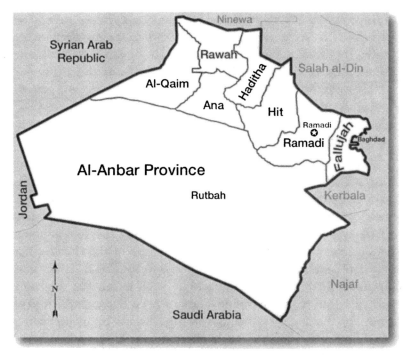

Districts of Al-Anbar Province

Al-Anbar is the most tribal of the 18 provinces of Iraq. The tribal system is poorly understood in the West, even though it is similar to the familiar, though defunct, Scottish clan system. In both systems, membership is based on kinship, loyalty is to clan or tribe ahead of the state, there are shifting rivalries and alliances among individuals as well as groups, and the leaders resist outside control, even while seeking support and patronage from the central government.

The two systems are also similar in that "sheikh" and "clan chief" are hereditary titles. However, this is where the systems diverge. The Anbari tribes do not practice primogeniture. A sheikh must be the son of a sheikh, but he may be any son of a sheikh. He is chosen by the consensus of the tribesmen; quite simply, he is the one whom the people trust and follow.

Furthermore, a sheikh's position is rarely secure. In this respect, he is similar to a Western politician. If his tribesmen (constituents) lose confidence in him, they will follow someone else—and he has many relatives and many rivals. His status and influence depend on his ability to bring patronage and security to the members of his tribe. They look to him for leadership, but he can only lead them where they are willing to go. Sometimes, tribal leadership is a matter of knowing the direction that the tribe is already going and getting out in front. Notably, in the interviews that follow, whenever an Anbari tribal leader made a significant decision, the announcement was preceded by an "education program" among his people.

Although the tribal system is deeply rooted in al-Anbar's history and actually precedes the introduction of Islam, in recent decades, two crises have endangered the system's continued existence. The first occurred when Saddam Hussein began providing state patronage to the tribesmen via their sheikhs. This development would seem to have enhanced the standing of the sheikhs, but Hussein simultaneously created the Office of Tribal Affairs and required the sheikhs to register with it. Each sheikh was assigned a classification reflecting the measure of his influence, which gave Hussein the ability to manipulate the sheikhs by manipulating classifications and patronage. In effect, the sheikhs became officials of the state. He also had his people register men without the requisite pedigree, thereby dramatically expanding the number of sheikhs. The result was the term "fake sheikh," as well as many tribal disputes that linger to this day.[4]

The second crisis occurred when al-Qaeda in Iraq began targeting tribal leaders, a tactic that intensified in late 2005. A number of sheikhs were assassinated, and many more either fled the country or were sent away by their tribes for their own protection.[5] Over time, the exiled sheikhs lost influence, while the younger men who remained behind in Iraq assumed many of their duties. Tribes were often (perhaps usually) internally divided in regard to which cause or faction to support during the insurgency.

For Americans serving in al-Anbar Province, there were additional complications. The title "sheikh" is also an honorific that is frequently

---

[4] Lin Todd et al., "Iraq Tribal Study—Al-Anbar Governorate: The Albu Fahd Tribe, the Albu Mahal Tribe, and the Albu Issa Tribe" (Department of Defense study, 18 June 2006). See also the interview with Sheikh Majed Abd al-Razzaq Ali al-Sulayman in this volume.

[5] See the interview with Col Michael M. Walker in the first volume of *Al-Anbar Awakening*.

used in addressing highly respected men or assumed by scoundrels seeking opportunities for personal gain at the expense of unwitting Americans. Also, a single sheikh may serve in many roles and represent different constituencies who have conflicting interests.[6]

Setting the Conditions for Insurgency

Everybody wanted to change the previous regime, but no one wanted it in this way. We really hoped that we could change the regime from inside Iraq, but it was too hard. No one could do it. Even all the other countries around the world accepted the idea that it wasn't going to happen from inside Iraq.

General Haqi Isma'eel Ali Hameed
Commander, 2d Region Directorate of Border Enforcement

Saddam Hussein led Iraq into one disaster after another. A year after assuming the presidency, he invaded Iran. The war dragged on from 1980 until 1988 with a devastating cost in blood and treasure. The economy was ruined and the national debt was impossible to meet. In 1990, just two years after the conclusion of the Iran-Iraq War, he invaded Kuwait, which resulted in the 1991 Gulf War. American-led Coalition air forces pummeled Iraqi infrastructure, military forces, and facilities for six weeks, and then Coalition ground forces drove the Iraqi army out of Kuwait in disorder.

Defeat opened the door for simultaneous insurrections in the Kurdish north and the Shi'a south. With 15 of 18 provinces in revolt, Hussein turned to the Sunnis for support. He warned that if the uprisings were successful, Iraq would become like Lebanon—a land of warring factions and utter chaos. Sunni fears of Iran and suspicion of Iraqi Shi'as were confirmed when Iraqi Shi'a forces of the Supreme Council for the Islamic Revolution in Iraq crossed the border from their safe haven in Iran to participate in the southern uprising. The Sunnis chose to support Saddam, and their response was swift and

---

[6.] For a detailed example, see William S. McCallister, "COIN and Irregular Warfare in a Tribal Society" (pamphlet, published by the *Small Wars Journal*, 2007), 30 (online at http://smallwarsjournal.com/documents/coinandiwinatribalsociety.pdf).

brutal. The largely Sunni Republican Guard crushed both uprisings with great slaughter, which included the use of chemical weapons in both the north and south.

Even though these actions left both Iraq and its leader weakened, Hussein refused to comply with the international economic sanctions. Instead, he tried to game his way out of them and failed, for more than a decade. In order to maintain his grip on power at home, he made major departures from Ba'ath Party ideology by embracing both the tribes and religion.

In Ba'ath socialism, the individual's duty to the state comes before his duty to his tribe. Therefore, tribalism was not only regarded by the Ba'athists as backward, but also as a threat to the government. Nevertheless, in shoring up his Sunni power base, Hussein granted greater autonomy and state patronage to the tribes. And, though Anbaris were not immune from the economic pain of international sanctions, Hussein ensured that they suffered less than most Iraqis. Government officials and military officers received extra rations, government cars, subsidized loans, and access to specialty shops with luxury goods. Furthermore, the sanctions increased the profits to be made from smuggling, which became a pillar of the Anbar economy. Anbaris used their transnational tribal connections to smuggle scrap metal, sheep, and oil into Jordan and Syria, where they were relatively expensive. They returned to Iraq with cigarettes, alcohol, and electrical appliances. These same smuggling routes and connections eventually served equally well as "ratlines" during the insurgency.

Regarding the second change, a religious revival transformed Iraq in the 1990s. Iraqi Shi'as had become more religious following the 1979 Iranian Revolution, and Iraqis of all sects and ethnicities had witnessed the religiously inspired enthusiasm of Iranian troops during the Iran-Iraq War. By the 1990s, religion was increasingly supplanting Ba'ath Party ideology, which had lost its relevance. Hussein disapproved of this trend, but unable to turn back the tide, he decided to co-opt it with a national "Return to Faith" campaign. Piety became a facet of Saddam's public image. The government closed bars and cinemas and spent large sums on mosques, clerics received salary increases and new services, and compulsory Quranic classes were instituted at all levels of education and even within the Ba'ath Party. Consequently, mosques became social centers, and clerical prestige increased until imams rivaled local sheikhs and party leaders in social influence. The secular Ba'ath Party was Islamicized, most people became more religious, and some became Islamic radicals.

As 2003 approached, Hussein prepared for the Gulf War of 1991. More specifically, he prepared for a repeat of the domestic uprisings that followed the Gulf War. Believing that the Coalition would be stopped by international political pressure and that Americans were too casualty-averse to conduct the ground operations necessary to overthrow his regime, he foresaw the worst-case scenario as a protracted air campaign followed by a limited invasion. Therefore, the bigger threats to his way of thinking were domestic uprisings and the potential for Iranian intervention.

So far, no evidence has surfaced suggesting that Hussein developed any plans for a post-invasion insurgency. Nevertheless, his war preparations had an irregular element, which served equally well for suppressing an uprising or starting an insurgency. Specifically, he established irregular and paramilitary organizations, such as the Saddam Fedayeen and al-Quds Army, which were tasked with containing and suppressing an uprising until the Republican Guard could arrive and destroy those who were rebelling. Second, he gave large quantities of weapons to loyal tribal sheikhs for the purpose of guarding the borders and suppressing dissidents. And third, in early 2003, Hussein decentralized command and control of the military in order to ensure that commanders had sufficient forces, support, and authority to respond quickly at the earliest signs of an uprising. He thereby enabled them to conduct preliminary planning for guerrilla and terrorist activities without central direction.

As war appeared imminent, some government mosques prepared the public for war by preaching anti-American and anti-Israeli sermons and urged Iraqis to jihad and resistance if the Americans invaded the country. This message was reinforced when the Islamic Research Center at al-Azhar University in Cairo, most prestigious Sunni theological center in the Islamic world, announced that an American invasion of Iraq would compel all Muslims to jihad. This pronouncement further legitimized anti-Coalition violence even among Islamists who hated the Saddam regime.[7]

Meanwhile, actions (or the absence thereof) by those aligning again Hussein also set conditions for insurgency. In January 2003, U.S. President George W. Bush established the Organization for Reconstruction and Humanitarian Assistance inside the Department of Defense to develop plans for democratic governance and rebuilding Iraq following regime change. The United States developed a branch plan for insurgency, but it did not write a detailed contingency plan, and it allocated no resources for counterinsurgency in the final war plan.

Development of the Insurgency

In March 2003, the Coalition invaded Iraq in Operation Iraqi Freedom. To everyone's surprise, Baghdad fell in a matter of weeks. The first Coalition forces to enter al-Anbar Province were British, Australian, and American special operations forces who were searching for Scud missiles in the western desert, hunting Ba'ath regime leaders, and securing important facilities and infrastructure such as Haditha Dam and al-Asad air base. They were followed by conventional forces from the U.S. Army. Since al-Anbar was only lightly defended, there were a couple of sharp engagements but no major battles.

In post-Saddam Hussein al-Anbar, resistance was initially disorganized and engaged in by small groups or individuals. Still, most Anbaris were cooperative with Coalition forces.

In May 2003, Ambassador L. Paul Bremer III announced the de-Ba'athification policy and the dissolution of the Iraqi Armed Forces, which threw hundreds of thousands of Iraq's most capable men into the ranks of the unemployed with no hope of future prospects.[8] A great many of these men were Anbaris.

---

[7] Associated Press, 10 March 2003.

[8] "De-Ba'athification of Iraqi Society" (Coalition Provisional Authority Order Number 1, 16 May 2003); "Dissolution of Entities" (Coalition Provisional Authority Order Number 2, 23 May 2003).

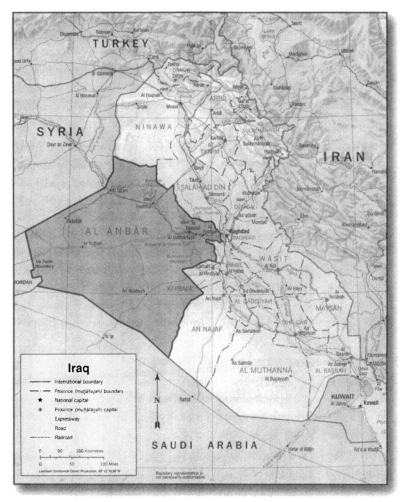

The number of armed groups proliferated and violence increased. These groups varied greatly in organization, capabilities, and goals, but they fell generally within certain broad categories. Sunni nationalists could be subdivided into two groups: former regime loyalists, who wanted the Ba'ath regime and Saddam Hussein restored to power; and former regime elements, who wanted the former regime restored without Hussein. There were also Sunni religious extemists, and another category, smaller than the others, of al-Qaeda-associated organizations.

The Coalition responded to the developing insurgency by focusing on tracking down former regime leaders. By the end of the year, Husay and Qusay Husseinwere dead and Saddam Hussein was in custody. The former regime loyalists became dispirited and splintered by rivalries. In defeating this segment of the insurgency, however, Coalition force methods contributed to the alienating the population and strengthened other elements of the insurgency.

Also in 2003, Abu Musab al-Zarqawi, an al-Qaeda associate and leader of Jama'at al-Tawhid wal-Jihad (Group of Monotheism and Jihad) moved his center of operations from the Kurdish north to al-Anbar, Diyala, and Baghdad. Over the next year, he kept a low operational profile while building his organization through the absorption of discouraged former regime loyalists and by attracting foreign fighters. In early 2004, he did not think that he was receiving sufficient support from the Iraqis, and in a communication with al-Qaeda senior leadership, he argued for provoking a sectarian war against the Iraqi Shi'as in order to radicalize the Iraqi Sunnis. The proposal was rejected because it would jeopardize Iranian support for al-Qaeda.

By October of 2004, al-Zarqawi agreed to subordinate himself to al-Qaeda's higher objectives, and he announced that Jama'at al-Tawhid wal-Jihad was incorporated into al-Qaeda. In return, he received access to al-Qaeda's global network of resources, personnel, propaganda support, and financing.

By early 2004, the former regime elements and the Sunni religious extremists had matured from splintered groups into organized forces that were able to engage in pitched battles. Incompatible goals prevented the unification of these two major categories of insurgents, or even the unification of the various factions within a single category. Nevertheless, the creation of local coordinating councils enabled short-term tactical cooperation.

Increasing cooperation brought about a rise in Islamic sentiment among the nationalists. The rank and file began to see Iraqi supporters of the Coalition as apostates as well as collaborators; the Coalition Provisional Authority was an enemy of Islam as well as an occupying power; and the Shi'a were heretics as well as agents of Iran. However, neither the nationalists nor the Sunni religious extremists were willing to support al-Qaeda in Iraq or endorse mass casualty attacks.

In April 2004, the insurgent groups felt strong enough to face U.S. Marines in open battle in Fallujah. They were no match for the Marines, but political pressure forced the Marines to halt their attack (Operation Vigilant Resolve) and withdraw from the city. The insurgents regarded this as a victory, and insurgent morale soared.

Subsequent negotiations between the Marines and insurgents resulted in the establishment of the Fallujah Brigade, which was intended to provide local control of security within Fallujah. However, the unit was compromised by insurgents and soon disbanded.

While events attendant to the Fallujah Brigade were unwinding in al-Anbar, Talal al-Gaoud was hosting meetings with U.S. Marine officers and officials of the U.S. Department of Defense in Amman, Jordan, in an attempt to negotiate an agreement between the Americans and Anbar's secular elites.[9] Talal al-Gaoud was a member of the al-Gaoud subtribe of the Albu Nimr tribe. The Albu Nimr rebelled against Saddam Hussein in the 1990s, and Talal al-Gaoud's relative, Fasal Raikan Najris al-Gaoud, was appointed governor of al-Anbar Province not long after the negotiations in Amman ended. While the negotiations did not result in an agreement, the meetings were an early indication that influential Anbaris were interested in engagement.

In November 2004, as Fasal al-Gaoud assumed the governorship, U.S. Marines and soldiers were storming Fallujah (Operation Phantom Fury/al-Fajr). The major insurgent groups suffered a severe blow. Thousands of fighters were killed or captured. The leadership spent several months reorganizing, and their men retreated into their remaining strongholds in western al-Anbar, unable to interfere with elections in January 2005.

However, antipathy for the Coalition led to a Sunni boycott of the election. Coalition diplomatic efforts during the remainder of the year focused on engaging Sunni leaders in the political process. These efforts, and a sense of hopelessness among insurgents following the storming of Fallujah, eventually bore some fruit. Sunni voter turnout

---

[9] David Rose, "Iraq: Heads in the Sand," *Vanity Fair*, 12 May 2009.

increased for the summer's constitutional referendum and the December 2005 election. These developments created a division between the more nationalist insurgents, led by Mohammed Mahmoud Latif, and the Islamists, led by Abu Musab al-Zarqawi.

The Rise of al-Qaeda in Iraq

Beginning in April 2005, insurgents stepped up attempts to target Baghdad, which led to Coalition military action against their strongholds in western al-Anbar. By the end of the year, insurgent participation in the political process was increasing, and nationalist motivation for the insurgency was declining. In-fighting ensued, which paved the way for the eventual dominance of al-Qaeda in Iraq the following year.

In late 2005, Operation Sayyad II had created a serious disruption in the al-Qaeda in Iraq network in western al-Anbar, which continued into 2006. Many other insurgents and emerging political groups used the opportunity to break away and seek political engagement with the faction under the direction of Mohammed Mahmoud Latif. Al-Qaeda in Iraq regrouped by early 2006, however, and it began targeting insurgent and tribal leaders who favored political engagement. This strategy was so successful that al-Qaeda in Iraq became the dominant insurgent group in all of al-Anbar. The magnitude of its success brought unparalleled power and created difficulties in maintaining the ideological integrity of the organization. Al-Qaida's murder and intimidation campaign also alienated large numbers of Anbaris, which created opportunities for both Coalition forces and insurgent rivals. The death of Abu Musab al-Zarqawi in June 2006 reinforced these opportunities, but it also allowed less volatile leaders to step forward within the organization, including Abu Ayyub al-Masri.

Al-Anbar Awakening

According to the Anbaris, the Albu Mahal tribe in al-Qaim initiated what became the Awakening in 2005 when they engaged in open warfare against al-Qaeda in Iraq throughout the spring and summer. This Awakening did not spread, probably because only local tribal interests were at stake. Nevertheless, tribes at the opposite end of al-Anbar were aware of it, and it seems to have served as a precedent.

The celebrated Awakening, which cleared the entire province, probably began in early 2006 and perhaps even in late 2005. It is difficult to determine a precise start date because the Al-Anbar Awakening began as the insurgency began: secretly and separately, with differing organizational structures, various capabilities, tactics adapted to local circumstances. Many of these stories and details can be found in the interviews that follow. By September 2006, the separate elements of the Awakening had coalesced and matured to the point where the movement was prepared to go public.

By the summer of 2007, al-Anbar Province was largely cleared of al-Qaeda in Iraq. Without the common bond of a common enemy, the Awakening began to splinter as the groups that had come together started to pursue divergent interests.

This is an outline of the backdrop against which the Awakening was set. The story of how it played out follows in the words of many of the brave Anbaris who made it happen.

In addition to the details in the preface on the editorial method applied across both volumes of this collection, here are some additional notes on the Iraqi interviews. The interviews in this volume were conducted between English and Arabic speakers who communicated through interpreters. Native Arabic speakers were integrally involved in each interview, using consecutive, and occasionally simultaneous, interpretation.

The single exception to these practices was the interview with the woman we has called Miriam (the first interview in the volume). The alternative procedures used to protect her identity are described in the introductory note to her interview.

Each interview was recorded on electronic recording devices. Upon the interviewers' return to Quantico, Virginia, the English portions were transcribed by a contracted transcription service. For publication, the transcripts were edited for clarity and abridged for relevance. Problematic passages were taken to the Marine Corps Center for Operational Culture and Learning (CAOCL), where native Arabic speakers listened to the original recordings and clarified the meanings. The resulting changes were reviewed and edited again, as necessary.

In the interviews, the Iraqis normally distinguished between Britons and Americans; however, they often used the terms soldier and Marine or Army and Marines interchangeably.

The Iraqis tend to use the word "division" in the same manner that English speakers use the word "unit." Therefore, only actual division-sized units are indicated by a capital letter.

The tribal system is hierarchical and contains words for confederations, tribes, clans, and families. As is the usual practice in interpreted conversation, tribe is most commonly used here.

Gary W. Montgomery
Colonel, U.S. Marine Corps Reserve

A View of
Daily Life

Interview 1

Miriam

Head of an Iraqi Women's
Nongovernmental Organization

"Miriam" is a pseudonym. All personally identifiable information has been concealed for her safety and for the security of her family. Her husband is a high-ranking Iraqi policeman who was targeted by insurgents. Also, Miriam is prominent in her own right due to her humanitarian and political activities.

In the first half of the interview, she discusses daily life during the insurgency and her efforts to support her family while concealing her husband. In the second half, she describes her interaction with Marine civil affairs and the activities of her nongovernmental organization.

Miriam was interviewed by Colonel Gary W. Montgomery and Chief Warrant Officer-4 Timothy S. McWilliams on 17 February 2009 at the Provincial Government Center in Ramadi. In accordance with Miriam's wishes, audio and video equipment were not used. Colonel Montgomery, Chief Warrant Officer-4 McWilliams, and an Iraqi interpreter made handwritten notes, and the separate versions were merged into a single draft. Miriam reviewed the draft and made corrections. Miriam was accompanied by three Iraqi women who occasionally interjected additional details, but the words reproduced here are primarily Miriam's. Also present were Captain Stephanie [surname deleted], a Marine civil affairs officer who was on her fourth deployment to Iraq, and two female Iraqi interpreters, one translating and the other taking notes.

Miriam: At the beginning, the Iraqi police worked openly under Chief Ja'adan.* In 2003 to 2004, they were coming to work freely and working very well. When the terrorists started in al-Anbar, they attacked the police first, causing a massive scare. During the night, al-Qaeda threw threatening notes onto their doorsteps or into their gardens so that they would find them in the morning

---

* Major General Ja'adan Muhammad al-Alwani, Provincial Director of Police, 2003-2004.

before work. The notes told them to quit working for the police and to go to a mosque, publicly declare that they are no longer police, and ask for forgiveness.

The terrorists called for jihad to get public support, but they misused the word. Jihad is for defending our home and family against people trying to take us by force. It does not mean cutting people into little pieces. The terrorists used the word as a cover for their evil acts. They used the word to win the sympathy of the people. It is a very big word. The terrorists targeted illiterate minds—a certain level of society—and used them as a front.

They threatened the Iraqi police and made them quit. Then when the policemen were unemployed, they offered them a lot of money to work for al-Qaeda. People who didn't cooperate got "the discipline." Whoever did not cooperate was taken from his house in a hood, stripped down to his boxers, and whipped with a bike chain or cable in front of the people to set an example.

The ugliest torture was committed by al-Qaeda. If the discipline didn't work, the people were abducted and slaughtered. The head was put in a container and thrown away, or the neck cut and the head placed on the back.

In 2005, our 16-year-old neighbor was killed during Ramadan. At the beginning of Allahu Akhbar,* he was hanged from a three-story flag pole. When the last note sounded, his body was dropped.

My cousin's husband worked at a police station. They drove a tanker through the station and detonated it. Everyone was killed or burned. He lived, but he was badly burned. His wife took him to a doctor for treatment. The doctor referred him to Ramadi General Hospital. However, she was afraid to go there because al-Qaeda had taken over the hospital, so she treated him at home. Al-Qaeda suspected he was there, so they sent some ladies to the house to find out. A lot of women joined al-Qaeda. These women were seamstresses, and they managed to get in the house under the

---

* A broadcast from the mosque that signals that eating is permitted.

pretense of discussing some sewing work. They saw the husband and informed al-Qaeda. The house was raided and the husband abducted. They put rocks on his legs and put him into the river.

Al-Qaeda brainwashed people. If we heard gunshots, we went inside our homes. It was a signal that they were going to do something. They announced on a loudspeaker why they were killing.

Al-Qaeda also incited hatred between the Shi'a and the Sunni. They accused everyone wearing a precious stone on his ring of being a Shi'a and murdered him. Sometimes they fired shots into doors to scare them.

One time they caught three men going to Baghdad and killed them. They killed three young, tall men who were wearing rings with precious stones. They said that because they were wearing rings with precious stones that they were Shi'a. Our [Sunni] men don't usually wear rings with precious stones. They tortured, killed, and mutilated them and then left their bodies on the street for three days. They told everyone not to touch them. But their families recognized them. They were former policemen. They weren't Shi'as, they were our men.

They killed doctors and leaders. They killed doctors and said that it was because they treated Americans. The doctors fled the country. They killed mullahs and said that it was because they liked Americans. Soon there were no men left to kill, so they started killing women and children. They killed women and said that it was because their husbands were policemen. They killed children and said it was because their fathers were policemen.

I cannot describe the horror we lived in. Those were very bitter days. Those days we lived in hell. We looked like ghosts out of a cemetery. We were very tired. We had a lot of complaints to take to the Coalition forces, but we were afraid. Some days we wished to be dead just to be rested. But I have [many] children. I was very tired.

My husband let his beard and hair grow so that they wouldn't think he's working. We had no income, and I started selling our property to pay the rent. I heard that this officer was killed, that officer was killed. I sent my husband to hide sometimes.

Al-Qaeda started rumors. On the streets, they accused Americans of being killers. People welcomed al-Qaeda into their homes as a custom, but they killed families, raped wives, and took over. If one of them killed 60 people, he was called emir.

Interpreter: Each al-Qaeda cell consisted of six people. If you kill 60 people, then you become an emir automatically. The cells didn't know each other.

Miriam: Each home they take over becomes a cell that doesn't work with the others. Every group of insurgents was in charge of some area. Al-Qaeda had their own patrol groups driving around making scary noises to terrorize neighborhoods and let them know they were there.

Fear made me very cautious. Sometimes if a door was opened, an entire family was killed—old people, women, and children. I had four huge locks on the front door. It looked like a protected holy place. I would only open the door for family. We had a way of knocking that was a signal.

Al-Qaeda started targeting college graduates. My father-in-law is a former [deleted] and a college graduate. We are an educated family. I had a family member at the government office. He offered me a job. So I covered my face and went for the interview. Women were not allowed to drive, so I taught my 11-year-old son to drive. He took me to work. He had a lot of accidents. He also used to take me shopping.

Three or four times I was stopped at al-Qaeda checkpoints. They asked, "Where is your husband? Tell him to come in or we will kill him." I started crying and told them that he ran away after he lost his job and that we are separated. So they let me go. The al-Qaeda commander in our area started watching me himself from a vehicle outside the fence.

I used to take my younger son walking. Females were not allowed to walk by themselves. They had to have a husband or male relative with them. So my son had to go with me.

Al-Qaeda controlled all fuels. The al-Qaeda group commander refused to allow them to sell fuel to me. I covered my face, but he recognized my eyes.

I felt like I had no life in Ramadi. I used to bring hairdressers home sometimes. But al-Qaeda asked why a male was in my home if my husband was not there, so I had to stop.

They were not mujahedeen; they were low-life people. A true enemy will face you and fight. These were cowards, cheaters, and backstabbers. They threatened my son at school. I told him, "If you see their cars, jump the back fence of the school."

Many of our original neighbors fled the city, and the insurgents lived in their homes in [other] areas. We are thankful for [name of prominent person, deleted]. He deserves a lot of credit. A friend of my in-laws heard of our situation and told [him]. He sent a force to get us out. He hired my husband back as a police officer. He worked six months at a station for [title deleted]. My husband lived in the station while I lived at home with the kids.

I was afraid of the Coalition forces and the insurgents. I used to leave the house at 6 a.m.. Before 7 a.m., there was a Coalition forces curfew. After 7 a.m., the insurgents were out. I used to carry a white flag with me. It was my husband's undergarment. The Coalition forces know the white flag. Nothing works with the insurgents.

This is the first time I've told my story without crying. I am happy. I just want to protect my family and love them. My husband and I were in love before marriage. That is rare here. Most marriages are arranged. If they killed us, I wanted them to kill me first. I can't bear to see him dead.

Our neighbors were on watch and asked questions. The neighbors were collaborating with al-Qaeda. Sometimes I disguised my husband as a woman or an old man. Every day was a different story. It was like living in a different movie every day.

The neighbors were asking questions, so we moved to a different neighborhood. I hid my husband in the back of my car. I took out the seat and put a blanket over him. There was no room to park the car at the new house, but our neighbors were so kind and let me park the car in their garage. The husband turned out to be a big insurgent. I told them that my husband was gone. I never told them the true story.

I asked my husband's boss to move my husband to [a different place]. Life was better there. Things were running smoothly there, and Ramadi was a ghost town.

The Awakening started with Sheikh Sattar Abu Risha because al-Qaeda killed many of his family. The police started coming down slowly. People started coming out.

We had the first woman's meeting on December 15, 2006, at the [place deleted] elementary school. Sheikh [name deleted] attended the meeting. He paid attention to the women's movement.

Captain Tina [pseudonym] of the Coalition forces was present at the first meeting, and she worked with us. We set up literacy classes for females. I worked with her, but I was also afraid. I stayed in the house for a week after the first meeting. I had a photo taken with Captain Tina, and it was posted all over town. She e-mailed it to my organization, and one of the women in our office let it leak out. Now women are going back to have pictures made with the Coalition forces.

After Captain Tina we got Captain Stephanie, and we met at the elementary school. Some women refused to shake hands with Stephanie, but she is very patient. She tamed them like taming wild animals: she brought them gifts and listened to problems. She won them over slowly. Stephanie opened literacy programs and classrooms at three places.

Stephanie is a great American woman. She taught us how to depend on ourselves. She gave us a financial mind. Our mindset was to get a degree, get a job, get married, cooking and kids. Stephanie taught us to do finances, fight gossip, depend on ourselves, and fight the insurgency. For example, a woman can't read. Her son comes in with money and says that he is on a holy mission. We should ask questions like, "What kind of holy mission? Who is telling you this?" The first thing is to teach kids morals.

Women who didn't like Stephanie are now trying to pull her away to their side. Stephanie distributes products. We call her "Santa" or "Mamma Claus."

Stephanie helped people love security. She helped women get jobs. She put rules on who should be hired: target unemployed college graduates to maximize employment.

In 2007, we organized as a united women's organization. We met at Sheikh [name deleted]'s house and discussed having more literacy classes. It's the only way to open the female mind. And women need to get more involved in their children's lives.

We opened our first classroom at a school. Stephanie asked us to make it succeed so the public would accept it and it would expand. We gathered new members in Ramadi, but the women were scared. We started with friends, and some came from Fallujah. We succeeded and now have 400 members in different parts of Anbar.

At the time, it was raging with insurgency. There were no rations available, except through Stephanie. She brought in a truckload of food and supplies—1,500 shares. Stephanie asked me to hand out the clothes today so that the kids could wear them tomorrow. I was fasting and it was hot, but I spent 12 hours handing out clothes. Some of the kids were so excited that they changed clothes immediately.

Stephanie is really great, comes all the way from America. I don't fear anymore. Stephanie showed me the way, how to love the responsible role that I take. She taught me not to fear but still be cautious.

We help women get jobs—jobs for widows, cleaning courtyards. If a woman can't make it, her kids do it, so that she still gets a paycheck.

The first meeting was with Donna [surname deleted] in [place deleted]. She asked for the number of widows. I gave her a record of each widow and the number of kids. We met with the director of social services in Ramadi. We identified the greatest need and formed a project. She was replaced by Lieutenant Carla [surname deleted].

Stephanie built women into leaders and gave them confidence. She inspired everyone. We are getting more organized and getting better government support. But we still need more support for the orphans.* There are 850 orphans just in Ramadi. Families shelter them, but they need help. We're collecting backpacks, mittens, shoes, caps, and sun block. We need classes in nursing, English, cooking, computers, making artificial flowers, painting on ceramic. We need a new hospital. There is no room in the existing hospital to deliver babies.

Iraq once had female doctors, judges, and scientists, and they were also good wives and mothers. We want you to separate us from Saudi women and the Gulf States. Twenty-five years ago, we had an Iraqi female minister. The world thinks all the women are like the ones in Saudi Arabia and other countries. We are not like that. Before Saddam [Hussein], women were free to get out. We had equal education. We're coming back. The wars, the insurgency, the Sunni and Shi'a conflict were a setback. The people who started the Sunni-Shi'a conflict were not Iraqis.

Chief Warrant Officer-4 Timothy S. McWilliams: Are you in touch with the rest of the world?

Miriam: We have satellite TV now. We're careful about what is on. Not all of the programs are good. We have the Internet. It's expensive though, about $50 a month. We're interacting with the rest of the world now. It's a sign of civilization. Iraqis are conservative but not extreme.

---

* In al-Anbar, the term "orphan" includes children with only one parent.

Iraqi Perspectives

Religious
Perspectives

Interview 2

Dr. Thamer Ibrahim Tahir al-Assafi

Muslim Ulema Council for al-Anbar
(Council of Muslim Scholars)
Professor of Religious Studies, al-Anbar University
Senior Theologian to the Sunni Endowment
Ramadi City Council Member

Sheikh Abdullah Jallal Mukhif al-Faraji

Head of the Sunni Endowment for al-Anbar
Regent Sheikh of the Abu Faraj Tribe
Ramadi City Council Member

Dr. Thamer Ibrahim Tahir al-Assafi is a cleric in Ramadi who chose a religious path after serving as a commando in the Iran-Iraq War. He is influential in Iraq and well-regarded among Muslim endowments in the Middle East and Southeast Asia. His nexus of influence is al-Anbar University, where his credibility is magnified by his combined status as a member of faculty, combat veteran, and cleric. He was an early proponent of engagement, and throughout the insurgency he used his sermons in the mosque and his lectures at the university to publicly call for moderation and restraint. He was shot in the shoulder during an assassination attempt against Governor Mamoun Sami Rashid al-Alwani, but he continued undeterred.

Sheikh Abdullah Jallal Mukhif al-Faraji is a former Olympic athlete, a cleric, and one of the original members of the Anbar Salvation Council. He is addressed as "sheikh" as an honorific. He is neither a true lineal sheikh nor a pretender. The true sheikh delegated most of his responsibilities to Abdullah, who is popular among his fellow Faraji tribesmen. His influence is concentrated around Ramadi and eastward toward Fallujah. During the insurgency, he used his influence to temper the insurgent movement, anti-U.S. rhetoric, and infighting among the various militias. He was wounded several times, including a gunshot to the arm during an assassination attempt against Governor Mamoun. The governor seems to regard him as a personal spiritual advisor and trusted agent. While recovering from the gunshot wound to his arm, Sheikh Abdullah was mistakenly arrested by Coalition forces. Brigadier General James L. Williams was instrumental in securing his quick release, an act which established a greater degree of trust and resulted in more Sunni leaders entering the political process.

Dr. Thamer and Sheikh Abdullah were interviewed by Colonel Gary W. Montgomery and Chief Warrant Officer-4 Timothy S. McWilliams on 12 February 2009 at Camp Ramadi.

Dr. Thamer Ibrahim Tahir al-Assafi: History speaks for people, for communities, so from us it necessarily is required to write down history. Whether we like it or not, we have been joined with you in history. We have to clarify for distant people and for later generations.

There is one overriding fact that you will have to know: there was no terrorism in Iraq prior to your coming here, except state terrorism. After the invasion of Kuwait [1990-91] and the total embargo that was placed on Iraq, it created a generation of people that was destitute and corrupt. They would be taken to court, and they would be imprisoned, and most of them were angry. Just before the time of Baghdad's fall to the Americans, Saddam [Hussein] freed all these prisoners in a general amnesty. Those people were set free among society.

After the fall of Baghdad, you noticed there was chaos, and you noticed that government institutions were looted, and particularly after the dissolving of the Iraqi army by [Ambassador L. Paul] Bremer. The internal security apparatus was dissolved, also. So there was a general freedom, and there was freedom of movement.

Saddam also opened the borders to allow foreigners to come in before the battle with the Americans, and a lot of them did come in. Most of these people were Syrians. Most of these people gathered in our province. We tried to get rid of them. We gathered a lot of money, and we hired vehicles, and we tried to kick them out. But they went out to the surrounding villages and hamlets, and there they organized themselves into cells under the guise of resistance to the Americans and the occupation.

After the fall of Baghdad, which was on a Wednesday, eventually we established a government in Ramadi with a new police chief. He chose new policemen. These policemen, some of them were bad elements, from among the people that Saddam let out of prison. I raised the issue with the police chief, and I asked him, "Why would you put bad elements in charge of the community?" He said, "Look, when I bring these people in here, I'm in charge of them. I keep watch on them, rather than turn them loose in society to create mayhem."

Negotiations ensued between the tribes of Anbar and the American forces. Coalition Forces were located primarily in Rutbah and the west of Anbar, and they wanted to come in from Baghdad, and they wanted to come in peacefully. An agreement was struck between some of the tribal sheikhs and the American forces for a peaceful entry. After they entered Ramadi, there was a big demonstration, a peaceful demonstration, because they did not approve of an occupier coming into their capital. The American forces did not respect the people who were demonstrating. They dealt with them rather violently. The people's reaction was to pelt the Americans with rocks and tomatoes, and it was a rather negative reaction. They provoked the citizens. That was the first thing that started hatred.

The next day, they demonstrated again, and the Americans treated them in the same manner, meaning their armored vehicles went right through them. A young man, an 18-year-old youth, threw a rock at an American tank, and the soldiers shot him dead. We are a tribal people, and in our tradition, we know revenge. If someone gets killed from your family, you have to kill the killer, or at least a relative of his.

When the Iraqi army was dissolved, they left a lot of armaments, including armored personnel carriers, heavy machine guns, and a lot ordnance. People took them and hid them in their houses, not to have a future confrontation with the Americans, but in fear of a confrontation with Iran. Keep in mind we are military-trained people as a society because of the battles—the Gulf War, the Iran War, the Kurds in the north. Most of us were in the army, so using weapons was something we could do with ease.

So these people whose youth was killed by the Americans, they formed a cell, and they started looking for revenge. They found out that placing an IED [improvised explosive device] is a simple matter, so a lot of cells began forming all over the place.

When the foreign Arabs came in, they came in with suitcases full of dollars, and they started organizing cells. They got in touch with the Iraqi people, and they started organizing them better. We had a weak police force, a weak army.

The Americans did not want to get involved unless they were directly attacked. If an American patrol was on the highway, and they saw a dead person, they would just leave him there. And this really started to create hatred toward the American GIs, because they couldn't care less what happened to Iraqis. If they were killed right in front of them, they did not get involved. So that reaction of the Iraqi people was like, we hated the Americans.

When the terrorists attacked the national mosque in 2005, Sheikh Abdullah was attacked, I was attacked, Sheikh Tarek was killed—the head of the Sunni Endowment. The American forces were 200 yards away. They were watching and did not interfere.

There was a gap between the American forces and the Iraqi people, and there was strong hatred. They did not improve the police. The police essentially got dissolved. There was only one unit, the highway patrol, and they stayed to themselves. They stayed in their headquarters. . . .

We had a huge conference with the American commanders and the tribal sheikhs to develop the Iraqi police and Iraqi army. In 2005, we had people gather to volunteer for the police, and two terrorists infiltrated the place and blew themselves up. The American forces did not even give first aid to the wounded. And the civilians who aided those wounded, the terrorists would catch them down the road and slaughter them. Another conference was held, and we interceded with them to develop the police and the army, and, again, they intervened. The terrorists said we deserved death, and many among us were killed.

Being clerics, we used to incite people against the terrorists through our sermons in mosques and speeches. The last election, the one in 2005, we defied the terrorists, and we went out to cast our votes. Afterward we were subjected to the wrath of the terrorists for the people that went out and voted.

Had the American forces allowed us to carry arms at that time, we would have eradicated terrorism much sooner. Any of us who carried a personal sidearm was arrested, while the terrorists had plenty of heavy armaments and were walking freely. So we were lost, and the American forces did not stand with us. There were many people that got killed by the terrorists, and the Americans did not stand with us, so our backs were open, so to speak. We could not get help, not even from the Iraqi government. Life became very difficult, because the banks were looted by the terrorists.

In the meeting, I accused the commander, [Brigadier General James L.] Williams, of being in cahoots with the terrorists, for looting the banks. I said, "Look, how can the terrorists go into a bank and take the money out, and you're right there—and you're not in cahoots with them?"

The province of Anbar became so paralyzed that even the employees of the banks could not receive their own salaries. Many fatwas were issued by the terrorists to close the universities. Ramadi became a ghost town. Universities, schools, factories, and institutions were all shut down, so we were pressed. The government did not pay us our salaries. Life became intolerable. So we started looking for salvation, no matter who it was.

Salvation came through the Anbar Awakening with the leadership of Abdul Sattar Abu Risha. I tell you frankly, we all disliked Sheikh Abdul Sattar Abu Risha. This being because he was not a religious person, so there was a distance between us. When Sheikh Abu Risha proposed the Awakening, we looked into it deeper, and we found it to be a really good thing to do. So I got Sheikh [Abdullah] Jallal [Mukhif al-Faraji], and we said this is the thing to do. We have to do it. And so we carried on, and with the help of Colonel [John W.] Charlton [USA] and Lieutenant Colonel Warner, we were able to get rid of the terrorists. The religious establishment started working hand in hand with the Awakening. When they liberated a street or a town, we used to go in and open the mosques that were closed by the terrorists. Some of the mosques were also closed by the American forces.

We lost many innocent people. Some of them were loaded down with blocks and put into the river. Some of them were taken out to the desert and beheaded. Some of them were imprisoned.

We were hoping after the Awakening—after getting rid of the terrorists—we were hoping that new building would take place, but it hasn't happened. A lot of money was paid out by the American forces to many contractors, but nothing came of it; nothing useful, that is. The streets that were paved got destroyed. They did a lot of painting of buildings and shops. We were not exactly happy about what these people did, all this money that was stolen. All the money was given to affluent people—tribal sheikhs and contractors—which could be considered as a sort of bribe.

We were hoping for the civilization of America to be transferred into Iraq. Maybe you're not a colonial power; this is new to you. We're hoping for many institutions. When Great Britain occupied Iraq, they left many institutions, bridges, hospitals. People can go right now and say, "There is the bridge that was built by the British. This is a hospital built by the British." When you leave Ramadi, or Anbar all together, what will your legacy be? It's total destruction. People will say you just came in, destroyed, and left. You're going to help us rebuild our country? A translator asked me a while ago, "If I come to Ramadi on vacation or to spend some time, where do I go?" I told him, "The street, where else? There are no hotels, no motels, there aren't even parks to go into." This is all I have to say.

Colonel Gary W. Montgomery: What was your impression of the foreign Arabs?

Thamer: We totally reject the foreign Arabs because we have prior knowledge of their doings in Afghanistan, in Chechnya, in Bosnia-Herzegovina, and in Algeria. They were hired hands, and Iran hired them. We knew that beforehand, but the security situation was really bad when they came in. The Ba'athists harbored them. I was just joking.

Sheikh Abdullah Jallal Mukhif al-Faraji: The most glaring mistake committed by Coalition forces was leaving the borders unattended. From these borders, the foreign Arabs entered. The second most glaring mistake they made was dissolving the army. Initially when the Americans came in, there was a peaceful coexistence between the people and the Americans. There was a great understanding between the tribal sheikhs in Anbar, especially [Ali Amar Limand], and there was no tension.

The foreign Arabs, when they came into Iraq, they changed the mindset of the Iraqi people and told them to use bombs.

I see things from a different perspective than Dr. Thamer, so I have a disagreement with how he sees things. I don't want Dr. Thamer to forget al-Ghazaliyah, Baghdad. He and I and our peers joined with the Americans. We killed four terrorists in Baghdad, so I don't want him to forget that they helped us in 2007.

Thamer: Yes, that's true, but that's after the inception of the Awakening. If it were before the Awakening, they would have killed us. . . .

Abdullah: And I liked Abdul Sattar Abu Risha, even though Sheikh Thamer hated him.

Thamer: Look, I hated him before the Awakening. We even met with him, and I told him personally that I hated him before the Awakening. But since the inception of the Awakening, no, I liked him.

Abdullah: Truthfully, Iraq had no foreign Arabs before. The reason the foreign Arabs came into Iraq is because they were following their arch enemy, the Americans. It's apparent that the United States will fight these foreign Arabs all over the world, and when they came into Iraq, that's where the battle took place, right here in Iraq.

Now, the American forces assaulted some Iraqis in their houses, and everywhere else, and that created a negative reaction toward the Americans. To be truthful, the U.S. forces didn't distinguish between who is a foreign Arab and who is an Iraqi, so they shot everybody. . . .

I represent the Sunni Endowment Organization before the Awakening and before the religious people. This is, right here, the telltales of them shooting me. Right here. He [Dr. Thamer] got shot, too. The governor, Mamoun, got shot. We were in the same building when they attacked. We took their own weapons, my force, and we fought them with their own weapons. I don't want to talk too much, but now I want to say this is the inception of the Awakening.

What Dr. Thamer explained is sufficient enough. We came in as the religious side with Sattar. We gathered this bridged duality of the religious people and the tribal people, and they were bound together. When finally the people realized that the clerics were in with the Awakening, they came in and joined Sattar. That's why the Awakening succeeded. . . .

And one cannot forget [Lieutenant] Colonel [Thaddeus] McWhorter [USA], [Lieutenant Colonel Michael] Silverman [USA], and Charlton. . . . They knew how to treat the tribal people. They knew how to treat educated people in the cities, and village people. They trained their minds, their military minds, their civil minds, to understand all this. Please, if you write down history, do not forget these people. I'm a religious person who speaks only the truth, and I don't know who is who, but I just tell you the facts as they are. They've established a great legacy for the Coalition forces. They were loyal to their country; they were loyal to their military.

Abdullah: I want to talk about politics, reconstruction, education, and economics. This election taught Iraqis to understand what an election is. There is a political awareness among the Iraqi people.

As far as education goes, we need an exchange of ideas, of views between us and the other religions, and not just religions, but civilizations. We've demanded the establishment of a university, an American university in Anbar, or anywhere in Iraq, so there will be an educational exchange between the United States and Iraq. We've demanded the establishment of libraries that will have all kinds of books—American, Arabic. We have demanded the establishment of an English-teaching institution, because we need these institutions. There are promises to that effect. We need an educational institution to rid the people of all the negative ideas in Iraq and the surrounding areas. We need a monument left for the American forces in Iraq, a hotel, a bridge [conversation with interpreter].

Interpreter: Again, he is speaking about the bridges that the British built.

Abdullah: When you cross over it, you say, "This is the British legacy." We need something to establish your legacy. What have you left? Sometimes it's paint.

As for economics, a lot of money was wasted, as Sheikh Thamer said, to specific people. About four to seven days ago, U.S. Forces Command in Iraq spoke of these financial mistakes. And the chief cause of it is corruption, whether among Iraqi society or the U.S. forces themselves.

At the end, I will wish you the best in writing history, but we don't want to forget what you went through.

Colonel Charlton knew how to treat people. When a person came to him raging mad, he used to smile in his face, calm him down, and deal with him positively.

Colonel Silverman knew how to treat Arabs, because he lived in the Arabian Gulf. So when they put him here in Iraq, he knew how to treat the Iraqi people, and he treated them well.

One other person is Major [Adam T.] Strickland, and another guy who called himself [name deleted for security reasons]. He was an American. Those people knew how to treat Iraqis.

Not to forget General [John F.] Kelly's role, because he used to shuttle between the tribal areas. We can never forget it. He knew how to treat people and to win them over. He would release detainees. He honored sheikhs. He would release a detainee as an honor to sheikhs. He supported those who are starting service projects.

They knew how to connect society with the rule of law. Everything about the military, they knew how to connect it. To be honest with you right now, I cannot think of everything good that you've done, because it doesn't come to mind.

And we cannot forget Brigadier General Williams, who I have mentioned, who was here before the Awakening in 2006. . . .

You must know the period between 2003 and 2009 is not an easy period. It was a very complex period. I want you to know that some of the clerics did side with the terrorists because they had religious tendencies. So we talked to them, and we told them the right way, and we won them over.

Sheikh Sattar even sent me to Oman to talk to Sheikh Harith al-Dhari and to tell him to stop all the fiery speeches, the negative things about the police and the army. We calmed him down, and we won him over, and no more fiery sermons. We said that we want security—the army, the police, everything—in our own country. We said, "Sooner or later, American forces will leave our country, and we will have to stay and rebuild it." He was somewhat satisfied with our suggestions, so for a year or two he did not say anything negative.

Montgomery: What part did al-Qaeda in Iraq play in the troubles here?

Abdullah: Their role was simple. They are the primary mischief makers in Iraq. They did not know what resistance meant. They did not know what jihad meant. They did not know what humanity meant. And I speak in front of the camera, and I say it forcefully. They did not know what life meant. They wanted to kill everybody that existed and everybody that did not agree with them. So, therefore, [inaudible], and that's why they had to be kicked out of this country and any other country. And I'm not saying this to be nice to you. And, if you get me madder, I will say much more. So, please, leave me be.

Montgomery: I think that we definitely don't want to get him angry.

Abdullah: I'll tell you what they used to do. They used to kill the doctor, who is in the business of bringing people back to life. They used to kill the children. They used to kill the women. They used to kill the engineers, whose job is to rebuild. How can you kill everybody?

You ask them the question, "Why do you kill?"

They said, "Well, this guy's not a Muslim."

"Okay, why don't you call him Muslim?"

"Oh, because he's a Shi'a, or because he's Kurdish, or because he's a Sunni backslider."

They had a reason for killing everybody. "This is a Sunni backslider. This is a Shiite. This is a Kurd. This is a policeman. This is a soldier." So they had a reason to kill anybody and everybody they wanted to. We tried to understand who the real enemy was. We just didn't know who it was. They consider a little baby, a woman, to be an enemy?

You may not know this; perhaps you do. The religion of Islam prohibits the killing of a child or a woman, even the cutting of a tree or destroying a building. This is not done in Islam. Islam means peace—peace and mercy for all people, not just for Muslim people. They used Islam as a cover, a pretense. I, being the head of the Sunni Endowment organization in Anbar, I say, and I declare it to everyone everywhere. And I would like to tell you, there are very few, and soon enough we will be rid of them. It is a dark spot in a bright room.

And, you know what? We can say frankly that there are some Christians who destroy the Christian religion also. There are very few of them, but they do exist. It's not only in Islam, but even in Christianity, though not the slaughter. Many sects pretend to be religious, but their aim is to kill people.

I said what I said, and I ask God for forgiveness. I wish success for everyone. I thank you for this meeting. And I'm ready and able and willing to start writing history as it is. History will record the bad deeds of the people who did evil. And good words will be written for those who are good people.

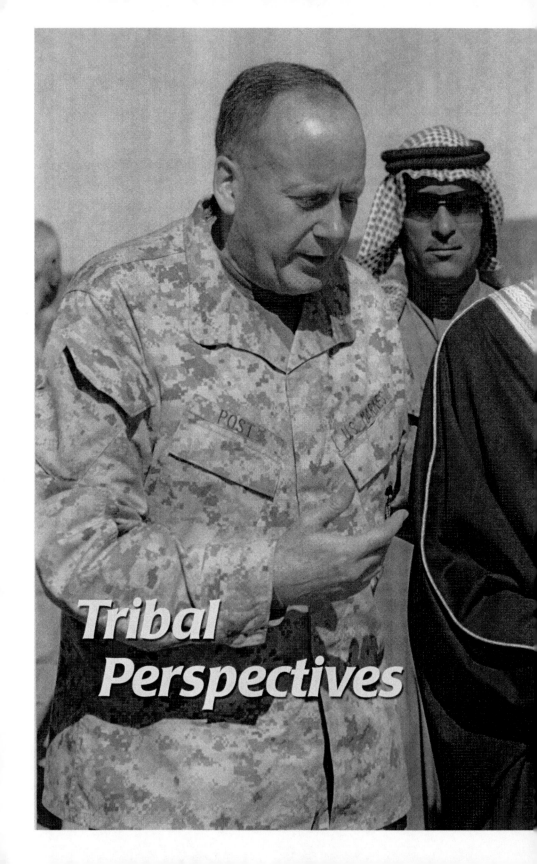

Tribal Perspectives

Interview 3

Sheikh Ahmad Bezia Fteikhan al-Rishawi

Paramount Sheikh, Albu Risha Tribe
President of Mutammar Sahwat al-Iraq
(Iraqi Awakening Party)

Sheikh Ahmad Bezia Fteikhan al-Rishawi is a brother of the late Sheikh Abdul Sattar Abu Risha, who was the founder and iconic leader of the Anbar Awakening Council. After his brother's assassination, he was elected to succeed him as paramount sheikh and president of the council. He was interviewed in his home in Ramadi, adjacent to the guesthouse where the Awakening was announced, by Colonel Gary W. Montgomery and Chief Warrant Officer-4 Timothy S. McWilliams.

Sheikh Ahmad Bezia Fteikhan al-Rishawi: We took the Iraqi commander to the American forces at K-160 [kilometer marker 160 on the highway], and we told them he was ready to talk. They said, "Bring him forth." Sheikh Khamis* wanted a guarantee from the American forces that if he brought the Iraqi commander, he would not be apprehended. They said, "No," and that was a promise. Sheikh Mohammed went along with them to K-160. Brigadier General Ahmed Sadag also went. They signed a peace treaty—no need for fighting—and he promised them he would discharge his soldiers. So the American forces entered Anbar with no fighting. That was 2003. A government was established in Anbar with the support of the American forces. Basic services, and everything else, were excellent.

Some people started inciting people to fight the Americans. They described those among us who cooperated with the Americans as stooges, and they gained a lot of popularity. They marshaled the people against us, so we left them. Right then and there, they started attacking the government of Iraq, the Iraqi police, and the American forces. And then, at that time, al-Qaeda came in. And that resistance, the foreign Arabs, the emirs, came in place.

---

* Possibly Sheikh Khamis Hasnawi al-Issawi, paramount sheikh of the Albu Issa tribe.

They killed a lot of personnel from the police. They destroyed the Iraqi army. They destroyed the infrastructure of the country. They attacked schools. They attacked university professors. They forbade involvement in any political dialogue. The situation became unbearable. The sheikhs and the brains left the province—professors, teachers, and doctors—they all went to Jordan and Syria. Al-Qaeda roved the country. We set up security forces around our compounds, and we stayed here. We did not migrate. They started lobbing mortar rounds on us in order to make us run away. We did not. We kept being friends with the Americans.

Infrastructure services were really bad. Education and health care were bad. Al-Qaeda took over the Ramadi hospital, the Department of Education, the university, the oil infrastructure, and they were the rulers. The governor of Anbar was protected by the American forces. Not many people stayed with him, except a few accountants who were working on the budget. Some of the budget was going to finance al-Qaeda via some contracts or projects. It wasn't given directly to al-Qaeda; it was channeled to them in various ways.

We realized that the people had had it with the situation. People started murmuring, saying that if we had obeyed the people who started work in 2003, the situation would not have deteriorated to this point. So they started the blame game, due to the losses that were inflicted among their ranks and their tribesmen. So Sheikh [Abdul] Sattar [Abu Risha] and I, we started thinking that we've got to get in touch with the tribal sheikhs and their cousins, the ones who were active, so we could incite them to fight al-Qaeda.

Sheikh Sattar told me, "Leave it to me. I'll take care of it." So he started moving, talking with the tribal sheikhs, one by one. He told them that he was ready to do something, and he gathered them for a conference on the 14th of September 2006. A communiqué was issued, containing 11 points:

First, to bring back the army in Anbar and to bring the tribal sons into the police and army.

Second, to declare war on al-Qaeda—and he described them as thugs and criminals.

To bring back the respect that is due to the tribal sheikhs.

The American forces were to be considered friendly, and attacking them was forbidden. That was the first conference ever held in Iraq with the American forces to be considered friendly.

To treat the Ba'athists humanely.

And no cooperation or negotiation with al-Qaeda.

To reopen the judiciary, and to bring the criminals before the law.

To be presented as government officials, as people who follow the law, and not as militias.

To enter the political system, and to enter into dialogue on a large scale, and to participate in the election.

These were the most prominent points that were announced at the conference.

Also, getting in touch with the Iraqi central government will be considered as reconciliation. And the formation of a council, which was called the Anbar Salvation Council, to take the place of the provincial pouncil that ran away to Syria. The central government refused that request, but they put eight people from the Salvation Council into the provincial council.

The central government agreed to let the people of Anbar enroll in the army and the police. The war on al-Qaeda started right then, and we began to take their men before the law. The American forces started organizing the police by taking their applications, screening them, training them, and, whenever we had a ready force, we established a police station with them. American forces helped us with training, with salaries, with transporting salaries, and with arming the police.

The war against al-Qaeda was waged first in Ramadi, and then in every other tribal area. Whenever we cleared a tribal area of al-Qaeda, we set up a police station. We elected a representative company from every area. We took these people, and we went to the city of Ramadi, and we attacked in Ramadi. That's how we liberated Ramadi. Tamim was also liberated. Malab was liberated. Albu Fayed was liberated. Tajiria, Khalidiyah, Amariyah, Fallujah, Saqlawiyah, Karma, Jazeera, the outskirts of Hit, Albu Issa. The city of Hit proper was liberated. Baghdadi city was liberated. The city of Haditha and all the adjacent territories, Rawah territory, Ana. Al-Qaim was liberated by the Albu Mahal tribe. They started before the inception of the Awakening. Al-Qaeda started a fight with them, so they counterattacked with their sons, and they were able to liberate their area.

We opened a new page with the tribes in the south. After the fight with al-Qaeda and the victory against them, we renounced sectarian violence, so we invited tribal sheikhs from the south to Anbar. There was a dispute among the Shiites and Sunnis, and we wanted to alleviate that. We wanted to cooperate with them as one people, as Muslims.

We opened up the highway. We put many checkpoints on the highway. Those people who were intercepting travelers—the criminals—we started fighting them, and we detained many of them and put them before the law. As you see, the highway right now is the most secure road in all of Iraq.

Tharthar, which contained many mass graves—the Tharthar area was attacked by the emergency response units. It was liberated. The Samarra road.

Al-Qaeda was broken, with the help of God, and they will not be able to conduct any military operations. You hear, now and then, about VBIEDs [vehicle-borne improvised explosive devices] or someone committing suicide. This is the choice that we gave them: you can either surrender to us or you can be suicided. They despaired of accomplishing any victories, so now they resort to suicide.

The organization concentrated on my brother, peace be upon him. They conducted 12 suicide attacks against him. The twelfth operation finally hit him exactly a year after the inception conference.

We changed the Awakening into a political entity. We became a political movement. We brought in people with high degrees: tribal sheikhs and their sons and relatives, tribal sons from the educated people who are able to lead, and we concentrated on them being clean and capable. We waged a campaign for the election, and we achieved significant progress. We encouraged the people to go and cast their votes. We encouraged the people to go and participate. We emphasized to them that their vote was very important and crucial at that juncture. We encouraged them for change. We obtained very good results in the election. We surpassed all the parties that used to be dominant. We overcame them. After the election results are announced, we will form alliances with the people that garnered enough votes to have a majority and form a government. This is the Awakening. . . .

I used to pay salaries to the police, who did not receive a salary for four months. Uniforms were imported from Jordan. I did not want them to look like militias by wearing civilian clothes. I wanted them to look official. We were careful not to conduct any military operations in civilian clothes, only in military uniforms. The martyrs who fell in battle, we used to go to their funerals and help their families monetarily. Weapons were short. We didn't have enough weapons, so we had to purchase what we could. These expenditures came out of our own pockets. At the time, we did not receive any support from the government of Iraq or the American forces.

Colonel Gary W. Montgomery: Where was the conference where they came up with the 11 points? What was the location?

Ahmad: At this house, right here.

Montgomery: So in this building we were just in. And I understand all of the tribes freed their own areas, their own tribal areas, but it happened in succession. Once a tribal area was free, did that tribe go to help another tribe, and so forth, or did they just each separately clear their own areas?

Ahmad: No, they elicited the help of other clansmen, from other tribes. But once they liberated a place, they left people from that tribe to be policemen in that police station.

Montgomery: So they did both. They protected their own area and also . . .

Ahmad: And helped other tribes. When we went out there, and we inquired about who was in al-Qaeda, we got a lot of help from the tribe's people in the area.

Montgomery: When they met with the Shi'a to get rid of their differences, who did they meet with? What was that like?

Ahmad: With many other sheikhs, al-Zargan sheikhs, al-Fetna sheikhs. They wanted to keep Iraq united, and they wanted to avert any internal conflict. It was a successful meeting.

Montgomery: Was that here, also?

Ahmad: At the guesthouse. No one was willing or able to undertake such an endeavor, to fight al-Qaeda in Anbar. No one was even willing to stand before the television camera and announce that he would fight al-Qaeda. We announced, right from this house, an open war against al-Qaeda, right on TV.

The organization got wind of it. They were right there. They had many weapons. They lobbed a lot of mortar rounds on us to get us to back off, but we never did. We never wavered.

Unknown: What actions did he think could have been done differently in the very beginning to possibly start this sooner? Was there anything either the Coalition forces, or the chiefs, or even the local government could have done to possibly get this going sooner?

Ahmad: As the American forces, per se, you could not have done anything. I'll give an example. If a contractor took money from you to build a school, he was killed because he was a collaborator. He says, "Look, please, look, I built a school." They said, "Yes, but you took money from the Americans," so they killed him. Therefore you all would have been very limited, if not at all.

As for us, we were able to convince the people that the situation was dire, and we needed to rise up against al-Qaeda and live like normal people, like advanced people. When we used to meet with the tribal sheikhs, we asked them—we lectured them, "Look, when are you going to have a normal life? When are you going to be able to get your dues from the government? When are you going to be able to send your children to school? When are you going to live a normal life, when these thugs are in charge? These people are wearing masks. They cannot build the country. People that can build government and sustain it are the police and the army. You cannot get your rights if you have no police and no army to protect you."

Unknown: You said that the Coalition forces had a hard time distinguishing, sometimes, between the Iraqis and al-Qaeda. How easy is it for you to distinguish? Are they still hiding out here, or have they left?

Ahmad: It is very easy for us to distinguish, and there are no foreign Arabs here now. It is hard for you to even distinguish between the guilty and the innocent, but we know them by their faces. This is a criminal, this is not. Some of the mistakes you made were in Bucca prison. It was better to have referred those criminals to the Iraqi justice system than to Bucca, because they started having a school, and they indoctrinated other detainees.

Interview 4

Sheikh Wissam Abd al-Ibrahim al-Hardan al-Aethawi

*Former First Deputy
Sahawa al-Anbar/Sahawa al-Iraq
Current President of Iraqi Popular Front*

Sheikh Wissam Abd al-Ibrahim al-Hardan al-Aethawi is a member of the al-Hardan clan, which is the paramount family of the Aethawi tribe and among the most respected families in al-Anbar and Salah ad-Din provinces. He was a member of the Tribal Affairs Council and among the founding members of the Anbar Salvation Council. He is not influential by way of a large following; rather, because he is from a very prominent family, he knows many important people and knows the background of many important people and significant events.

Sheikh Wissam was interviewed by Colonel Gary W. Montgomery and Chief Warrant Officer-4 Timothy S. McWilliams on 15 February 2009 at Camp Ramadi.

Sheikh Wissam Abd al-Ibrahim al-Hardan al-Aethawi: After too many killings had taken place, to the Iraqis . . . the nationalists rose up. I was the head of that movement. We gathered about 500 army officers from the last army, and we rose in 2005. I went to Sa'doun al-Dulaimi. He was the defense minister at the time. He was my relative. I asked him to give the fighters permission to carry arms. I was not successful in that endeavor. We could not get government's permission for them to carry arms.

Most of the officers left the country because they were subject to being eliminated. They were traced, and they were killed by the terrorists, many of them were. One of their leaders, Muhammad Ishmael al-Jabawi, was eliminated. He was from the previous Iraqi army. He was a leader in the national resistance. A general in the air force, Waji, was also killed. My brother, Mohir al-Hardan, who was a judge, was also killed. He was a deputy to the governor. Sheikh Naser [Abdul Karim al-Miklif] was also killed. Sheikh Jai

Tehan Abu Risha was also killed, and many more notables— nationalists who would serve the country—were eliminated.

Colonel Gary W. Montgomery: These were all outside the country?

Wissam: No, inside the country.

Montgomery: Inside the country?

Wissam: So those who remained immediately left the country.

Montgomery: Right, okay.

Wissam: The militias also had a role in making people flee the country, based on sectarian divide. Some people were displaced. So the last of the national resistance movement that I envisioned was left with very few people. You could count them on your hands.

I don't want to make the story too long, because if I am to talk about the Awakening and its history, it would take months. Sheikh [Abdul] Sattar [Abu Risha] called me by phone. He said, "Please, I want you to come to Anbar." I was living in a village. The name of the village was al-Mish Haniyah. That's where my grandfather lived. It's about 70 kilometers from here. I asked what he had in mind. He said there was a conference about to take place in Amman, and I told him I did not wish to attend any conferences, because they are to no avail. He insisted that I attend, or more likely, he pleaded with me. His cousin is my wife, so he kind of pressured me into attending. Sa'ad Hamid al-Douish, his cousin, also was martyred. His mother is also from the same family, the Tehan family. I brought Ali with me to Anbar.

When he saw me, when he laid his eyes on me at his house, he said, "We are victorious by the God of al-Kaaba." When I asked him what he had in mind, he said, "We have a huge undertaking, and nobody can take care of it, except you." Before he even said hello, which is customary in the Arab world, he started telling me what he had in mind. He said, "I want to fight al-Qaeda."

I said, "How many do you have?"

He said, "I have 7,000."

I knew for a fact he had maybe 70, not 7,000, but I told him, "Your 70 would be considered as 7,000."

So all night long, we sat down, and we were planning and plotting for this huge revolution we're about to undertake. My plan was as follows. The first phase of the plan was to start an educational program toward the tribes. The second one, when the people finally saw that I was involved in it, they became courageous.

It was hard for the tribal people to come into Abu Risha's compound because he was considered an agent of the Americans. When I sent for groups to come in, a lot of times, out of four you may get two killed on the road. That's because too many terrorists were about on the road looking for people that would cooperate with us, and they would eliminate them. The difficult places, both topography-wise and infested with terrorists, were Albu Aetha, Albu Faraj, Albu Beit, and Albu Bali.

I planned to make a nucleus of 50 men in each tribe. Those 50 men would be ready after we went to the conference in Jordan and announced the revolution against the terrorists. They would be ready to move right then.

Okay, this meeting started with me and him in the evening. It ended up in the morning with 10 more people. The notables would be Hamid al-Hayess, Shalan Nouri, Jabar Ajaj, Muriad Maieshi, Abdul Sattar, and a name I cannot recall. He is from the Albu Gharraf tribe. Sheikh Fara Sabar Deri from the Ghali tribe, and Sheikh Khalid Araq.

After the killing of Sheikh Khalid Araq al-Ataymi, who is from the Albu Aligasim tribe—they severed his head, they left him out in the open. His head may have never been recovered. We used that as a pretense to start the revolution. This guy was killed merely because he wanted to start a revolution, even though he had not even begun it. He wanted to start fighting terrorism. The name of his organization would be Anbar's Revolutionaries. We used his tribe under the pretext of vengeance. We elicited his tribe to help us. Their tribe also, because it is a part of Albu Aetha, wanted to do something, but they are not politically savvy. They do not have the political will, but we elicited their help nevertheless.

So Sheikh Sattar provided me with an office, with a computer, with papers to write on. His brother, Sheikh Ahmad, who was living in Dubai, wired me $5,000. At the time, Sheikh Ahmad was not known. And I started putting the group together for the revolution against al-Qaeda. Sheikh Ahmad was asking me to stay with Sheikh Sattar, because he did not have staying power, and if I left, he would be hanged.

The first people I tried to get were the religious clerics. I implored them that there was no sanctity left for travelers or for anybody else. Notable among them were Abdul Malik al-Saidi and Ahmed Al-Kubaisi. I exhorted them to Islamic principles. The second people I tried to get help from were the tribal sheikhs. Through the Internet, we got a fatwa to start the fight against terrorism.

The commander of the American forces at the time was constantly in touch with Sheikh Sattar Abu Risha, but I didn't meet them. The most important part was to finish off terrorism so that people would become free again, regardless of who we cooperated with.

So we started preparing for that conference we spoke of, and we let it be known that 90 percent of the tribal sheikhs were in Jordan. From over there, from abroad, we faced stiff resistance to the initiation of a counterterrorism undertaking. They accused us of trying to take over the tribes, trying to be sheikhs. They said, "You are not sheikhs. You cannot do this. You cannot do that." They mocked us. They said, "You're trying to take on al-Qaeda—the ones who fought America?" They laughed at us. They said, "You people are simple-minded. You cannot do what you think you're going to do."

Montgomery: Who told them this?

Interpreter: The sheikhs, the 90 percent of sheikhs that were living in Amman. Do you want me to ask him that? That's what he just told me.

Montgomery: No, if that's what he said. I just missed a word.

Interpreter: The sheikhs, the tribal sheikhs who were living in Amman, who were scolding them that he tried to take our place. They said, "How are you trying to fight al-Qaeda? And besides, you're not even real sheikhs. We are the sheikhs. You're trying to use our place. You're trying to pretend to be us."

Montgomery: No, I missed the word Amman.

Wissam: Even in Syria, even in Jordan and Egypt.

The Marine commander at the time pledged his support to the undertaking.

Montgomery: Does he remember his name?

Wissam: The 14th of September 2006, if you look at that date, you'll find his name.* There was a common interest between us and them, and that is security for all. I asked the commander at the time to help us by removing the concrete barriers, because they sectioned Ramadi into too many places. So he immediately said, "Yes, I will give you fuel, water, rations, remove the barriers." He said, "This would be a good step forward, the people will find out we are here to help them, not to harm them as the terrorists have done in the past."

What I'm speaking of at this time is the day before the conference. On the eve of that conference, a civilian vehicle came to Sheikh Abdul Sattar's. I think it was from the CIA [Central Intelligence Agency]. I was not able to meet with them. After the meeting, he informed me of all that went on because it was his habit to inform me of everything. He told me, "This is the speech that we have to give," and as I understood, the speech was from President [George W.] Bush. These are secrets that nobody is privy to except me and Sattar.

I was able to read the speech. Sheikh Sattar was not able to read it because he was illiterate. He did not finish school. And I told him, "If you read it at the conference, you will be laughed at, because this translation is verbatim, and they can tell this is not our writing. It is American writing." I changed quite a bit in the speech that we received from President Bush. The substance of the speech was left intact, but I changed the wording to grammatically correct Arabic that would be easily understood by the participants of my conference. Had it been left the way it was, there would have been a misunderstanding.

---

* Major General Richard C. Zilmer was commander of I Marine Expeditionary Force (Forward) at the time.

On 14 September 2006 we started.

Interpreter: And he did say a while ago, the speech contained something about the rebuilding of Iraq and pulling the troops out.

Wissam: We readied the place for the conference I'm speaking of. There were no television stations present at the time, so we brought a very simple camera to the conference. In that conference, we made a committee, which I personally called the Awakening and the Anbar Salvation Council. We chose 41 people to represent the governing council for Anbar, which was not present at the time. Sheikh Sattar was chosen as governor, and I was his administrative deputy. Sheikh Hamid al-Hayess was the head of the Salvation Council. Many more names are documented.

Here the political phase started. How do we implement the decision? The tribes began fighting, each one in its own territory. Each tribe knew who was a terrorist, so he was either killed, given to the government, to the police, banished, whatever. I admonished them not to kill as al-Qaeda was killing because if that was the case, then we'd never see the light of day; meaning give them to the law. Let the law take care of them. Most of the people in the Awakening did not have political savvy. They did not know the law. They did not have political awareness, and I warned them that should they kill anybody, they might end up in detention centers. [conversation with interpreter]

Interpreter: The Awakening started in Jazeera, in all these places he mentioned, except Albu Beid and Albu Bali. He mentioned Albu Aetha, Albu Diyad, Albu Faraj. Okay, Albu Faraj was the first to raise the surrender flag, so Albu Bali and Albu Baid—Albu Aetha, Albu Bali. Okay, so those are four places: Albu Aetha, Albu Beid, Albu Bali, and Garban.

Montgomery: And those are where the bad guys surrendered?

Interpreter: No, the bad guys surrendered in Albu Faraj.

Wissam: In Sufiyah and Street 17, the terrorists were entrenched. They were killing in the street. No man could raise his head. One day, when we were meeting, Sheikh Jassim Suwadawi from Albu

Soda—and there was another person with him, who came from Shamiyah—they came in, and they pledged their allegiance to the Awakening, and they asked for help. We gave him very simple assistance, a few rifles. Why? Because we were not helped by the army, by the government, or by the Americans. We were simply that involved, and we were told, "The enemy is behind you, and the sea is in front of you."

Interpreter: Meaning "between a rock and a hard place."

Wissam: The first cell was constituted to fight in Shamiyah with the leadership of Jassim [Muhammad Saleh] al-Suwadawi. I was called "the engineer of the Awakening." As far as Sheikh Jassim al-Suwadawi is concerned, believe me, he has many chapters. I lived them. He got involved in many battles with me. He had a great role, and he will never be given his just dues.

Now we come to the Americans' role. Now we come to the promises that were made by the American commander, as far as lifting the barriers, giving out fuel, kerosene, gasoline, what have you. We got in touch with Baghdad, specifically with Methal al-Alousi. We had no way of communicating with the prime minister. Methal al-Alousi was a friend of mine. We told him what we were undertaking. And he said, "You are heroes. Tomorrow I'm getting my bags, and I'm coming to join you."

We got a date to meet with the prime minister, [Nouri Kamil Mohammed Hasan al-] Maliki. The political entities started pressuring the American commanders in Anbar not to help us. We met with al-Maliki, and a verbal confrontation ensued, and we threatened him. If we were not given any assistance from them, we were going to push the terrorists into their territory, close the borders, and let them worry about the terrorists. Mowaffak al-Rubaie, the national security advisor, was writing, and he never said a word. But two days later he came on television and said, "Men of Anbar, we are supplying you with men and materiel."

When the people got wind of the fact that the government was about to help us out with men and materiel—meaning guns—they said immediately that we sold out to the government. Now we're lining our pockets, we're taking ammo and not giving it to the people. We're taking weapons and not giving them to the people, meaning the revolution is not genuine anymore, meaning his speech was full of landmines.

I got in touch with Methal al-Alousi. I said, "Okay, when are you coming? Bring your bags and come join us."

He said, "Look, we were told by President Bush, 'Whoever goes to the governor's office is to be shot.'"

I asked, "Why?" The political entities in Baghdad understood our Awakening to be against them, and that we were about to go into Baghdad and take care of them. So there was pressure from these political entities on the ambassador, and the ambassador on Bush, and back.

We came back, and the American commander at the time in Anbar had switched his thinking 180 degrees. I asked him about his pledge to help us. He said, "Look, I cannot help you. As far as Jazeera goes, I'm not going to help you with logistics, or weapons, or what have you." As for the governor's office, he said, "Do not advance against it."

Interpreter: I think I'm misunderstanding, because he said there is no help coming through for Jazeera. Do you want me to ask for that again, because he's saying now that "six months later we were able to liberate the governor's office in Ramadi."

Montgomery: Yes, make sure you're understanding.

Wissam: [Conversation with interpreter.] These were his instructions. You can go ahead and fight in al-Jazeera, but if we find any terrorist weapons, he would take them himself and not assist us with any kind of weapons.

The one thing that you have to understand is that the Americans were not sure of the loyalty of the Awakening people because the people that were working with the Americans told them, "These men are just wearing masks. They're going to turn against you, and they're going to kill you." It is a fact that some of the police were members of al-Qaeda.

Everything was confused in the meantime, except the determination of the Awakening people. Many problems ensued between the Awakening and the Islamic Party, so the American command suggested a meeting between us and them. The Islamic Party became wary of the Awakening. . . .

It's a long history, and it cannot be recalled in one hour. I went to al-Rashid. There was a conference there, and they said, "Here comes the engineer of the Awakening." So all the television reporters came and gathered around me because they were trying to make a documentary on the Awakening.

As I said, they suggested that we meet with the Islamic Party representative, along with the American command. Sa'doun Dulaimi, who was not at the Ministry of Defense at the time, advised me not to enter the meeting. I asked him why, and he said, "Because those are politicians, and they spin everything. You will never be able to advance an argument with them, because they will overwhelm you."

I told him there was no problem. We'd meet in Fallujah. The meeting was between me, Sattar Abu Risha, the governor, and his deputy. They took us from here via helicopter. . . . We didn't know what the future held. Are these guys going to dump us somewhere? I'm being frank. Sheikh Sattar was sitting right next to me. He said, "Look, any moment, these guys are going to push us out of the plane, because these guys like the governor." In the helicopter, with our garb, and the wind was flowing violently, so we were disheveled, but when we got to Fallujah, [Major General Richard C.] Zilmer greeted us. He had a complete team from the American embassy.

I had written down in a small booklet 24 points on Mamoun [Sami Rashid al-Alwani], who was the governor. Sattar asked me, "What am I to say?" I said, "Just start anything, and I will take over." That is because he was the head of the Awakening, and I was his deputy. He went in, and he said, "Greetings my brother, and this is Sheikh al-Hardan, and he will inform you about everything."

The discussion was bitter and sorrowful. When I confronted Mamoun with the 24 points I had laid out, he said, "Should I answer?" I said, "No, you answer one after the other." I said, "Write down one by one, and then answer." He said, "I don't have a pen." I said, "Your deputy has a pen."... When his deputy said, "I don't have a pen, either," I told Commander Zilmer, "Look, this is a very hot province, and this man is incapable of defending himself or carrying a pen. How can we leave him to be a governor?" It was the knockout punch to Mamoun. He came to me, and he pleaded with me to be his friend.

Zilmer suggested we form two committees to govern—five people from the Awakening and five people from the Islamic Party. After that, we kissed and made up, and we took pictures, and Zilmer went home. But then Mamoun abrogated the agreement. They started a division between me and Sheikh Sattar through his brother, Sheikh Ahmad, who was the closest to the Islamic Party, which led me to stay away from Sheikh Sattar for three months. From that day on, the Awakening was either infiltrated or sold—however you want to characterize it—and it ended with the killing of Sheikh Sattar.

These are the highlights, and there are a lot more. I was involved in a battle against al-Qaeda. The Americans helped me with it. So there is a lot more to be said, but I'm going to tell you when the film is over, so you're not recording.

Interview 5

Sheikh Jassim Muhammad Saleh al-Suwadawi

Contesting Sheikh of the Albu Soda Tribe
President of the Sufiya Awakening Council

Sheikh Abdul Rahman al-Janabi

Member of the Awakening

Sheikh Jassim Muhammad Saleh al-Suwadawi served as a warrant officer in the Iraqi air force for 30 years. He was an ordnance expert who specialized in armaments for MiG-23 and MiG-29 aircraft. After the true, lineal sheikh of the Albu Soda tribe fled the country, Jassim became the de facto head of the tribe, primarily because of his actions during and after the battle of Sufiyah.

Sheikh Abdul Rahman al-Janabi is a kinsman and a member of the adjacent Albu Mahal tribe. He served as a company-grade officer in Iraqi special forces during the Iran-Iraq War and was wounded twice. After leaving military service in 1991, he was recalled to the army and served as a company commander from 2001 to 2003.

Sheikh Jassim and Sheikh Abdul Rahman worked closely together before, during, and after the battle of Sufiyah. In the first interview, they provide an overview of events leading up to the battle, the battle generally, and subsequent developments. In the second interview, they give detailed descriptions of tactics and techniques employed during the battle and subsequent operations.

Estimates vary widely as to how many al-Qaeda fighters attacked the Albu Soda tribe on 25 November 2006. Coalition estimates are much lower than those of the men who were actually under fire, but all agree that Sheikh Jassim and Sheikh Abdul Rahman were heavily outnumbered.

Sheikh Jassim and Sheikh Abdul Rahman were interviewed by Colonel Gary W. Montgomery and Chief Warrant Officer-4 Timothy S. McWilliams on 12 and 20 February 2009 in the Albu Soda tribal area east of Ramadi city.

Sheikh Jassim Muhammad Saleh al-Suwadawi: After the disbanding of the Iraqi army and some other ministries, I had nothing to do. I had no job. I tried to help the Coalition forces, but it was difficult.

On 5 November 2003, I met a guy named Ayham al-Samarie to coordinate activities with the Coalition forces. He was the electricity minister. It was difficult to meet as frequently as I wanted due to the inherent danger of traveling to Baghdad and terrorism being rampant. I tried to elicit the help of the government of Iraq and Coalition forces through Ayham al-Samarie, and I tried to establish a covert chain of command. We gave periodic reports to Coalition forces and to the Iraqi government from November 2003 until September 2006.

On 28 September 2006, one of my brothers and three of my tribesmen were kidnapped. Then I declared open hostilities against the terrorists, and I established checkpoints in my territory.

I'm a member of the Tribes Council in Iraq. In September 2006, I had only 17 people fighting with me, so I got in touch with Sheikh Sattar Abu Risha and Hamid al-Hayess to get their help. I did not resort to them because I was defeated. No, I wanted to get permission to carry arms in my own territory. I met with General [Richard C.] Zilmer at the time. I met with Lieutenant Colonel [James] Lechner [USA]. I tried to get the help of Coalition forces. I tried to get better arms for my men, but there was somewhat of a mistrust in the Coalition forces to my aim because they thought it was foolish for 17 men to try and take on the entire terrorist apparatus around here.

The way I got through to Sheikh Abdul Sattar and Sheikh Hamid al-Hayess, I used to swim the river to get there safely, and come back by swimming the river. The distance was about 200 or 300 meters. It was very tiring, and one time I almost drowned, but, with the grace of God, I survived. I resorted to swimming the river because the place was infested with terrorists, even inside my tribe. They tried to kill me several times. They set up a lot of ambushes around the river to try to catch me and dispose of me.

The first thing I ever got from General Zilmer and General Murthi [Mishin Rafa Farahan], the commander of the Iraqi Army 7th Division, was a handwritten note saying it was okay for me to cross the river using a boat. . . . There was a combined American and Iraqi army checkpoint on the other side. That's why I wanted that authorization, so I could show it to them. That paper was dated 28 October 2006. . . .

On 20 November 2006, Coalition forces came in at night and arrested my men who were manning the checkpoints. There was no coordination between me and Battalion 1-9 of the Army. They didn't have prior knowledge that I had set up checkpoints to prevent the terrorists from lobbing mortars on them. My brothers and my cousins pleaded with the Americans that "we are here because Sheikh Abdul Sattar, Sheikh Hamid al-Hayess, and Sheikh Jassim put us in here. They need us in here to fight terrorists." They still handcuffed them and brought them in to meet with me.

Interpreter: He did say "with the permission of Lieutenant Colonel Lechner," too, that they were in there.

Jassim: The last thing I did, I sold my last cow to purchase a Thuraya phone to get in touch with Sheikh Abdul Sattar and Sheikh Hamid al-Hayess to coordinate with them. After they verified with Sheikh Abdul Sattar, Lieutenant Colonel Lechner, and Sheikh Hamid al-Hayess, they said, "Okay, you're okay." So they untied their hands and let them continue.

On the 24th of November, I negotiated with some of the chieftains in al-Qaeda to try to avert mayhem. It's because I squeezed them. I prevented them from accomplishing their missions because I set up the checkpoints, and I prevented them from going about in my territory. So they wanted to defuse the situation and try to convince me to let them do what they wanted to do. . . . They negotiated with me to lay down my arms, and they offered me as much as 1 billion Iraqi dinars.

At the time, they had already decided beforehand that if I couldn't turn an agreement with them right then and there, they would kidnap me and do away with me. They had prepared 17 vehicles loaded with men and weapons to kidnap me. The meeting took place at Sheikh Hamid Jabour's house. I wanted to delay the confrontation with them to a later time when I could better equip myself with men and materiel, but I kind of sensed they were up to no good. I had five armed men with me, and we pulled out of the meeting.

We wanted to renegotiate in a week so as to reassess our situation and to avert conflict. But at the same time, one of the Albu Mahal tribe was assassinated—which is adjacent to me—by al-Qaeda. The Albu Mahal are my cousins. They are my children's uncles. They are relatives.

I went back and reproached them. I said, "Look, you've opened another wound. You've just killed one of my tribesmen from Albu Mahal. We've just agreed that there will be no killing. Therefore, no agreement, no peace with you, period."

The next day, 25 November 2006, there was a huge attack by 850 armed men, armed with all kinds of weapons, from al-Qaeda and some other militia groups. They lobbed between 62 and 67 mortar rounds on my tribe that day. Afterward, they came in with their light machine guns. We fought back with the 17 men that I had. I suffered seven casualties, which I considered to be my brothers, but they were my tribesmen. And we killed more than 90 people from al-Qaeda. Among my tribesmen, I suffered 10 more casualties, consisting of women, older people, children—innocent people. The terrorists came into their houses and just slaughtered them.

The battle took place from 1:00 in the afternoon until 9:00 at night. We exhausted our ammunition. They were able to penetrate my house and my brother's house and burn them to the ground with all the furniture in them. They burned 11 vehicles that belonged to me and my brothers. At 10:00 at night, Coalition forces intervened, 1-9 Battalion.

We were able, with Coalition forces, with the Iraqi army, with my men—they were called Jassim's Militia at the time—to raid the places where the terrorists were concentrating. We were able to capture quite a few terrorists, and from interrogating them, we were able to get a lot more. Some of them I turned over to Coalition forces; some of them I turned over to the Iraqi justice system.

When Lieutenant Colonel [Charles] Ferry [USA] found out that I could confront the terrorists, he had enough trust in me, and I gave him prior knowledge as to where my target was. He started assisting me. Through that, I was able to clear the area little by little.

Colonel Gary W. Montgomery: When you're outnumbered so very much, how do you fight that many men? What tactics do you use? Were you at a house? What was the battle like?

Jassim: We used rooftops and ground emplacements, and we picked them off. We knew who they were because they were wearing masks. Our faces were open. We used maneuver to our advantage. Whenever we got pushed back, we pulled back. Whenever the force was overwhelming, we pulled back to other secure places until nighttime. And they were more busy picking up their wounded and dead comrades than trying to fight. By nighttime, they were finally convinced it was a lost battle. They were busy picking up their men because they didn't want to be identified. In addition, American jet fighters joined in. With the sound, I guess they got scared.

At 1:30 p.m. I called some security organizations. I told them there's a big fight in my area, but the American infantry did not join in, but the air force did join in late. After the terrorists pulled out, two of their vehicles were burned by the jets. . . .

I started an education program, trying to educate people to the fact that we were a small band of men who defeated a huge number of men. That is because God granted us the victory because we were in the right and the terrorists were in the wrong. So I was able to bring in many people on my side. Eastern Ramadi has about 12 tribes. Within three months, I was able to enlist many of these tribes into the police fold.

Sheikh Abdul Sattar asked me to gather the tribal sheikhs on 22 February, along with Colonel [John W.] Charlton [USA], and Abdullah [Muhammad] Badir, of the 1st [Iraqi] Division. I must try and praise him. There is a lot of praise for him because he participated in helping me establishing security in this area. . . .

In March of 2007, we started to change the tone of things from combat to providing infrastructure services to the people. So we started a council like the al-Jazeera council, and we nominated four people from each tribe. From 44, I was able to garner 41 in the council. Through that council, and with the help of Coalition forces, we were able to provide the people with many services. Through that initiative, we were able to provide the people with drinking water, with many services, and with jobs, because the area had been neglected since 2004. Through the Coalition forces, I was able to get enough projects going, such as pumping stations, paving roads, repairing and refurbishing schools, clinics, building schools. We were able to put people to work. We were able to put engineers to work . . . to repair the electricity and water. . . .

And now I will turn it over to Sheikh Abdul Rahman. He will give you the highlights. I really have done a disservice, because I didn't even mention his name, even though he really is one of the heroes that I depended on in the fight. . . .

Sheikh Abdul Rahman al-Janabi: On 17 September 2003, to be exact, Brigadier General Ibrahim Sijil Said, my uncle, got in touch with me. We used to work internal security in the former regime. Later, he was kidnapped by al-Qaeda, along with his son and my other cousin, and got killed. He wanted me to help him due to my extensive contacts with other tribes in the middle of Anbar, and in order to not let the Iranians penetrate into Anbar or Iraq as a whole. I agreed with him, and he told me there were some people in Baghdad who would support us. After he got their agreement, I went to Baghdad, and we met with them. (I don't want to mention who those people were.) We agreed to cooperate with them, and we formed a cell. We called it the Eagles Cell, and both I and my brother, Sheikh Jassim, belonged to it. From that point, we started our work, and we expanded it, providing the security apparatus with information about the terrorists. And that was 5 November 2003.

February 2004, the martyr Fatha, who also coordinated and cooperated with us; he used to carry my Thuraya phone because I couldn't bring it to Ramadi, and the GPS [global positioning system], he used to keep it for me, too. He was killed right in front of his house in 2004 in al-Dour by a terrorist squad. From then on, we worked with great caution and excluded any unit that had an Iraqi interpreter.

We still suspect that those interpreters are the ones who related information about us to the terrorists. One of the mistakes that Coalition forces made was using local interpreters instead of bringing interpreters from the United States. And we tried to alert them to the fact that those interpreters were duplicitous.

We worked until the ominous day of 29 April 2004. I call it ominous because my brother and three of his children were kidnapped that day. He was kidnapped on his way to Baghdad by a cell headed by Omar Hadid in Fallujah.

To tell you the truth, not only al-Qaeda fought us. All the armed militias fought us. They issued fatwas against us, and they sent out a lot of leaflets. That's why our work became very difficult and inherently dangerous for us and our families. Our support was minimal—you could say nonexistent—from our Coalition partners.

Now, not only were we supporting our families from our meager resources, but we were supporting the families of the martyrs who were killed supporting us. Coupled with that, we were not working our regular jobs, because the terrorists did not allow us to live like ordinary people. They fought us, and our resources, and our working areas. . . .

We attempted an uprising against al-Qaeda many times, and I will mention one. It was at the end of 2004, beginning of 2005. I met with the electricity minister of Ayad Allawi's government, Dr. Ayham al-Samarie. He mentioned a tribal uprising against al-Qaeda, and he said that he would provide me with support through Coalition forces in Baghdad. Indeed, we started that endeavor, Sheikh Jassim and me, and we made many contacts in Anbar and Baghdad, and Salah ad Din, Diyala and Kirkuk, in Baghdad, and Latifiya. We were trying to establish a public base to fight terrorism, but because of his frequent travels and lack of knowledge of the support people, and the change of government from Allawi to another government, that project was abandoned. . . .

All along, from 2003 until the uprising, terrorists were constantly picking at the people who got in touch with us, and, as we say, "It reached up to here." When they kidnapped my uncle, Abdul Sattar Sijil—that was the 18th of October, 2004—that's when my fight began with them officially. With the help of Sheikh Jassim Muhammed, I succeeded in saving my uncle from their hands. We wounded one of the people who kidnapped my uncle.

In July or August 2006, they kidnapped my brother. I rescued him and found him between life and death due to the extensive torture that he suffered. After all of that was done to us, Sheikh Jassim and I started gathering information relating to these terrorists and their places, their emplacements, and their arms, until the day that I call the ominous day, when his brother—

Interpreter: He wants to say something. The brother of Sheikh Jassim was kidnapped on that day.

Jassim: There was a general consensus among the people in the street that those people were resistance fighters, so we started a campaign of education that these people, if they are truly resistance fighters, why are they kidnapping our men? So during that, we were able to garner a lot more information about the terrorists.

Abdul Rahman: In that operation, Sheikh Jassim Muhammad had only a pistol, but he was able to save his brother. He fought them with his pistol and wounded one, but they got away.

On 20 November 2006, that's when Sheikh Jassim made the courageous stand in open warfare against them and placing checkpoints all over the place—him, his brothers and his children—despite the objections of some of the tribal chiefs in the area. Those sheikhs were in cahoots with the terrorists.

This movement that Sheikh Jassim started, started the Awakening in eastern Ramadi and the tribes of Ramadi, along to the Abu Risha sector, along to al-Fallujah from the side of Ramadi. . . . He got in touch with Sheikh Abu Risha, God bless him, and he officially provided him with support, and Sheikh Abdul Sattar was in the forefront in giving the blessing for this initiative. He and the tribal sheikhs called him the Lion of Eastern Ramadi, and well deserved.

At the time, al-Qaeda started planning an offensive against the sheikh's tribe. They perpetrated many assassinations of people that were close to him, but he remained steadfast despite all the obstacles and challenges. He spent all of his resources in support of that initiative. He did it so people could live in security and safety.

Again, the offensive began on 25 November 2006. At 1:30 in the afternoon, the criminals started their offensive with probably more than 850 fighters. They started by lobbing more than 67 mortar rounds. But the courageous fighters, despite their low numbers, were able to withstand and thwart the offensive.

At the time, I was at the funeral of a sheikh from the Albu Mahal tribe, Salman Adnan Hallawi. When the fight started, ... my uncle from Albu Mahal tribe came in support. Only six men came with him from the Albu Mahal tribe. I was one of them. Two of them were martyred. And from the fighters that Sheikh Jassim had, there were 17 fighters, and some of them were martyred. From the information we gathered after the battle, the enemy suffered about 90 dead and 170 wounded.

Right then and there, the barrier of fear was broken in all of Ramadi, so open warfare against the terrorists took place. We had a great role in clearing the areas I'm about to mention—Sheikh Jassim and me. The sector from eastern Ramadi to Khalidiyah, al-Jazeera, Albu Beid; al-Jazeera, Abu Ali; wal-Karma; Ibrahim Ibn Ali, which is located east of Karma toward Baghdad. Our fight against the terrorists continued up until now, and right now, we are fighting them in seven provinces.

Second Interview

Jassim: In order to protect my tribesmen from outside terrorists and from internal terrorism within my tribe, I had 17 fighters. I placed points at the entrances of the tribe. Their main objective was to search vehicles coming in and going out.

Two simple attacks took place upon the people that were manning these checkpoints. They lobbed some mortar rounds at the tribal area where we live. This took place about a month before the main battle. And we had skirmishes with small arms between the members of my tribe and the terrorists.

We had small Motorola radios, and that's how we communicated. I had four checkpoints. Each had one radio. At no given time was there less than two to four people manning each checkpoint. They changed shifts day and night. My men carried AK-47s [assault rifles]. Each one had 30 to 40 rounds. One PKC [machine gun]. So for the 17 fighters I had, I had 16 AK-47s and one PKC. They were very vigilant all the time. . . .

The attack began, and they entered the area from three different points. There was no equality in the forces. We had 17 fighters, while they had about 850 fighters on their side. Even in the weaponry, there was no parity, because 850 fighters would carry a lot more than 17, and ammunition as well.

After sunset, some of my men started pulling out from their positions because they ran out of ammunition. Because of my men pulling out, the terrorists were able to penetrate the area. They started killing children, old men, and women. They burned two houses that belonged to me. They killed cattle and sheep. They burned vehicles. Even electric generators—they started shooting at them, and burning them, and destroying them.

I had a Thuraya phone, and I was getting in touch with my men in the field and the American forces as well. The battery ran out in the Thuraya. Coalition forces were able to locate exactly where the battle was taking place through the GPS [global positioning system] in the Thuraya phone. They sent fighter planes to fly over the area. The Coalition forces were asking me for exact locations of the enemy, but when the enemy penetrated my area, everything was intermingled. In military terms, when everything is intermingled, there is no specific target, so the battle is lost. So I told them, if they want to hit the terrorists when they pull back, start hitting them, so we would inflict heavier losses on the enemy than on ours. And indeed, they were able to burn three vehicles after they pulled out, with all the occupants in them, about 15 kilometers from here.

We assessed our losses after 9:00, after the battle. We found that we had 17 martyrs from the men, children, and women, and seven of my fighters were also killed. Those seven were missing, I should say. We couldn't find their bodies. They had tied up their corpses, and they were pulling them behind their vehicles for about 20 kilometers. Five of them were my brothers. They were dragging them.

We found many of the enemies' corpses on the battlefield, even though they had taken many with them. Some of their corpses stayed on the battlefield for about three days. We tried to exchange corpses with the enemy, but it did not take place.

The Iraqi army and the 1-9 [battalion, USA] came into the field at 10:00 at night. They set up positions within the houses of my tribe, so we started raiding the enemy's hiding places, day and night. . . .

Because of my military background—I had 30 years in the military and had studied psychology—I was supervising the interrogations myself. I would send a raiding party for five people. My men would bring me 30. Believe it or not, I put the people in a room like this, the 30 of them. In addition to the information that I had already gathered on them, I knew who was a terrorist and who was not just by studying the expression on their faces. I was accurate most of the time. So the people I let go were honorable people, and they carried arms with me, not against me.

What I used to do with them, I used to gather them in a room like this, and I would make a speech about the evil of terrorism and the destructive nature of it, and after that, they would believe in my cause. After two or three days, they would come back to ask me to let them become policemen. Within a very short period of time, we were able to organize 12 tribes against terrorism, despite the knowledge there were some sleeper cells entering the tribes. . . .

Abdul Rahman: I want to give you an abbreviated synopsis of what happened to the plan. The sheikh, when he laid out the plan in advance, he did not imagine the amount of force that was coming against him. His plan was a defensive one, for a very small force. . . . But because of his dogged determination, with the help of the Almighty, the whole, full-fledged battle took place on his hands.

Some of the men who sympathized with him but could not help him, they helped him a little, either directly or indirectly. I'll give you an example. When al-Qaeda came to attack, they did not expect the Albu Mahal tribe to resist them at all. They thought they would have safe passage, but the Albu Mahal attacked them and sniped at them.

So the plan, as it was set up, was defensive in nature; but as the battle developed, it was spontaneous. The battle itself imposed on us what we had to do. Initially, he relied on his own resources and his cousins' resources, but as the battle developed, he started asking for help from Abu Risha, from Coalition forces, from the Iraqi army.

Montgomery: We say that no plan survives contact with the enemy. You always have to adjust.

Abdul Rahman: Exactly. After the battle, we considered three months to be the golden months, because the battle developed square-by-square, and it was to our advantage. First, we were able to win the people over against al-Qaeda. Through the good people, we were able to educate the people about terrorism and against it. We encouraged the opening of police stations so the law can take hold. Despite the fact that the youth were reluctant to join the police because of fear, our education and our lectures got them into the fold, and we were able to open the first police station. It was named Karameh, which meant "dignity."

After that, smaller battles took place all throughout al-Jazeera. They saw the example of what we had achieved with small means. They rose up, and they helped clear al-Jazeera. I got in touch with Mohiad, Ibrahim, and Ahmed, and through the media I was able to announce that this tribe had joined us and that tribe had joined us. Despite the fact that maybe one or two of the tribe came with me, I said the whole tribe was with me. So people starting enlisting on our side, because they're saying, "Look, the whole tribe's with them." That way, I won them over, and I was able to outwit the al-Qaeda through the media.

After the battle, we did not just lay back and say, "Okay, it's over." We kept gathering intelligence on their cells. We found many a weapons cache, because the terrorists had relied on them—like you see a fighter coming from Diyala to here, his weapons are already here, but we had already confiscated them.

We used the media to our advantage. If we had a 10 percent success, we said it's 90 percent.

Montgomery: Right. Information operations.

Abdul Rahman: Yes. So, you see, when a tribal sheikh started talking about a success, even if only 2 percent was true and 98 percent was false, well, when the terrorist heard it, it's grand, it's big. So they started to flee the area by themselves.

We used the counterattack. Instead of waiting for the enemy to attack again, we pressed the attack on them. When they got confessions from detainees as to the existence of other places, despite the fact that they have no communication gear, no vehicles to travel with, they would conduct four raids a night on these targets.

There was a well-known saying that Sheikh Jassim was going to get a chopping machine that would chop the terrorists to pieces, so everybody knew to avoid Sheikh Jassim. The truth of the matter, everyone was dealt with fairly, either through the Albu Risha, Coalition, or Iraqi army, the government, what have you. But the general consensus was Sheikh Jassim was chopping people up— just to let the terrorists get wind of it and instill fear in their hearts.

After the battle, the sheikh formed a cell to gather intelligence and another unit to raid the terrorists. At the same time, he extended his hand to the central government and established law and order in his territory. He told them, "Look, I am a tribal sheikh, but I cannot be the police. I cannot be the interrogator. I cannot be everybody. Let's divide the jobs, one for each."

After the success of this battle, many a tribesman came in from al-Jazeera and from the surrounding areas, trying to learn from the sheikh's experiences.

One of the misinformation campaigns that I conducted, I would pledge that a person is good. I'd sign it, and put my seal on it, and give it to his people, saying, "Look, there is nothing on your man or on your son. Let him come back." And when he came back, we detained him.

I would like to relay one incident that took place. The terrorists came into this man's house, who's from the Albu Mahal tribe, and they took his rifle so he could not shoot at them. After the battle, we went out in the sector that I was in. We found a dead terrorist, among many, who had the man's rifle next to him. So we took the rifle, and we gave it to its rightful owner.

Jassim: The three months that followed the battle, we were surrounded. We were under an embargo. We could get no medicine, no food, no water, no fuel, and it was a very severe winter. If they got wind of anyone supplying us with fuel, food, anything to sustain life, they would kill him. With my meager means, I bought three boats. We started buying things to sustain life, fuel, food, medicine for the sick and all of that, from al-Jazeera, through the three boats, because Jazeera was more peaceful, more stable than us. . . .

Whenever I wanted to go on a mission, say, a raiding party, I used misinformation. Like, I'd tell Coalition forces that I'm going to the Albu Alwan area on a raiding party at night, and I asked them for lights so they can identify my men. That night, I changed the plan. Why? Because these phones are easily infiltrated, and they would know my plan ahead of time, so I used misinformation. I kept them guessing at what I was doing. And I changed the plan right when we were working toward the objective, so that nobody knew there was a change of plan, and without informing Coalition forces of my change of plan.

Montgomery: Wasn't that dangerous?

Jassim: Yes.

Montgomery: Did Coalition forces ever shoot at you because you weren't where they thought you'd be?

Jassim: No, no, because we had the chemical lights.

Interpreter: He's talking about the chem lights that the Coalition forces supplied him with. So that was their signal. Because they carried them, they knew who they were.

Montgomery: That's what I thought.

Jassim: Twice I had raids on terrorists, and I did not find the targets, so I knew the Motorolas were infiltrated. It could be infiltrated easily. That's what made me think, what if those people have it? . . .

So at times, when I told the Coalition forces I'm going here, I changed my plan and went there. And that's where I found the targets. Not here, but there.

One time Lieutenant Colonel Ferry asked me why I changed plans. I told him why: "Because I think these radios are infiltrated. The terrorists could easily listen to the Motorolas." Indeed, 10 of these Motorolas were found with the terrorists. Some of them had the Iraqi army signal, and some of them had the Coalition signal. . . .

I was able to enlist the help of one of the people of the Albu Fahd tribe. I gave him a Thuraya telephone, and he would call me and tell me where the terrorists were, and we'd raid them. He used to come from his bedroom, and you know the Thuraya telephone is not very effective from inside buildings, so I used to hear his voice breaking up, but still, through his talk I was able to know exactly where the terrorists were located.

I set up a task force, no more than 30 fighters. I obtained some chem lights from the Coalition forces. We used to used this road right here, which is called Seda Road. I was in constant communication with my men from the beginning of the raid until coming back. I'd give them the exact location of the target, and within an hour, they'd call me and say how many men they got and how many weapons.

The Coalition forces wanted to join me in many raids, and I refused. Why? Because Coalition forces, when they go, they use vehicles. Vehicles make noise. Noise alerts the enemy to run away, so I prefer to go dismounted. So I preferred the Coalition forces to be at least 300 meters away from my raiding party, as a backup.

And the roads we took to get these people were infested with IEDs [improvised explosive devices]. These IEDs were rigged with wires and a battery to initiate an explosion to kill my men. Because of my military background, working in the air force, I was able to show my men how to disarm these IEDs by cutting the wires. They used to bring me terrorists, and along with them they used to bring IEDs on their shoulders. . . . The terrorists surrounded themselves with IEDs.

Montgomery: On the roads?

Jassim: On the roads, right. . . .

Some of the terrorists were very close to the encampments of the Americans. Why? Many a terrorist camped right here [pointing on a map to a neighborhood adjacent to an American compound], close to the Coalition forces. Why? These areas right here, nobody can stay in them except with the permission of Coalition forces. So what we did, we got the Coalition forces' permission to get into this area close by them, and we found many terrorists.

This is also a camp of the Coalition forces [pointing to another place on the map]. These houses right here [points to adjacent neighborhood], we found many a terrorist. They have many ways of hiding—misinformation—you cannot count them. . . .

Montgomery: Did you have to go at night?

Jassim: Day and night.

Montgomery: Did there seem to be more in one place, or about the same number coming from all the directions? Was there like a main attack and supporting attacks, or was it equal all the way around?

Jassim: Let me explain to you. [He points to various locations on a map as he describes the disposition of forces and scheme of maneuver.]. . . . All of them wore face masks, and they were in succession. The guys that wore red head bands were on suicide missions. Then yellow bands, and then black, and their clothes were black. There were terrorists coming from Hit, from Baghdad, from Fallujah, from Diyala. They all joined in this attack, and it was a huge attack. Why did they concentrate so much in this attack? They theorized that if I succeeded in clearing this area right here, all the surrounding areas would follow suit, so they wanted to finish me off right here. But thanks to the almighty, their thinking was faulty.

Montgomery: When they attacked, were they on line or were they moving like we do, in groups that are in formations, or was it sort of disorganized? What did it look like?

Jassim: The attack took stages. Like I said, those terrorists who came in on a suicide mission, when they achieved an objective, others came in and took their places, and so forth and so on.

Interpreter: It's not exactly the answer to your question.

Montgomery: No, but it helps. . . . Did you have anyone carrying ammunition up to the checkpoints before they ran out?

Jassim: No, I didn't have any men resupplying my men. Everyone relied on his 30 or 40 rounds. I was not able to buy ammo. Nobody ever gave me any ammo. People with ammo were afraid to sell me any, because terrorists were killing them.

Montgomery: What about your wounded? Did you have wounded, and what did you do with them?

Jassim: Yes, Coalition forces were able to treat my wounded and took some of them all the way to Balad, and I thank them for it.

Montgomery: You faced a very highly coordinated attack.

Jassim: Yes indeed. It was a military plan, and it had plenty of intelligence, and I tell you, some of the intelligence came from my own tribe. They got the exact location, who was carrying what in the checkpoint, and the numbers of my men. They had already known beforehand they did not have a whole tribe fighting them, just 15 or 17 men against all of them, so they imagined it was very easy to finish us off, and quickly. We were able to capture or detain some of the men who were relaying information to them and who let the terrorists stay in their own houses prior to the attack. They are still being detained. They confessed to everything they did, and hopefully they will get their due from the justice system.

Montgomery: Did you have any thoughts of trying to fall back across the river?

Jassim: Some of my own relatives fell back and crossed the river.

Interpreter: And I asked him why your relatives?

Jassim: Because they were fearful of being slain and their heads cut off. These men did not have any weapons, and they were afraid that, because they were my relatives, the enemy would capture them and chop off their heads. Some of my relatives—men, women and children—they had no weapons, but they killed them just because they were my relatives. This cousin right here, they killed his sister and they chopped off her head, just because she was my sister, and they cut off her breasts. . . .

Unknown: Did he have enough time, advance knowledge of the attack, to do any defensive preparations? And if he did, what did he do to prepare?

Jassim: I didn't have any. No, I had no prior knowledge as to the exact time of attack.

Unknown: Could you ask him, of the terrorists, how many were foreign, how many were Iraqi?

Jassim: Due to the fact that we found no identification papers on them, we did not know who they were, but I estimate there were about 50 foreign Arabs. We found some corpses that, from the looks of them, were not Iraqis.

Montgomery: Then when you brought in the captured prisoners from these raids, for interrogation, you said you looked at them, and a lot of times you could tell with good accuracy who was an insurgent and who wasn't. What were you looking for?

Jassim: When I gathered these men—and based on the intelligence that I'd already gathered—when I asked one of them a specific question, I saw his hands shake a little bit, or he couldn't look directly in my eyes. I knew, and he was afraid. These were some of the signs that I used to identify the terrorists from the nonterrorists. I used to look at their features, everything in their faces—even their ears. And I would ask him a question—how far in education did he go? If he had no education, I knew he was influenced by the terrorists. The uneducated were easily swayed to be on the terrorist side, and so I would concentrate on him and ask him more questions because they used ignorant people, uneducated people.

Interview 6

Sheikh Aifan Sadun al-Issawi

Fallujah Representative
Iraqi Awakening Political Party

Sheikh Aifan Sadun al-Issawi's father opposed the Iraqi nationalists of the 1960s because they were interfering with family and religious traditions. In 1967, he killed a man at a meeting in Fallujah and fled with his family to Saudi Arabia, where King Faisal provided him with land, homes, and support. He subsequently died during a visit to Helwan, Egypt, and his family believes that he was poisoned by agents of the Iraqi government.

Sheikh Aifan was born in 1972 in Ar Ar, Saudi Arabia, on the border with Iraq. He studied computers and mathematics in college and worked in Saudi Arabia until 2001, when he moved to Iraq to take care of his mother after her second husband died. Nine of his brothers still reside in Saudi Arabia, and two live in the United States.

Sheikh Aifan is the nephew of Sheikh Khamis Hasnawi al-Issawi, the paramount sheikh of the Albu Issa tribe. Sheikh Khamis exercises leadership of the tribe, but he is aged and not very active. Consequently, Sheikh Aifan tends to represent the tribe in dealings with Coalition forces.

Sheikh Aifan was interviewed by Colonel Gary W. Montgomery and Chief Warrant Officer-4 Timothy S. McWilliams on 14 February 2009 at Camp Ramadi.

Sheikh Aifan Sadun al-Issawi: As we feared, there was a war. We believed there would be a war, so as a normal precaution, we all armed ourselves and prepared for it. I was almost certain the Iranians would enter Iraq.

The collision came quickly. Baghdad was finished, but Fallujah was still under control. We contacted Abdul Dureb, the director of security in Fallujah. He asked me to visit him, so I went to his office. I found about 50 people there. They were foreign Arabs. I remember one of them. I knew him. He's from the Emirates. There were Syrians and Tunisians—a lot of people. Some were Fedayeen Saddam. I heard Abdul Dureb tell the Fedayeen Saddam, who were wearing black uniforms, to take these young people [the foreign Arabs] and prepare them to fight. He told me that we all had to fight. I told him that Iraq was finished, to just stand by because fighting was useless. After that, I left.

A few days later, I heard that he had disappeared, and the Coalition forces had arrived at K-160 [highway kilometer marker 160]. The tribal sheikhs had a meeting in our guesthouse. As I recall, they had many ideas, but in the end, we decided to let the Coalition forces enter the cities. We made an invitation to meet the American force at K-160. We negotiated with them. We even had lunch together in the desert. We said, "If you want to go inside the city, come on in, but without fighting." We had a deal, and they came to Ramadi and Fallujah, and the surrounding cities like Habbaniyah. They made a temporary camp at the big bridge by Fallujah, but they didn't enter the city.

I stopped to talk with them. They had an interpreter, an Egyptian named Ennis. And there was a captain named Hickey. They were my points of contact. I told them I would give them advice on how to behave when they went into the city. I also told them about an Iraqi army base in front of Taqqadum, Habbaniyah. It was full of weapons. Any weapons you can think of, it was full of them. It was so big you needed a car to go around it. It was huge. Captain Hickey told me, "We'll go together, and I'll see it." We went in two helicopters, and I showed them the location. They were surprised. When we came back, they told me they would send a force to surround this camp, but they didn't do anything after that.

After the Americans went into Fallujah, people started going into the bases and taking weapons because they were not secured. I took about 80 RPGs [rocket-propelled grenades], PKCs [machine guns], and other things.

The Americans had no experience with our culture. The British, when they went to Basrah, they knew the area, because they've been there. They knew how to deal with the sheikhs and with the people. They had ways of communicating with the sheikhs and the people.

But the Americans, when they got inside Fallujah, they started to arrest people. They arrested sheikhs.

They shot me by mistake when we had a meeting in Karma. They shot me in the left leg. My tribe took me to our hospital. You know that I am a son of the sheikh of the Albu Issa tribe, so many people know me. Everyone was surrounding the hospital to find out what's happening to me. And it was at the beginning. It was a new thing. So when they heard that the Americans shot someone, everyone was surprised. In our culture, they go to find out what's happening.

Then the Americans visited me in the hospital and said they would take me to Germany for treatment. We have our habits and our traditions, and it was too great a favor. The Americans were a new force in our lives, and it seemed strange, so I refused their offer. They went to the government people in Fallujah to get them to make me accept their offer, because the wound was a bad one. The bones were broken. So they put some Iraqi security people around me in the hospital to protect me. I was bleeding, and it was a very, very dangerous situation. They gave me blood transfusions to stabilize me so they could fly me to Germany. The Americans visited me in the hospital and said that if they didn't take me to Germany, my leg would have to be amputated.

Some of the sons of Albu Issa, my tribe, were very brave people. They took me from the hospital by force. My friends, my sons, my people—they know me in the tribe. They surrounded the hospital. They went to the policemen who were protecting me and locked them in a room. Then they took me to Amman, Jordan. My brothers came from Saudi Arabia to Jordan, and they were waiting at the border. They put me in Khalidi Hospital, which is the best hospital in Amman. They took care of me over there, and they operated on my leg. They replaced the demolished bone with a platinum tube. They found that my blood had been poisoned, and they thought the bullet that shot me contained some kind of poison. I stayed there about four months. After six months, I came back to Iraq. I was on crutches. I had a very hard time.

So I arrived home from Amman one night, and the second night, the Americans surrounded the area where my house is. They even had helicopters over my house. They arrested me and my brothers—Sheikh Barakat, Sheikh Jamal, and their sons. So the whole group was about nine. They took us to Fallujah town.

General King* was responsible for the campaign; his headquarters was in Baghdad, but he was responsible for this campaign [conversation with interpreter]. He was upset with me because, maybe, first because I refused their offer and went to Jordan. And he was upset because Barakat, my brother, refused to shake hands with him.

Then they took us to Abu Ghraib jail. I stayed there nine months without being charged with anything. We didn't know the charges, and I was very sick. There were demonstrations in Fallujah to release me, a delegation of sheikhs interceded for my release, and many things happened like that. But any time they asked General King to release me, he refused very strongly.

Then Jalal Talabani, the Iraqi president, asked President [George W.] Bush to release me. So they came to Abu Ghraib jail, and they took us by helicopter. They took us to the Iraqi president, Jalal Talabani. We stayed in his palace as his guests for about three days. Then they put us under house arrest for about six months.

Colonel Gary W. Montgomery: Could you describe what it was like being imprisoned in Abu Ghraib?

Aifan: It was like a grave. I wore the same clothes for nine months, and I was very sick, and it was often very cold. We didn't know what was happening outside. There were always mortars falling on the jail. They put us in a tent, and many of my friends inside the tent were killed by mortars. There were foreign Arabs with us. Abu Ghraib jail was very bad. They scared us with attack dogs during interrogations.

And this lady—you know the pictures?** When the thing happened in Abu Ghraib? This lady with the short hair? I know her personally, and she knows me personally. I was one of her prisoners.

---

* Possibly then-Col R. Alan King, USA.

** Probably Pvt Lynndie R. England, USAR, who was shown in many of the infamous photographs from the prison.

But when some of the Americans came and learned that I can speak English and saw me on my crutches, they sympathized with me. They took my detainee number, and after one or two days, they came back and said, "You have a big, big problem. We know you are a good man, but we can't help you. We need to help you, but it's a big problem." [inaudible] I had the crutches, so [inaudible]. They allowed me to go to my house in Fallujah, on one condition—that I won't leave Iraq.

During the time we were in Abu Ghraib, the situation was getting bad in Fallujah. Fighting started to increase between the Americans and some fighters in Fallujah. So when we were with the president of Iraq, Jalal Talabani, he talked with us in the presence of some of the Americans. They said, "We're going to release you to cool things down in Fallujah." So it's a deal. When I came back to Fallujah, the situation was very critical, and the insurgents were rising up.

After we went home, the Americans visited me in my home. There was no one being visited by the Americans in his home. It was strange, because the insurgents, if they had any suspicion that a guy had any relationship with the Americans, they cut off his head. The leaders of the insurgents in Fallujah at that time were Abdullah al-Janabi and Omar al-Hadid. These were the top leaders of the fighters there. There were a lot of foreign Arabs with them. After the Americans visited me, the insurgents posted a lot of papers around saying that I was an agent for the Americans.

Then I was meeting the Americans at the center called FLT [Fallujah Liaison Team], which is from the American and the [inaudible] hospital in Fallujah, which is on the highway.

Montgomery: Is that the small compound just east of the Jordanian hospital?

Aifan: Yes. It had some old rooms that had been used for the Iraqi army, but I rehabilitated it and made some offices for the Americans, so they could use it as an office for reconstruction or compensation for the people. People were coming to ask about their compensation. If someone was hit by the Americans, or his car was burned by the Americans, he came, and the Americans paid him for it. And the Americans, for history and to be honest, they helped the people too much.

The head of it was Major Gregory [G.] Gillette. He is a lawyer who was responsible for the Civil-Military Operations Center. And there was Colonel [Colin P.] McNease, Colonel [John A.] Toolan [Jr.]—he's a general now. He was the top leader of the forces in Fallujah. He is a very close friend, a very dear friend. McNease and Gillette were very close friends to me.

So I was going to this place daily. I helped people get compensation, and I was still on crutches. Then the Americans did the paperwork for me to get compensation for my leg. They asked for the invoices from Khalidi Hospital in Amman. They saw how much it cost me, and they paid me back.

I started to develop a stronger relationship with the Americans, so the insurgents made me a target. They couldn't hit me, because I have my own people who protect me, so they couldn't face me face to face. But they kept me in mind as a target, watching for me. We kept each other afraid of each other. Then they hit one of my cars, and they killed one of my people.

So I called a huge meeting in Fallujah. I collected all the people—the imams of the mosques, and the sheikhs, and everyone high level in Fallujah. I have a videotape of the meeting.

Montgomery: Do you remember what time this was, approximate date?

Aifan: I have the tape, and I have the date and the time.

Montgomery: Was it between the battles of Fallujah, or was it before the fighting started?

Aifan: Before the big fighting in Fallujah. There were some people who were insurgents or mujahideen, but they were not against me. They attended this meeting. There were armed people around all the roads. They went all over the area. I held this meeting in coordination with the Coalition forces. I let the imams start to talk and tell the people that the insurgents who come from outside Iraq and cover their faces, they are not mujahideen. They are criminals. And they warned people that they were letting surrounding countries, like Iran, Saudi Arabia, and Syria, interfere inside Iraq.

Sheikh Hamza [Abbas al-Issawi, Mufti of Fallujah], God bless him, was the head of the imams in Fallujah. He attended that meeting. After that, he was killed. They killed him in front of the mosque. Sheikh Jamal [Shakir al-Nazzal] and Sheikh Kamal [Shakir al-Nazzal] were the top imams in Fallujah. Sheikh Kamal was killed.* Sheikh Jamal fled to Syria, and he's still there.

After this meeting, the fight between us was announced. We started to coordinate and work with the Coalition forces, and we started to target the leaders of al-Qaeda. We killed some of the big leaders.

I started fighting al-Qaeda publicly in 2005. During this time, from my cousins, my families, and my tribe's sons, about 37 were killed because of this fighting. In 2006, after the big battle in Fallujah, the situation was getting very bad, and people were going after to the foreign Arabs. People wanted to live peacefully, so they started to follow al-Qaeda. There were just seven people being faithful and staying with me. I was surrounded, so I couldn't even leave my house. If I wanted to go outside, it meant too much security, and I might have to fight at any second. So I started to not go out much. Even my uncles, who are just across the road from my house, told me, "Don't come to us, because you are a suspect. They might kill us because we know you."

Montgomery: What year is this, you're talking about?

Aifan: The end of 2005.

Montgomery: Okay.

Aifan: At the start of 2006, they ambushed one of my cars. We tried to visit Sattar Abu Risha. No one could visit Sattar Abu Risha at that time, because whoever visited him would be slaughtered.

I had a good relationship with Sheikh Sattar and Sheikh [Hamid] Jabour. So I went to Sheikh Sattar's house, God bless him. I found just two people with him. We approached his house and waited on the highway, going back and forth until the highway was completely empty.

---

* Sheikh Hamza was assassinated on 29 November 2005, and Sheikh Kamal met the same end on 7 February 2006.

Interpreter: Because his guesthouse is very close to the highway, less than 100 meters.

Aifan: We left Sattar's house after lunch. We took the old Habbaniyah road to Fallujah. Al-Qaeda was at the Boston and Ira intersection.* There were about seven cars waiting for us, and we only had three cars. We faced them and started fighting. Of my people, four were killed and one was very seriously shot. We killed one of them and seriously wounded three.

The four who were killed had been in one car, which was disabled, and we had killed one of them [al-Qaeda]. We kept going until we reached home with our wounded man. The situation was very bad.

I took my family to Amman, Jordan. I have my own house in Amman, so I stayed with my family—my wife and my children—in Amman. And even Sheikh Sattar fled to Amman for a little while. He visited me, and we talked about the situation, saying "what are we going to do?" Then Sheikh Khamis [Hasnawi al-Issawi, paramount sheikh of the Albu Issa tribe] and Sheikh Khalid, my uncles, fled to Amman. They refused to fight al-Qaeda. They came to Amman and lived with me in my house. I stayed about four months in Amman.

The Americans visited me in Amman. General [David G.] Reist—and there was colonel—

Interpreter: There was a colonel who was responsible. He doesn't remember his name.

Aifan: He visited me in Fallujah, and it was very bad. We are still in 2006. He wanted me to come back and fight al-Qaeda.

Sattar came back, and he started fighting al-Qaeda. Then Sattar called me and said, "Hey, look, I'm in Ramadi, you are in Fallujah. Let's cooperate and start fighting al-Qaeda and finish them." The biggest problem that had kept us from fighting al-Qaeda was that we didn't have weapons. The Americans at that time took any weapons they found, anywhere in any house. So I made a deal with

---

* Boston and Ira are the Coalition names for these two roads.

the Americans. I will come back to Fallujah from Amman, but keep away from my weapons. We had a deal with them. So that's why I came back and started fighting.

The first day I came back, I was attacked by mortars. You know the news in Iraq—everybody knew that Aifan was back, so they started shooting at me with mortars. The Americans made a brave stand. They stayed with me at my house for a long time. There were many attacks on my house, and they were on the roof. They stayed with me. We fought together on the roof of the house.

So al-Qaeda started to expand their shooting. They started shooting all the houses around me, and it was an advantage for me—expanding the fighting, so it's not just me. Because if I stay alone, and I fight alone, and they're targeting me alone, they will hit me. I would be a very easy target. So it's better for me to expand it and make it bigger.

And the other advantage, if I expand the battle, there will be too many people with me. So we expanded the fighting for the Albu Yusuf, Albu Jamali area, Albu Khalid—around my house, around my area.

Then al-Qaeda sent a letter to Sheikh Khamis, my uncle. The letter was delivered by Sheikh Abdullah Shuesh, one of the Albu Issa tribal sheikhs. The letter said, "We want to meet Sheikh Khalid and stop the fighting." So Sheikh Khalid met them. They said, "We don't have problems with you, the Albu Issa tribe. We have a problem with Aifan, and Aifan is an agent. Either you kill him, and the problem will be finished, or bring him to us, and the problem with you will be finished."

After this situation, my cousins sympathized with me. Some of my cousins joined me, and they are heroes. I had eight PKCs. The Americans helped me with some ammunition, so I started getting stronger. The first operation I did was in a center for al-Qaeda, and I did it with the help of the police.

I had three black BMWs, and I was always changing cars so nobody knows which one I'm riding in—three of them, same type, same color, everything. So they put some IEDs [improvised explosive devices] on the road. One of my cars was blown up. With me was Mushtar, my uncle Khalid, Othman, and my uncle Majid. Mushtar lost both legs, Othman lost one leg, and the driver was killed.

The Americans helped. They took them to al-Asad by helicopter. And then I took them to Amman to take care of them, to Germany, and now they are back, but without hands and without legs.

After they were wounded, their families turned against me, but I kept fighting. Al-Qaeda sent a tanker of chlorine against me. They blew it up in the first checkpoint, which is very close to my house. My mother was killed—her name was Turkiyah—and five children were killed, and one of my guards. This gave me another great push to fight them. I still kept my arms on me, and we joined the American operations to fight al-Qaeda. And we kept fighting until God, by his blessing, gave us the victory.

In 2006, the Awakening was announced publicly. I think I'm a person who was close to Sattar and Ahmad Abu Risha, and they made a very big sacrifice. The Americans supported us very strongly through the projects they put in our areas, and also through the police and the Iraqi army, which we started with them and the Americans trained.

In 2006, I established an ERU [emergency response unit] battalion in Fallujah, and I was the leader. It is a very strong, very well-trained battalion, and it protects Fallujah. And thanks for that.

In my house, I have hundreds of pictures. If we spent three days or a week just talking about writing, you would not understand exactly what was going on as well as if you saw the pictures, the videotape. We filmed our operations. We documented everything. I have pictures of the Iranian we caught in 2006. Two people who tried to kill me in 2007, I have a picture of them. Three weeks ago, they sent a guy with a vest.

Interpreter: Three weeks ago?

Aifan: To blow himself up. And I still have one guy, a foreign Arab. He's Yemeni. I have him in my jail now. You know, we can't just kill him. If I kill him now, they will be happy, but other people will come after a couple of years and take me to court and punish me because I killed him. It's happened. We have law. We should send him to the court and the law, and if the court decides to kill him, they can kill him in the street.

Interpreter: I told him, "Sir, if somebody came to kill me, I would slaughter him, I would kill him."

Aifan: When we were fighting with PKCs, face to face, we killed many people.

Interpreter: Yes, in fighting.

Aifan: Yes, one from Sudan, one from Saudi Arabia. Me, I killed them.

Interpreter: During battles, yes.

Aifan: But if we catch someone, and we know we have rules and our religion, we can't kill him. A Syrian, if he killed my mother, and I catch the guy, I can't kill him.

Interpreter: In our religion, if you catch someone, it's not good to kill him. He's helpless. He's hopeless. So for that, he said, he's had for two months now a guy that has been arrested, and he can't.

Aifan: Eleven times they tried to kill me. Last year, they killed my captain and two of my guards. They came to my checkpoint and said they were British priests. They came to my area, and they had American uniforms and a British badge. He was Tunisian, I think. His face looked American, and he made himself American. He said, "We need to talk to Sheikh Aifan." But I went to Jordan that morning, and he came to my gate at 1:00 in the afternoon. When they told him I was outside Iraq, he went crazy. They were sure I was at home. He said, "I need to talk to whoever is the chief of security around Shcikh Aifan. Who is it? I need to talk to him." Captain Mahmoud was my security guy. When he came to him, he caught him like this, and he blew himself up.

There was a woman with pistols. When they came to detain her, she blew herself up.

Montgomery: You said he made himself look American.

Aifan: Yes.

Montgomery: Do you know where he was from?

Aifan: He was Tunisian.

Montgomery: Tunisia, Okay.

Aifan: The Americans know about that. They did an investigation. He was from Tunisia, and he had a fake police badge.

Interpreter: And he looked white, with blue eyes.

Aifan: Yes. A week before that, they sent two kids with vests to the mosque on a Friday, and they were waiting for me to enter the mosque to blow themselves up. But we ambushed them behind the mosque and caught them. We called the Americans. They came and took the TNT and all of that stuff, and we sent them to jail. They are in jail now.

Montgomery: Do you think they're after you now for political reasons, or out of revenge?

Aifan: Before, they tried to kill me because we fought al-Qaeda, and I am sure they will keep looking to kill me. I have heard the Americans say, "He is a target for the rest of his life," and they gave me letters for the American government saying that "he did this and that, and he helped us. We think he deserves to be an American citizen, he and his family, because he will remain a target for the rest of his life—him and his kids."

I have four kids. I didn't put them in school. They will kill them, and you know they will kill them, especially now.

When we fought al-Qaeda, we didn't have a big problem, because we fought al-Qaeda, and 1920 [Revolution Brigade] fought al-Qaeda, the Islamic Party fought al-Qaeda, the Islamic army, the mujahideen army—all these groups fought al-Qaeda the same as me, so that we destroyed al-Qaeda completely, on the ground and on the table. Underground, we still have sleeper cells. On the ground, under your eyes, we destroyed al-Qaeda.

Now we face a big problem. Some of those groups who fought al-Qaeda with us had a different agenda. Yeah, they fought al-Qaeda with us, because we had the same enemy. But after they finished al-Qaeda, they started looking to kill us, because we are "agents" who work with the Americans.

Me and my people, we didn't fight al-Qaeda because we have religion or ideology or something. We fought al-Qaeda because they are bad people. They killed people and did evil things, so we fought them. I don't care if they pray or don't pray, if they believe in God, or have some other reason. I don't care. But the Islamic Party, the Islamic army, the mujahideen army—all these groups, 1920—they have ideologies, different agendas. Some of those groups have foreign agendas, maybe from Iran or Syria.

Now we're a bigger target, more than when we fought al-Qaeda, because now I am sure 1920 are bad people. They tried to kill my people. And the Islamic Party, I know they mean to kill me. I am sure. We have proved it.

Interpreter: Before, you saw them. Now, you don't see them.

Aifan: Now, some of the people who were in those groups are in the government. He is captain or major or something, so that he has the ability to move very freely, and they can watch me, and they can listen to my radio. So it's very, very difficult.

Interpreter: More risky now.

Aifan: I am sure they will keep on targeting me because I am not in one of those groups. And they'd fight with me. And they always visit me.

Interpreter: To join them?

Aifan: Yes, they told me, "We will make you a big head," and "Come with us." "You are the sheikh."

Yes, I am the son of the sheikh. But everything ends—everything. The soldiers, the leaders, the mayor, the governor, the minister, [Prime Minister Nouri al-] Maliki, Jalal Talabani—for some reason, they will all be changed. But I will still, for all of my life, be the son of the sheikh. I am a good man. I have my respect and my people. I think my level is very high—the highest.

Interpreter: Of course, they're going to lose their positions, but your position is for life.

Aifan: If I am poor, I am the same Sheikh Aifan. If I am rich, then I am still Sheikh Aifan.

Montgomery: So you don't need them, but they need you.

Aifan: Yes, sure. We are still a big target. I can't move, except with my guards, with my armored vehicle. I have very high security around my house. It's difficult.

I have a Saudi passport. I have a Jordanian passport.

Interpreter: I told him, "You have a passport, why don't you leave?" He said, "What about my history? This is my history, my life."

Aifan: My people, my tribe. I can't just leave.

Interpreter: He has to be faithful for them. It's easy for him; he has his passport.

Montgomery: What would happen to your tribe if you do leave? Would a brother take your place here?

Aifan: No, I don't think so. We should be honest. Life won't stop if I leave, but I have a thousand people who trust me. They follow me blindly. A thousand people. Leave Iraq now?

Interpreter: It's not faithful to leave them.

Aifan: It would be a black point in my history if I leave them. We have to be willing participate more in the government. We have to have balance in the government—the government of Iraq and Anbar—because these people's rights are my responsibility. I should take care of them.

God's will made me honored. I am the son of the sheikh, and I am the leader, and I am the youngest one in the family. I have 16 brothers, and 14 brothers are older than me, but God chose me. And the people chose me. They came to my house. They didn't go to my brothers' houses. So if you see, if you know my life and how hard it is, and how the people came to me and asked for my help, you can't just leave them. It would be unfaithful to leave them and run away.

Montgomery: I think with so many brothers, and so many brothers who are older than you, I guess it's not like in Europe with the nobility, where the oldest brother gets the title. How are you chosen from among your brothers?

Aifan: They chose me. Nine brothers are Saudi, and they were already in Saudi Arabia. Three of my brothers have no interest in the tribes. They are businessmen, and they are not ready to spend one hour listening to the people. And Barakat, who is the oldest, I have not agreed with him for the last five years. He is very hard, and he's against me being a friend of the Americans or making any relationship with them. He was against the fight against al-Qaeda. He lives in Jordan. He was just back for a couple of months. So the people look for the guy who guided them, who showed them, who made something a fact—not some big shot, but someone who helped them.

I am not strong through my muscles; I am strong through my people. When I make a celebration in Fallujah, thousands of people attend. I think you saw the celebration for the Awakening that was on TV. It was the biggest celebration in al-Anbar by attendance, because people love me, and I am very strong through them. I am not strong through my money, or the Americans, or through my muscles. When I am upset, I stand up, and hundreds of people stand up with me. That's what I'm working for, and I'm ready to sacrifice all my life for these people.

Montgomery: I understand better now, and it sounds to me like it's not even something like a formal election so much as the people just sort of begin to follow the person whom they trust most and have the most confidence in, among the brothers. They are drawn to you.

Aifan: And because I'm the son of Sadun, and I was the closest one to my father in his behavior. I was very similar to my father. When they saw me, how I behaved, they said you look like your father. I'm very proud of that.

Montgomery: What was it like in Fallujah between the two battles? And what was the effect of the battle of Fallujah?

Aifan: They hated the Americans. It was a very big mistake. They could have taken care of it a better way. From the beginning, if they dealt with the right people, they wouldn't need to fight by themselves here.

Montgomery: Since we've been here, since 2003, what are the biggest mistakes we've made, and what have we done right?

Interpreter: In Fallujah particularly, or in Iraq, sir?

Montgomery: In his opinion, and in any regard—wide open question.

Aifan: The biggest mistake was the incident in Abu Ghraib. After that, there was something—American soldiers raped an Iraqi woman. I think you remember this story. Even if the Americans punished him, and I am sure the main government didn't agree with these mistakes. But sometimes you have to be responsible for what you've done.

And the other mistake, which made these mistakes go on and on, was that the Americans dealt with the wrong people. They didn't mean to do it, but they believed—because they are honest, they believed anyone—so they dealt with the wrong people. It's not the Americans' mistake.

We can't—I should be honest—we can't trust the Americans completely yet. We have a theory. The Americans don't have continuous friendships. They always have their interests. Their relationships with people are based on how much benefit they can get from a person. When we were fighting al-Qaeda, the Americans were in my house every two days. I even met President Bush. [Barak H.] Obama—I saw him; [David H.] Petraeus [USA], all the generals.

Each MEF [Marine expeditionary force] changed. The generals invited me to celebrations, and we made relations stronger between us. The situation got better in Fallujah. When General [Walter E.]

Gaskin [Sr.] and General [John R.] Allen left, General [John F.] Kelly came in. Kelly visited me one time in my house, and General [Martin] Post, I didn't see him except in a general celebration. Now they are gone, and new generals are coming, and I don't know them.

This is a big mistake. It means the advantage of having a relationship, a friend, is finished for me. We have a good situation. It's safe. But a new person could say, "That's it—we don't need him anymore." I still have very good relationships with some of the Americans, mainly the leaders and generals. I should be in the meeting if they came, and they are leaving. At least call and tell me. This is a mistake.

Even I—and I'm very close to the Americans—am starting to be distanced from them. The government of Iraq, Nouri al-Maliki called me the "American sheikh." They know I have very strong relationships with the Americans, which makes me happy. I don't feel ashamed of it. I used my friendship with the Americans to build a secure Iraq.

This is what we have achieved, because it's God's wish, and with his blessing and the work between us and the Americans. Now I'm involved with the police, and we're taking care of the security situation in Fallujah and the surrounding area. And we are cutting out this cancer, al-Qaeda and the insurgents. And we won the election, thank God, and I am a provincial council member. Maybe I will be more than a provincial council member in the future. Maybe.

And we have deals on the table. Sheikh Ahmad [Abu Risha] was in Baghdad yesterday, and we have a meeting every day with someone on [inaudible] politics. We are working. Maybe we can get something bigger on the table. We keep going, working to build and secure our Iraq.

And a big mistake, which they will regret—the Americans pull out of the checkpoints very fast. This is a killer mistake. We have a lot of police, with good equipment and weapons, but they are compromised. We have some bad people among them. They change their faces.

Montgomery: Among those who are manning the checkpoints now?

Aifan: In the police. We detained some people who planted IEDs against the Americans. We caught them in the act. When they were detained by the police, they stayed in jail two days, and they released them, because they were placing IEDs against Americans, not against Iraqis.

And I'm very sure and very confident that there are policemen using police vehicles to place IEDs. And I'm very sure that the insurgents and al-Qaeda have keys to the checkpoints, and they can get through without any questions. This is a big mistake. But the Americans do it very fast.

Maybe it's Obama. I told him, when I talked to him. I gave him a letter. If you become president, be alert. Don't pull out very fast. I personally talked to him more than 20 minutes, but he is still young. He's going on with it.

Montgomery: During the fighting against al-Qaeda, was the Awakening a single organization, or several organizations that were fighting at the same time? Throughout Anbar, was there coordination between the anti-al-Qaeda fighters in each city across the province?

Aifan: There were many people that were fighting. There was the Islamic Party, 1920, [Interpreter and Aifan simultaneously naming various groups].

Some people from al-Qaeda changed their faces. They are in the Awakening now. They didn't join us because they believe we are good, but to protect themselves. They saw who's winning, so they said they were with the Awakening. But when al-Qaeda was in, they were al-Qaeda.

Montgomery: There are always people like that.

Aifan: People without any principles, like these people, you cannot trust them. The proof of it is the bad people infiltrating the police. And the proof of that is the incident when they killed Sheikh Abdul Sattar. The guy who planned it and did it was in his security detail, and he was captured.

Chief Warrant Office-4 Timothy S. McWilliams: The colonel asked about the period between the battles of Fallujah, from April 2004 and November 2004. Could you tell me what was going on in Fallujah during that time?

Aifan: After the first battle of Fallujah, they established a security force. They were all faithful to al-Qaeda. They were al-Qaeda, and they proved it. After that happened, there were no police on the street; just the people who wear masks and their drivers, which is al-Qaeda. It was a very big mistake.

I told Colonel Toolan and Colonel McNease, "One of these days, the Fallujah people will fight you with these weapons that you gave to the police," and that happened. They used police vehicles and the guns from the Americans to fight the Americans.

The Americans didn't listen to advice. The Americans don't trust anyone. They have the principle, "don't trust anybody, so you can protect yourself." They came to my house and slept in my house. We fought shoulder to shoulder. I have a long history with the Americans. And yet when I visited the FLT every Monday, they searched me.

One time I remember, at the center of operations in our area, they spent eight days in my house. They brought the screens and the satellite, the big chairs, and everything. We spent eight days in my house, like my brothers.

Interpreter: And they're still searching you.

McWilliams: You mentioned Abdullah Janabi and Omar Hadid, and I've heard they've done some terrible things. Can you describe some of those?

Aifan: They put evil thoughts into the minds of the people of Fallujah. They established the Shura council in Fallujah. They gave authorization to kill anyone who worked with the Americans and anyone who volunteered to be a policeman. And they were thieves. Abdullah Janabi owned buildings and factories in Syria. Omar Hadid was an outcast. In the Saddam [Hussein] regime, he was accused, and charged, and wanted in many sex crimes.

Who were the people who joined al-Qaeda? Violent and irresponsible people. He had no value in society. His mother or his sister was a prostitute. He's homosexual. He found a chance to control the people, and he was being humiliated by the people, so he joined al-Qaeda. So al-Qaeda are bullies. They were all named with their mothers' names, not with their fathers'. Did you find any sheikhs, any high-level people, who were involved with al-Qaeda? No way. Only outcasts joined al-Qaeda.

The most important thing is that we woke up from this bad dream.

Interview 7

Sheikh Ali Hatim Abd al-Razzaq Ali al-Sulayman al-Assafi

Heir Apparent to the Paramount Sheikh
of the Dulaimi Tribal Confederation
and
Head of the National Salvation Front Political Party

Born in 1971, Sheikh Ali Hatim Abd al-Razzaq Ali al-Sulayman al-Assafi is relatively young, which is typical of leaders of the Awakening movement. He is also the true lineal heir of Sheikh Ali al-Sulayman, who was one of the most powerful sheikhs in al-Anbar during and after the transition from Ottoman to British rule (described in the writings of Gertrude Bell).

The role of paramount sheikh is nominally filled by his great uncles, Sheikh Amer and Sheikh Majed, who serve as co-regents. The former resides in Ramadi and the latter supports from Amman, Jordan. Sheikh Ali Hatim is the de facto paramount sheikh, though he declines to claim the title publicly out of respect for his uncles.

After the assassination of Sheikh Abdul Sattar Abu Risha, the Awakening movement fractured and Sheikh Ali Hatim formed his own political party.

Sheikh Ali Hatim was interviewed by Colonel Gary W. Montgomery and Chief Warrant Officer-4 Timothy S. McWilliams on 16 February 2009 at Camp Ramadi.

Sheikh Ali Hatim Abd al-Razzaq Ali al-Sulayman al-Assafi: We went through a difficult period that rattled us during the Saddam [Hussein] era. Before Saddam, we knew Ali Sulayman and two more sheikhs, and that was it [referring to his lineage]. During Saddam, we had 460 sheikhs. This would be considered interference in our independence.

The second difficult period that we experienced was the uprising of the sheikhs opposing al-Qaeda. I want to emphasize the fact that we did not bring al-Qaeda into Anbar. There were mistakes on both sides, on the tribal side and on the American side. There was a gap between the American forces and the tribes. There was no meeting of the minds, so to speak.

In 2004 al-Qaeda began to appear, and we warned General [Charles H.] Swannack [Jr., USA] at the time. Their presence after 2004 intensified, and if you look in the al-Qaeda ranks, you will find a lot of lowlifes. Their aim was to destroy the Islamic religion by attacking the Christians and Shiites, not just the Anbari sheikhs.

In 2005, we met with the defense minister and the interior minister at the time, and we asked them to institute a force to protect the western desert. We proposed to them that we had 2,500 fighters, and we were willing, able, and ready to attack al-Qaeda. We got permission to institute this force, but we found cowardice in our own men. I asked why, and they said because they were intimidated by al-Qaeda and its brutality.

At the beginning of 2006, the Albu Mahal tribe in al-Qaim, that was the first spark, between Albu Mahal and al-Qaeda. They instituted a company called al-Hamza Company, but they got no help, neither from the Americans nor from the Iraqi government. Al-Qaeda started buying people, buying their consciences, and this is what we warned about. The reason being there was a lot of unemployment, so they exploited that factor. We exploited the spark that took place in al-Qaim. We started educating the people here and tried to incite them to stand up to al-Qaeda. We succeeded in taking some people from Anbar to Baghdad to demand support from the government, because support was almost nil. We were followed by al-Qaeda, and the first attack occurred in a place called Sadiyah, in Baghdad.

Interpreter: I asked him what time that attack was on his person in Sadiyah.

Ali Hatim: In the beginning of 2006. And before that, they attacked me right here in my guesthouse. They totally wiped it out. Sheikh Amer [Abd al-Jabbar Ali al-Sulayman al-Assafi] was at the guesthouse at the time. Nevertheless, we insisted on finishing the endeavor that we had undertaken.

About mid-2006, we had a conference, which the American ambassador [Zalmay M. Khalilzad] attended, and some other notables. We gathered the most important sheikhs, even from the south of Iraq, and we proposed raising arms against any militias, whether Iranian-backed or al-Qaeda. Very few reacted positively, because they were fearful.

I tell you that right now, there are some new people who rose up that were unknown before. There was a movement called Anbar's Revolutionaries, which started three months prior to the Awakening. The first confrontation that they undertook was in the Rahman Mosque, right here in Ramadi. They detained 12 people, nine of whom were emirs of al-Qaeda, and they executed them. The second incident was in Haditha. They detained two people. They brought them to the Tash area and executed them.

We got in touch with Abdul Aziz al-Kabasi, the intelligence chief in Baghdad, and we asked him for a copying machine so that we could make leaflets to incite people to rise up against al-Qaeda. To be truthful with you, we tried to stay away from working with the Americans because we didn't want it to look like an American initiative, because people were opposed to that. We wanted to show that it was wholly Iraqi and to incite them and to bring them into the fold.

Montgomery: About what time period was this?

Ali Hatim: About two months before the inception of the Awakening. That was with the agreement of the American command in Baghdad. We got the American commander in Baghdad to agree to the wording that we were using, because the situation was not really solid here. It was probably a secret endeavor that we were undertaking.

The second spark, like I spoke of al-Qaim and the Albu Mahal tribe, the second spark, there was an officer who was traveling along the highway. His wife was the daughter of Hamid al-Odda, who was the sheikh of the Albu Ali Jassim tribe. Al-Qaeda was questioning him, and they got hold of his wife's hair and pulled her out of the vehicle.

We exploited that, and that was the second main spark that took place. We used that incident, of pulling the woman by her hair, to give the people passion, saying, "Arise! Look! This is your cowardice! This is your complacency! This is your ignorance! This is what it has done! Look what we have descended to!" So we poured gasoline on the fire, so to speak.

Colonel Gary W. Montgomery: Where was the incident?

Ali Hatim: Close to Jarash, which is here in Jazeera, here in Ramadi. The officer's name was Hamid Zivin.

The true campaign that took place against al-Qaeda, to be honest with you, was started by Hamid al-Hayess, long before Sattar Abu Risha. Right at Hamid al-Hayess's guesthouse, that's where the meetings took place and the incitement to fight off al-Qaeda. Hamid al-Hayess got hurt the most by al-Qaeda. That was the step that we took forward in calling the revolution against al-Qaeda. We used what we call our right, which is tribal right, to fight al-Qaeda. So Sheikh Hamid al-Hayess asked the tribal sheikhs to gather, to incite people, to bring people into the fold to fight off al-Qaeda. There was no safe place to go, except Sheikh Abdul Sattar Abu Risha's house. And we made many decisions that were very dangerous, and they were dangerous to implement. That is because al-Qaeda possessed lethal weapons, and we lacked support from anybody, Americans or the government.

And you know something? When we started talking about this initiative, many of the sheikhs thought we were a little bit mad, because here we are trying to take on al-Qaeda. They thought we were crazy, and most of them ran away. And you know something? I'm willing to confront them to their faces and show them their cowardly stance. Right now, when they meet with the Americans, they boast about how courageous they were, but the fact of the matter is that their own people know who they were and their cowardly stance.

So when we decided to have that meeting I talked about a while ago, we got in touch with Sattar Abu Risha, and I said, "You are welcome. My house is yours." So the Awakening revolution—now we're into the Awakening phase—was started by Sattar Abu Risha, Hamid al-Hayess, and me, and we also have some heroes. Notable among them is Mohayed Maish, Fathal Maklef, and there was a brigadier general. His name was Hamid Ibrahim Jazza. Sorry to tell you, he was detained by the Americans. Americans killed many al-Qaeda members. Another person that was with us, his name was Shalan al-Nouri. Some other men had the heart to join with us. And open warfare against al-Qaeda started. Now, thanks be to the Almighty, it started.

Afterward, we turned our attention to Nouri al-Maliki, the prime minister. Hamid al-Hayess and I and some other men, we met with al-Maliki, and it was a very long meeting that lasted from 10:00 in the morning to 6:00 in the evening. When we went, we asked him for many things. We asked him to create emergency response units, a police force, bring in the army, and without hesitation he did. He had a long meeting with his security staff, and they fulfilled all our demands.

The Awakening was basically a conference, and we decided, okay, after this conference, what is it we're going to do? What is the end result of this? So the end result was the Anbar Salvation Council. I'm going to speak frankly. The Anbar Salvation Council was to be in the forefront in the fight against al-Qaeda, and to lead Anbar Province, and to have people from that council appointed to the governorship, and to lead the government. At the time, there was no provincial council. At the time, the Islamic Party had run away from the province. It was like a vacuum. It is well known that the Islamic Party used the vacuum that it had created to take over the government in Anbar. People started coming to our side, seeing the government of Iraq was helping us, and seeing what we accomplished. I'll tell you something, the American side was important, even though it was a little bit late.

We had a conference in Baghdad to nominate someone who would lead the Anbar Salvation Council, and we nominated Hamid al-Hayess and Sheikh Sattar Abu Risha. Hamid won by 70 points. Sattar Abu Risha pulled out, and he said, "Look, I'm going back with the Awakening," and here the division took place. What we started was a great step, but what took place was the division that we had really feared. I don't know what it was, maybe a different point of view or whatever, but there was a difference.

Montgomery: About what date was that?

Ali Hatim: At the end of 2006, beginning of 2007, right about there.

Montgomery: You were attacked twice, once in Baghdad and once in your guesthouse. Could you describe the attacks?

Ali Hatim: I was traveling from Jadriyah to Sadiyah, visiting my in-law, and we had four vehicles. Once we made a right turn into Sadiyah, hell broke loose, fire from everywhere. I had four men killed and many more injured. Most of the vehicles were disabled, except one. I don't know how I was saved, except by the grace of God, because it was a one-sided confrontation. They had six vehicles. They had PKCs. They had heavier machine guns. I don't know how I was saved.

The second confrontation, after we came from Baghdad, we started going about in Shamiyah and Ramadi proper and holding education sessions with the people. One day, we're meeting—we tried to incite them to fight, not intelligence gathering. We were not really military commanders who knew what to do really. All that we wanted to do was fight, fight, fight. One day we're meeting with my people in my guesthouse, and a young kid came in. He was about 15½ years old, at about 7:30 in the evening, and he stood right in front of me and started pushing a button, like he was drugged. You could see the wire coming right here from his cuffs, so he started pushing, pushing, and nothing happened. I guess it malfunctioned. So my men came in and took him out to the ditches and killed him. And the American forces came in the next day and detonated his explosive payload.

But we insisted on finishing the undertaking we had started. We had accomplished something great. We had contacts with the Iraqi government, but to be truthful with you, between us and the Americans, there was a gap. That was during the time of the general who preceded [Major General John F.] Kelly.* To tell you the truth,

---

* The time frame before MGen Kelly arrived was February 2007 to February 2008, during which time MGen Walter E. Gaskin Sr. was Multi National Force-West commander.

we did not concentrate on the gap between us, because we were really busy doing what we had to do. We did what we could to strengthen the security apparatus in Anbar, to strengthen the institutions in Anbar.

We had some confrontations with the Islamic Party. We started demanding to know the Anbar budget. We tried to find out where the money went from the budget of 2006 and 2007. The money belongs to the Anbaris. They are the rightful owners of that money. And I tell you frankly, we insisted on kicking out the Islamic Party, even if we had to resort to the use of force.

The American command, to be truthful with you, before Kelly, was exasperating the situation, not making it better, and we gave up on it. It almost came to a confrontation between us and that general I spoke of. It is not really a good thing to bring a military man, who only wants to assert his dominance through the use of force. You have to bring someone who has the political savvy, the knowledge of the people, the tribal inner workings of the people, because Anbar is a tribal place.

We got an invitation from [Mahmoud Dawud al-] Mashhadani, who was the Iraqi head of the parliament. He asked us to be patient and not to have any conflict with the Islamic Party. At the same time, there was a change of the American command in Anbar. That's when General Kelly came in and took charge, him and General [Martin] Post. We really did not know who they were. When we met with Mashhadani, the head of the Iraqi parliament, we threatened them that within a month, if the Islamic Party was not removed, it would be subject to confrontation, maybe attack.

The first meeting between us and Generals Kelly and Post took place in Habbaniyah. I'll tell you something, if there are generals like Kelly, kind and important—General Kelly and General Post worked with us using our mentality, not the Marines' mentality. There was a consensus that there was a huge difference in the command between the one that preceded Kelly. And Kelly himself listened to us, tried to understand the problem, and solved it. Maliki wanted to see us, and we met with al-Maliki to solve this dispute. Kelly invited us for a lunch, and he asked us to be patient and said, "You have my support for anything you face." We found that Anbar Province was open to all: the prime minister, the Iraqi parliament, and the American command. For that, we met, we thought, and he helped us in many things, like how to solve our problems before we use force. So after the confrontation with al-Qaeda, the confrontation with the Islamic Party was the most notable, and I'll tell you, General Kelly was able to defuse it.

You know what really makes us mad? It is seeing that the Americans were able to spend money and fulfill projects much more than the Iraqi government, or I should say the Anbari government that's headed by the Islamic Party. What the Americans have done is great. What they have been able to accomplish is great, but also the flip side of it is, "What if the Americans had the Anbari government's money?" They would have accomplished a lot more.

President [George W.] Bush's visit to Anbar was an important thing as a political message, but not in substance. Nothing really came out of it. [Barak H.] Obama's visit to Anbar, along with the two senators, the Democratic senator and the Republican one, was an important one.* We met with them, and we gave them a clear message. The true test right now for the Americans is to leave Iraq standing on its own feet, not lying on its back.

And to tell you the truth, rockets, scientific things like genes and the science of genes, and stuff like that, are not as important as leaving Iraq standing on its feet. The true test for America is to leave a new Iraq, as we were promised. I'll tell you what, the true test of democracy came in this election, not the one preceding it, nothing before that, ever.

There are three things to note that were of very great importance. The first is the appearance of al-Qaeda in Iraq. It was something that was not imagined. The second thing was that the Americans

---

* Then-Senator Obama, who was at the time the presumptive Democratic Party nominee for president, visited Ramadi on 22 July 2008 as part of a congressional delegation that also included Senator John F. "Jack" Reed, a Democrat from Rhode Island, and Senator Charles T. "Chuck" Hagel, a Republican from Nebraska.

stood with us, how they backed us up. That was not imagined. And the third thing was Maliki's stand, and how he did not look at himself as being Shiite. He stood with us, regardless of his sect.

So there were three noted things that were of great importance that one must look at, after which we had two meetings in preparation for these last elections. I went to the council in Baghdad, and two VBIEDs [vehicle borne improvised explosive devices] came in and attacked us. They brought down the building on us and, thanks be to the Almighty, I was saved.

General Hickman* paid me a visit, the deputy ambassador paid me a visit, and many more people from the American command and the embassy came in and paid me a visit. Even at those precarious times, we still insisted that Iraq would be clean and clear of al-Qaeda.

I think the reason I was attacked was because, two weeks prior to the attack, I had made a statement on the air that the trouble and the problems were neither the Americans nor the Iraqi government, but it was the Iranians. I also said that there is no connection between the Iranians and the Shiites of Iraq. So, with the help of the Almighty, we are on this steadfastly. The rebuilding of Iraq, getting Iraq rid of all the militias. I espouse no chair, no position, nothing, just the service of Iraq.

Montgomery: I'd like to go back and ask two questions about what you said earlier. First, at one point you were facing al-Qaeda, who was armed with lethal weapons, but you could not go to the Americans because then it would look like you were their puppets. So how could you fight under those circumstances? What do you do to fight? It sounds like you're organizing, but how do you fight?

Ali Hatim: It's not the fact that the people would think we are American stooges. No. There was a huge mistrust between us and the Americans due to the fact—if you remember the attack on Fallujah?

Montgomery: Yes.

Ali Hatim: There was a huge gap between us and the Americans.

---

* Possibly Col William B. Hickman, USA.

That's why we didn't want to ask them. As far as your questions, "How did we fight off al-Qaeda," we were able to buy weapons. Everything was on the market. To buy a PKC [machine gun] was like 500 bucks. We were able to buy French weapons. We were able to buy heavy armaments, Dushka—a Russian Dushka antiaircraft [heavy machine gun]. So there was plenty of it going around. And due to the distrust that existed between us and the Americans, had we asked the Americans for weapons, they would not have given them to us because of the fear factor. They did not know who we were.

Just to let you know, it's a known fact that Iraq is awash with weaponry. That's one thing.

And the second thing that we counted on, the fact that the Americans would come on our side once we started the fight—and this is exactly what took place. To tell you the truth, if you look at the Americans' role, and what they did in here, they were more interested in the welfare of the Iraqi people than the government of Anbar was. Tell you some facts—the way they stood behind us, the way they supported us, the way they kept overwatch on the police apparatus, on the security apparatus. One thing about it, they even counted the gasoline, how to disperse it among the police, who took it in turn and sold it. So the Americans kept watch over everybody and anybody. They really kept everybody in line, and if it weren't for them, it was chaos.

Montgomery: You're leading into my second question. You said there was a change in the American approach when there was a change in command. Could you give some examples of how things were changed, before and after?

Ali Hatim: The difference between the two commands, the first guy was sort of moody. He tried to please some people, very few people, mostly the people that were outside, by giving them contracts that really didn't matter too much.

Montgomery: Outside where?

Ali Hatim: Outside the country, to the sheikhs who lived maybe in Syria or Emirates or Jordan. So he was trying to please these people, rather than to do the right thing in Anbar, like I said. He was moody. He didn't have the political savvy. He did not know how to work the Anbar people.

Whereas General Kelly, no, no, no—he started using reason with us. He helped us. He did everything possible to defuse the situation against the Islamic Party because, I'll tell you what, if the confrontation had taken place between us and the Islamic Party, not even 100 American tanks would have defused it.

We had intended to finish off the Islamic Party. The thing we detest the most is Islamic Parties in Iraq. I'll tell you a synopsis of how he treated Anbar. He treated it like his own garden. He paid a great deal of attention to the cowards who ran away from here, the people who stayed in Jordan or Syria, or what have you. He gave armored vehicles to some people—some people who did not deserve it. He put people who did not deserve to be in leadership ahead of the real leaders. They purposely wanted to insult, dishonor, and create disputes between people. So he really did not—this is the first commander.

Montgomery: Isn't that what Saddam did, created new sheikhs?

Ali Hatim: Yes.

Montgomery: So it's the same thing again.

Ali Hatim: And this is what we refused to accept.

I'll tell you something else. Sheikh Sattar Abu Risha, Sheikh Ali—we did not kill anybody with our own hands. It was the fighters from the field who did the killing, yet Sheikh Sattar Abu Risha was made too prominent. He was given much more prominence than he deserved. I'll tell you the truth, and I'm going to speak frankly, he was given too much money under the guise of various projects, meaning arming of the people. But truthfully, just to be frank about it, it was too much money, much more than he deserved. It has to be noted and has to be acknowledged that Sheikh Sattar Abu Risha made a great stand. His stand against al-Qaeda was well known, but not as much as the Americans made it to be. For instance, the fighter in the street, to me, was much more deserving of attention than Abu Risha.

When General Kelly came in, he leveled the field, so to speak. He spoke with everyone equally. There was equality in his treatment. And this is what really we're looking for, this treatment. Do not treat me better than Sheikh Hamid, or Hamid better than Sattar, or Sattar better than so forth and so on—everybody equally.

Montgomery: That prominence is probably what got him killed, though, isn't it?

Ali Hatim: I think you're probably right. The way that his prominence rose may have led to his demise, but Sheikh Sattar Abu Risha had to be fair with his own self, because a man has to be truthful to himself and to the Almighty, too.

When I went to Jordan and tried to get the sheikhs to come back to Iraq to fight, you could see cowardice in their faces: "No, man, leave me alone. I'm not going back."

When the American soldiers go back to the United States, they don't go back there and boast about what they did in Iraq. They simply did their duty, and that is what we did. We did our duty to our country, to our province. The American government provides medical coverage. They pay salaries to their men. In other words, they're taken care of. It's well deserved.

Whereas these sheikhs, when they come back here and say, "Well, look, I am and I am and I am," and they start boasting about their doings, which are false. General Kelly, when he came in, he realized who was who, and he gave each his due. I hope that the new general, who is taking General Kelly's place, will follow in his footsteps.*

What we started in Anbar, we finished in Baghdad. Sheikh Hamid al-Hayess took 24 fighters and went to Hamdiya, and he fought off al-Qaeda. We started many Awakenings in Baghdad. I'll tell you, in one section of Baghdad, the Americans were paying as much as $52 million a month for the Sons of Iraq. In Abu Ghraib, we took part. In southern Baghdad, we took part. Ameriyah, Ghazaliya, also

---

* MGen Kelly was succeeded as commander of Multi National Force-West by MGen Richard T. Tryon on 9 February 2009.

Adhamiyah. We went forward toward Salah ad-Din, Taji. We used our tribal affiliation and interaction to push this initiative forward. And what was great, when we traveled about in Baghdad, in Salah ad-Din, everywhere else, we found that the American response and cooperation with Iraqis was as good, maybe even better.

I admonished and reminded Obama of the fact that you've accepted the fight in Iraq, so you must pull out responsibly. Do not go out of Iraq as losers because that will be a sad reflection on your legacy, so pull out of Iraq responsibly. Make a responsible pullout, not just because you vowed in your election campaign that you're going to pull out of Iraq—not just to fulfill that vow. No. Make it a responsible pullout, even though, to be frank with you, we are opposed to occupation. We don't want to be occupied, but at the same time, we have to look for a responsible pullout. The most volatile place in Iraq is Anbar Province. But we have to think with our heads and not be emotional.

What we notice right now, the Obama administration is trying to repair things inside the United States. But to be honest with you, the United States proper is affected by what takes place around the world. Obama's emphasis is to go to Afghanistan and do what is right in Afghanistan. Well, let me tell you something: Anbar is much more volatile than Afghanistan. Considering the undercurrent of animosity that exists among various entities, the only reason it is contained right now is because of your presence. It's like a car. You lift your foot off of the accelerator, and the vehicle dies.

I have said what I said as a warning and to be remembered in future years. The security situation right now in Iraq is relevant to many things. Therefore, if we have an irresponsible pullout, it might do more damage, and the situation will become much more dangerous than in 2005.

Interview 8

Sheikh Majed Abd al-Razzaq Ali al-Sulayman

Co-Regent
Dulaimi Tribal Confederation

Sheikh Majed Abd al-Razzaq Ali al-Sulayman is a descendant of Sheikh Ali al-Sulayman, who was one of the most powerful sheikhs in al-Anbar Province during and after the transition from Ottoman to British rule (described in the writings of Gertrude Bell). He is a great uncle of Sheikh Ali Hatim (interview 7 in this book), who is the heir apparent and de facto paramount sheikh of the Dulaimi tribal confederation. Sheikh Majed and his cousin, Sheikh Amer Abd al-Jabbar Ali al-Sulayman al-Assaf, initially served as co-regents due to Sheikh Ali Hatim's youth, with Sheikh Amer residing in Ramadi, Iraq, and Sheikh Majed supporting from Amman, Jordan. Now Ali Hatim has matured, but he continues to honor this protocol out of respect for his uncles.

Sheikh Majed and his family fled to Jordan after coming under government scrutiny following a failed coup against Saddam Hussein in the 1990s. King Hussein of Jordan gave him sanctuary, and he began working with exiled Iraqi opposition groups.

Sheikh Majed was interviewed by Colonel Gary W. Montgomery and Chief Warrant Officer-4 Timothy S. McWilliams on 25 February 2009 in Amman, Jordan.

Sheikh Majed Abd al-Razzaq Ali al-Sulayman: The first one who contacted me, and we are still very close, was Dr. Ayad Allawi. He traveled here to Amman, and I met with him. Two Americans were with him. I don't know who they were. Apparently he informed the Americans in London about Sheikh Majed, and they were astonished and surprised to meet Sheikh Majed here in Amman. I met with Ayad Allawi and the Americans for about two or three hours, and Ayad Allawi was translating for me. They said, "We'll meet you later," and they went back to the States.

A month, two months later, I traveled to London. I met with the opposition in London, [Ayatollah Sayed Muhammad Baqir] al-Hakim—not this Hakim that's here, but the one who was assassinated—Massoud Barzani, and Ahmed Chalabi.

[Conversation with interpreter on what time frame Majed is discussing.]

Majed: That was in the year of 2000. They were talking about the next movement, and where they're going to go, and how they're getting ready to overthrow the regime, and they decided to go and meet in the north of Iraq. I objected to that. I told them, "Look, if I want to enter Iraq, I will not allow myself to get in from the north. If I want to assist, I will enter Iraq from the right road, which is from Jordan to Trebil, and from Trebil to Anbar."

We talked for a long time, and there were so many warnings and objections. You have to be frank, because we're talking about history, and I have to be right in what I'm saying. The only one who spoke who was a patriot to Iraq was Ayad Allawi. He was not sectarian at that time.

I came back to Amman, and we continued our meetings here in Amman. I had a phone call from Dr. Ayad Allawi and Nouri Badran, who was the first interior minister during Ayad Allawi's era. I think that was in 2001 or the end of 2000. He said, "There are highly important VIPs coming from the States, and they want to meet you in person. They want to meet you in Abu Dhabi in the United Arab Emirates."

I traveled to Abu Dhabi, and we met continuously for two or three days. They introduced themselves, but I don't think they gave me their real names. I understood from Nouri Badran that one of them was the assistant to the CIA [Central Intelligence Agency], and the other one was a very important person in the Department of Defense. So we met for two or three days, and they even showed me the plans on how they're going to enter Iraq on a map. This was a long talk. And they told me that a person would be coming from the United States to coordinate with me in person.

At the beginning of 2002, a person came from the States, and I met him here in Amman. His name was George. We used to meet from hotel to hotel for security reasons, and he used to go to the States and come back, but we continued our meetings. He asked me, "What's your influence on the military officers in Anbar Province?". . . I told him, "I'll contact the officers in Anbar in person, right in front of you now." And I said, "I will show you that most of them are not supporters of Saddam Hussein." There were about nine Americans sitting in that meeting. Some of them spoke Arabic. One of the American gentlemen, called Yahir, was translating for me. And I contacted three generals in Anbar. They were listening to what I told them on the other line. One of them was in the Republican Guard, one of them was in military industry, and one was in the artillery. I spoke to them, and they said, "Please, sheikh, assist us in overthrowing this regime today, not tomorrow. We have had enough of Saddam Hussein's regime."

The year 2003 came. We continued meeting during that time. I went to London and back again, and I went over to the United Arab Emirates again. George came back—a very nice gentleman. I think George stayed with me here for two months. We met three or four times a week with his groups, as you know, and we kept looking at Iraqi maps, how to enter Iraq. I showed them how to enter Iraq from the Saudi side, and I even showed them the Iraqi checkpoints. And I told them, "What we need now is to have some people working for us inside Iraq, so they can tell us the Iraqi military movements, the Fedayeen Saddam movements. To check the movements between Abu Ghraib and the border with Jordan, to keep an eye on the borders—the Saudi border, the Jordanian border, and the Syrian border."

The first people we used for formation were the sheep smugglers because nobody keeps an eye on them or thinks of them as spies. They brought their sheep, they kept an eye on Iraqi military movements, and they passed the information to us.

There was a gentleman we met once a week because it was so dangerous at the time to send any written messages. Another gentleman came with George later on, by the name of Roy. George told me that we needed to get some Thuraya satellite phones into Iraq. There were some military guys with them, but they were wearing civilian clothes. At the time, as you know, anyone who had a satellite phone in Iraq would be executed on the spot.

He said, "Let's smuggle 100 satellite phones into Iraq."

I said, "No."

He said, "Let's smuggle 20, 25, up to 30 at a time."

So we used these cell phones between the Syrian border and the Saudi border. They watched the H-3 base and H-2 base, and they kept an eye on the Iraqi checkpoints. They kept passing information every hour.

And we used to meet in hotels for our safety: the Holiday Inn, to the Sheraton, to the Four Seasons—no, the Four Seasons wasn't open—the [Radisson] SAS Hotel. And we used to contact them at 10:00 every night. We used to call everyone, and then we expanded the area. We took it from just the borders to all the way to Ramadi. The first cell phone I handed over to my cousin, Sheikh Amer Abd al-Jabbar, in Ramadi, and that put his life in so much danger. And I handed some to our guys in Fallujah, and some into Abu Ghraib—nearer to the Abu Ghraib base.

Then we had another meeting in London. That was January 2003. I wasn't very happy about that meeting, which was between us, the oppositions. They wanted to go back to the States, and I decided to come back here to Amman. At the meeting, there were the Shi'a Iranians and the Kurds, al-Hakim and Chalabi, Massoud Barzani and Jalal Talabani. They were insisting on dissolving the Iraqi army, and we were objecting to that. We really objected to their idea of dissolving the Iraqi army, and they asked me, "What is the solution?" I said that the Coalition forces enter Iraq, we call it a military coup, and all will be accountable then. The high officers during Saddam Hussein's era, and the politicians, and the Ba'athists, put them aside—the high ones. And the country continues with its organization, with the ministries as they are. Those guys went to the States, and I came back to Jordan.

To be frank, Ahmed Chalabi had a lot of influence in Congress and the Department of Defense. And at State, they talked about the same subject, and Ayad Allawi was objecting to dissolving the Iraqi army. I came back here to Amman, and we continued meeting with our friends. It's a long, lengthy talk. I've got it summarized.

The day that they were warning of invading Iraq from Basrah, the plan changed completely in the last minutes. Roy and George and the other friends took me and some of the opposition from Amman, and they put us on a Jordanian base called H-4, I think, nearer to the Iraqi-Jordanian border. I think 40 of us were there—me, Ayad Allawi, and his groups. Some of the sheikhs from the south were there as well. We stayed there for about 15 or 20 days, I think, maybe 15 days. The war had started by then, and they were telling us how to put on gas masks. I received a phone call from here in Amman. The American embassy wanted me and Dr. Ayad Allawi for an urgent meeting at the American embassy. My people stayed there. We had satellite channels as well at the H-4 base. We were advising the Iraqi military, the Iraqi civilians, "Do not fight the Coalition forces. They are a Coalition of liberation." And we had some Iraqi military officers, generals from the opposition, supporting us as well. One of the generals was Salim al-Imam. He was an ambassador and a soldier. And there was another guy called Ahmad Shabib, who was a military guy, too. And the third one was Ibrahim Janabi. They stayed at the H-4 base, and we came back to Amman.

When I got here to Amman, I was surprised with the news that they attacked Barzan's farm, which was a big disaster to me. The house they attacked was my sister's house, and I lost my sister and her children. I lost 22 members of my family in that attack. My sister and her children and her grandchildren all died in this attack. I was devastated. They hit my old house by mistake, and I think somebody passed wrong information to them. They told them, I think, that this was Barzan's farm and that [Saddam] Hussein was hiding in this house.

I remained here in Amman, and I had my sister waking me up for three days. I received a phone call at 12:00. They said, "Get ready. We are ready to move into Ramadi." Prior to that, the Americans asked me, "What do you think if we start bombing the military bases in Ramadi—in Anbar Province? What do you think of that?"

I told them, "Please do not shoot even one bullet in Anbar Province. I can assure you that once you enter Anbar Province, nobody will resist you, neither the tribes nor the military. And I am responsible for what I say. And anything that happens in Anbar Province, I will be responsible." At that meeting, when I said what I just said, the Iraqi ambassador to Egypt was attending that. His name is Raad al-Alousi. But I advised the Coalition forces, "Do not bomb the province, above all else."

So we left Amman. I think we left Amman about 9:30, 10:00 in the morning, and we were accompanied by our Jordanian friends to protect us. When we got into Iraq, we were very disappointed. I saw that the Trebil border crossing had been looted. There were no employees there. The border was open. There was a big picture of Saddam Hussein at the border. We shot at it with our weapons until it fell on the ground, and we continued into Iraq.

Roy and Ibrahim Janabi entered Iraq before us, and they were waiting for us at the K-90 [highway kilometer marker 90] area. The tribes were waiting for me in my guesthouse, and I was in contact with them all the way by satellite phone, just making sure I was traveling all the way to Ramadi. There were American forces all the way to Ramadi. When I introduced myself to them, they let me go through immediately.

I think we got to Ramadi at around 8:00 in the evening. Ayad Allawi and his group, and Roy and his group, were astonished and amazed at the reception and the welcome that we received from the tribes when we got there. This was recorded by Ayad Allawi on his own camera. There were about 2,000 or 3,000 people from my tribe, and all of them were armed. They were dancing and celebrating. And all the sheikhs were waiting for me, too. We had dinner, and Dr. Ayad Allawi remained in my guesthouse for three or four days. Then he moved into Baghdad after it was secured.

Roy and his group contacted me. They said we needed to have other meetings regarding Anbar Province. I said, "Prior to having our meeting, tomorrow morning I have a meeting with all the tribes of my province. And during our meeting, we'll appoint a governor for the province." The Americans did not believe that we could do that so quickly, and it was the first province in the whole of Iraq. We appointed Abdul Karim Burjis al-Rawi as the first governor for Anbar, and we appointed the first chief of police. His name was Ja'adan [Muhammad al-] Alwani. So what we did, the main thing is that we stabilized the province. We appointed the governor, we appointed the chief of police, and 10 days later, all the government offices reopened, and everybody started going back to work.

So when I went to meet with the Americans, they were very happy about what we had achieved in the province. They called it the first step for democracy and liberation. After 15 days in Anbar, I insisted on reopening and securing the border crossing points by putting sheikhs and Anbaris in charge of the Trebil and Tanf border crossing points.

I remained in Ramadi, and I had several meetings with a general who lived in Saddam Hussein's palace. When we entered the palace, we saw it had been looted completely. The Thurayas had been looted. Thieves looted the whole place. It was a really difficult time that we passed through.

After being in Ramadi 25 days, they requested me for a meeting in Baghdad. Ambassador [Jay M.] Garner was there. All the overseas opposition was there. Some of the opposition from inside Iraq was there, too. That meeting took about three or four hours. "What's next? What's the next step now? What are we going to do?" We said it again, the same as I said it before, "Everything should remain as it was prior to the liberation."

But we faced the biggest tragedy by changing Garner for [L. Paul] Bremer. Bremer came over, and the first thing he did was dissolve the Iraqi army and create an armed enemy against us. This is what we were warning against prior to the liberation. He dissolved all the Ba'athist parties. This is the other disaster he made. He dissolved all the government institutions and ministries. What he did is just like putting a bomb in this room, and the bomb explodes the whole room. He decimated everything.

I wasn't very happy at all then. I was not optimistic. I went out with my American friends to take me back to a meeting with Bremer in a palace in Baghdad. There were 12 of us, me and Adnan Pachachi, Massoud Barzani, Ahmed Chalabi. Ayad was sick. He didn't attend the meeting, but he sent his representative, Nuri Badran. Hoshyar Zebari, the foreign minister, [was there, as was] [Ayatollah Sayed Muhammad Baqir] al-Hakim, the one who was assassinated. We discussed a lot in that meeting regarding the mistakes that he was making by dissolving the Iraqi army and the government institutions, but he insisted on his decisions. The Iranian Shi'as and the Kurds had brainwashed him, and I could not change his mind at all.

The border now became open to everybody who ever wanted to enter in and out of Iraq. Nobody was controlling it. Millions of people entered from Iran. Hundreds of thousands from al-Qaeda and the terrorists entered from Syria.

They wanted to form a governmental committee. Roy contacted me, and the general, and they asked me to come and meet them at Saddam's airport. The road was very dangerous, but they said, "There is an important meeting. You have to attend." They said to enter the palace through the Radwaniyah side. They took me in armored cars. I think there were about six cars. And for history, I have to be straight and frank about what the Americans did. Each American sat on one side, just to secure my life.

I entered the republican palace at the airport, and this was the first time I had entered this palace. All of the government's members, who they wanted to choose, were there. Ghazi al-Yawer was there, as were Pachachi, Allawi, Chalabi, Hakim, Massoud Barzani, and Jalal Talabani. There was seating for groups of people. The Americans, with their arms and their body armor, secured my life, standing next to me, protecting me. And somebody came and asked who I am. It was the British ambassador there. I don't remember his name.

He said to me, "We're going to have a meeting with Bremer now."

And I said, "What for?"

He said, "Once you have the meeting with Bremer, he'll tell you why he wants to talk to you."

It was a lengthy talk with Bremer then, and he was snobby. I told him that I will not be a member of this governing council, and he asked me why. "Because," I said, "you are forming the council wrongly."

And he said, "What am I doing wrong?"

And I told him, "The first mistake you made was dissolving the Iraqi army." I told him then that all the weapons that Saddam Hussein bought for the last 30 years had been looted. I told him, "Go out on the street and see. They're selling weapons on the pavement in streets of Baghdad. This is the first thing." And secondly, now you're starting to form a government on a sectarian basis by choosing from Shi'as, Sunnis, Arabs, and Kurds. I would rather go back and help build my province. That's better than being a member of your government."

So I left. My American friends, who I used to meet here in Jordan, asked me about the meeting. I told them what happened, and they were very sad then.

So I went back, and we made a governing council in Anbar Province. The borders were open. The terrorists started coming in. Every day, there were demonstrations against us. There were no schools at the time. There was no army. There was no Ba'ath Party. There were no security forces. There for two or three months, I was calming people. None of them were receiving salaries, so I was trying my best to keep them quiet.

The governor at the time was an intelligence provider. He said, "We have stores and warehouses full of cement, wood, and metal. I will sell all this stock and get the money for the government before somebody loots it." Then people started looting and stealing what they wanted from the stores. He sold it, and he collected some money. We started paying salaries and calmed the situation.

Then the governing council was formed in Baghdad. I went to Baghdad and used my influence to appoint some Anbaris as guards just to keep them quiet, so they could receive salaries, and the Americans assisted me then, too. We employed about 2,000 or 3,000 Anbaris. The teachers, the lecturers—we managed to get them some salaries, too, with pressure, of course, from the American general.

After that, people started to lose trust. They had enough of people lying to them. They regarded me as if I was the one who contacted President [George W.] Bush and told him to invade Iraq. That's the way people looked on me. The first bomb in Iraq exploded in my guesthouse. As a family, I don't know how God blessed us, and none of us were killed. Some of my guards and people outside were killed. About 25 houses around my guesthouse were demolished completely. The car was a Toyota Land Cruiser, and it was filled with 500 kilograms of TNT. So the American forces came into al-Anbar straightaway and surrounded our area. They were shocked at the amount of TNT that was in this car. With that amount of TNT, they could have demolished half of the city. Anyway, we got out of it safely.

I went to Baghdad for a meeting, me and my bodyguards. I had a license from the general to carry weapons. On the way back from Baghdad (al-Qaeda had taken over Fallujah), I had about 16 or 17 cars in my convoy, and they're all similar, so they didn't know which car I was in. We got to the Saqlawiyah district, and they opened fire on us. Hundreds of thousands of bullets were shooting at us. My guards were brave. Straightaway, they came out of their cars and laid down on the ground. We had PKC [machine guns] with us, and we resisted. It was a valiant resistance. I continued on my way, and my bodyguards stayed and fought. They told me to just leave and go, and there was another car guarding me. I think the Americans heard what was happening. Two Apaches [helicopters] came over, and al-Qaeda ran away. I didn't see, but my bodyguards told me they killed seven al-Qaeda. Of my bodyguards, I think five or six people were injured. Eight of my cars were demolished completely.

We got back to Ramadi, and we continued our work. One day I was calling the governor and coordinating with him. Since my guesthouse was bombed, we were sitting in one of our houses. There was a gentleman trying to get in, and my bodyguard asked him, "Who are you?" He told them, 'I came to see Sheikh Majed, to ask him to appoint me to the police or the army or on the borders." They let him in. It was a shortcoming of my bodyguards. They didn't search him. The important thing is that he entered my house. I was on the phone, speaking to the governor. About 30 of us were sitting there. Sheikh Amer was sitting next to me. My cousin, God bless his soul, Sulayman was sitting there. And Sheikh Ra'ad was by my side as well, and my people were sitting all over.

He asked, "Who is Sheikh Majed." They pointed at me. They just told him in good faith. I asked him straightaway—a boy of 24 or 25 years old—I asked him, "Where are you from?" He said, "I'm a Dulaim," but he said it in a different dialect from Baghdad. I started wondering who this guy is. He started pressing a button. It was winter, and he was wearing a coat. God saved us. He tried to detonate a bomb.

He asked one of the guys who was sitting there, "Is there a toilet around?" We said, "Yes, there is one on the right." My cousins and my nephew said, "There is something wrong with this guy. I think he is full of explosives." Straightaway I told my guards, "Don't let him come in." He went to the toilet. I think the wire wasn't connected to the suicide belt, so he went and connected it. He came running toward me. My bodyguards caught him by both arms. They took him outside the house and threw him into the street. As he fell down, he exploded. Even from a distance, it broke all the glass.

[Rest break. Conversation omitted, except for the following exchange]

Majed: One thing I would like to mention in your record—you must write it: when I appointed Abdul Karim Burjs al-Rawi as the first governor, I appointed Ahmad Abu Risha as one of his bodyguards—the head of the Awakening.

Interpreter: I said, "Oh, did you appoint Ahmad or Abdul Sattar?" He said, "No, I appointed Ahmad, because Abdul Sattar was a road gangster. He was robbing in the streets."

[end of break]

Colonel Gary W. Montgomery: Could you tell us how the Awakening came about?

Majed: The Awakening—I'm going to speak frankly—the Awakening wasn't built by one person. Unfortunately, credit was given to one man, and from others it was taken. This is the biggest mistake the Americans made, too.

Al-Qaeda started to enter Ramadi city. We don't have it in humanity, not in Islam, not in any other religion, that somebody can come and cut off someone's head. Al-Qaeda started to prohibit people from doing things and to allow other things to be done in the name of Islam, as if they were messengers from God, and it was all lies and wrong. They started to steal.

They did what they did in Fallujah, and I warned the people of Fallujah about them, too, and I told them at the time. I warned the people of Fallujah that al-Qaeda members are not Islamic. They are members of the Iranian groups, and they want to shove us in front of the Americans. This is an Iranian strategy: that we, the Sunnis, are against the Americans and against humanity, and the Shi'as are a peaceful and poor people. Nobody believed me.

When people started to recognize al-Qaeda for what they were, after they destroyed and damaged what they did, it was too late to say, "I'm sorry." They started to realize what I said was right about al-Qaeda, and I told them afterward.

Let's start about the Awakening, how it started. The first thing al-Qaeda did, they started attacking the women. And we, the Arabs, as you know, when you pull a woman's hair, it's a big thing. This can start a war. And there was a woman from the Albu Ali Jassim tribe. She was the daughter of one of the sheikhs. I won't mention names. So the tribes started to rise up after they attacked this woman.

We, all the sheikhs, had a meeting here in Amman. We met to start a revolution, to start the Awakening. We went to [Prime Minister Nouri al-] Maliki and got his advice. He said, "I will not accept the Awakening unless it's blessed by the al-Sulayman tribe." I've got a letter.

I think General [John R.] Allen came to see me at the time, and he asked me, "What's your opinion?" I told him, "What you are doing now, you should have done three years ago."

And, as we say of someone who dies, we just say "God bless him." Sattar was with them, too. Everybody knows the reputation of Sattar, I'm sure you know, and of his brother Ahmad. So we, the sheikhs, discussed among ourselves who will head the Awakening. I tell you frankly—and this is being recorded, so I'm speaking frankly—if any other sheikh denies it, it's on record. They say, "The right job for the right man, and the bad will be accountable unto the bad." So we chose the bad one, which was Sattar, because he was a troublemaker, and he had a bad record, so we chose Sattar. And, as you know, his tribe is a very small tribe.

And in the circumstances that occurred, everyone started to rise up against al-Qaeda. So we sent an e-mail, and I have it here with me. I sent an e-mail to the prime minister, Nouri al-Maliki, advising him that the al-Sulayman tribe blesses this movement, and he can supply them with weapons. And all the Dulaimi tribes signed it, supporting this move. Even General Allen was happy about it.

We held a forum in Ramadi. The whole tribe started supporting it. Each tribesman started to fight against the people within his tribe who were with al-Qaeda, from Fallujah to Rutbah, to Rawah, to al-Hit, to al-Anah, al-Qasiyah, to al-Qaim. Each tribe fought al-Qaeda. This brave work was done by the tribesmen. But unfortunately, it was credited to only one or two people. This is what is not fair.

After we finished, and we cleared al-Qaeda—and thank God we kicked them out—the head of the Awakening, one or two of them, started to abuse it for personal gain, to gain more contracts, only for financial gain.

Now, as you know, the Awakening has been breaking down because al-Qaeda has been kicked out. Each tribe is proud of its achievement, and unfortunately, some of them have been directed into financial gains only. And if you remember, I spoke to General [Martin] Post directly about this matter when he came here. I told him to stop that work. I advised him to stop supporting a few men because it will reflect badly on you. Because the tribes know what is up. They know me, they know you, they know each and every one of us. And they know what you earned and what your financial capability was two or three years ago. Now, after two or three years, I see the difference in them, how much they changed. Now, they have wealth. They're worth millions of dollars. Previously, most of the people who became multimillionaires were road gangsters. They were robbing cars on the highway. So they have been awarded more than they deserve. Now we have to stop the support—quietly and gently, because, as you know, the tribes are very sensitive.

Saddam, with all his power, wanted to play on problems among the sheikhs and open doors for himself. You have to keep this in its history, and keep the tribes to themselves. Each sheikh and each tribe has his history and his position. Saddam made some sheikhs in the '90s, and you know them. And when the Americans came over, they made two or three fake sheikhs, and they're all playboys and road gangsters. This is one of the negative things being done. And, as a friend, I warn my friends in all frankness and honesty.

Montgomery: How can Saddam—or in two or three cases, the Americans—how can they make a sheikh?

Majed: I'll tell you. Saddam opened an office for the tribes, and he started to register the sheikhs: A, B, C. Then, he mixed it up. B became A, C became B. He started mixing the names of the sheikhs as he liked. This is history. You cannot play with history, but he wanted to play with history. The older tradition has its life, has its history.

Now when the Americans came, at the beginning, when we sat with them, they used to call and meet only the main tribal sheikhs in al-Anbar, that is, me and the governor, and the general who used to sit on the panel. And this has all been documented, I'm sure, documented by you. I am the head of all the tribes. [Interpreter—name deleted], for example, is from this tribe, so I bring the head of that tribe. I don't know what Saddam did by changing the names from A to B, B to C and all this, but it does not work with us, because we go back to history, and we know who the head of the tribe is. So in our way, when we met with the Americans, we were on the right path. But once I came to Amman, chaos started—and al-Qaeda. Unfortunately, the Americans don't know our tradition. Everybody who was wearing a scarf like me, they called him sheikh. If he is a sheikh, yes, but any sheikh we meet, go and ask him for his history first.

Montgomery: You mentioned that Sattar was the right man for the right job, and at the same time, you also said that he was from a small tribe. Was it important that he was from a small tribe?

Majed: They are very small. Ask the whole province about the Abu Risha tribe. They are one of the smallest tribes.

Montgomery: What I'm wondering is—

Unknown: Was that part of the criteria for him being chosen?

Interpreter: No, it was the criterion because he was a gangster.

Montgomery: But to start a revolution, wouldn't it be better to have a sheikh from a big tribe?

Majed: Okay. I'll tell you how we chose him. We were hesitant. First of all, we went to Sheikh Tariq, and he said, "Look, I'm a tribal head, and I've got a history. I cannot be a cowboy in the street. It doesn't suit my position."

So we chose someone. He was a son of a tribe. Sattar, God bless his soul. He's dead now. He was a brave man. You have to be fair. And he was not like Ahmad, who loves financial rewards. And he used to talk to everyone. And he educated and civilized himself. He left the past behind, but unfortunately, he was assassinated, and God bless him.

Montgomery: I guess that a small tribe minimizes the risk to other people, doesn't it?

Interpreter: I asked the sheikh, "Was it you chose him because of a small tribe or because he was a gangster?" He said, "That's why, because he was a gangster, and that's why we chose him."

Montgomery: I've heard that some of the inspiration for the Awakening came from a very local uprising in al-Qaim that did not spread anywhere, but it kind of gave an example that people refer back to frequently. What do you think about that?

Majed: I told you before that the Awakening revolution started when al-Qaeda attacked the woman that I mentioned earlier.

Montgomery: And that was in al-Qaim?

Majed: No, it was in Anbar—it was in the Albu Ali Jassim tribe. There was a conflict in al-Qaim, because some of the tribes—if you walk in one path, it's okay, but once you start walking in several paths, you will be discovered. As you know, al-Qaim was the first place al-Qaeda entered. Then they started fighting among themselves. But it didn't last long. It was quieted immediately. But the Awakening started from Ramadi when they took this woman by the hair.

Montgomery: The reason I'm asking these questions is I've interviewed a lot of people, and, as you said earlier, each tribe had its own Awakening, so to speak.

Majed: It's so, it's so.

Montgomery: But when I'm interviewing people, sometimes I hear the same facts from each person, and sometimes I hear things that were more important locally, but not for the whole province. So I ask other people to see if this was a province-wide thing or a local thing.

Majed: I'll tell you why. When you talk to each tribe, it's talking about itself, because each tribe knows who's the infiltrator in the tribe, and they know who's the thief in the tribe. But when I speak, I speak on the whole of the province. The effort we started when we, the sheikhs, met—all of us—in Amman here, we wanted to gather and unite all the efforts of the tribes in one group. And we moved in the right path.

Iraqi Perspectives

Interview 9

Sheikh Sabah al-Sattam Effan Fahran al-Shurji al-Aziz

Principal Sheikh
Albu Mahal Tribe

Sheikh Sabah al-Sattam Effan Fahran al-Shurji al-Aziz is the principal sheikh of the Albu Mahal tribe in al-Qaim, on the Syrian border. He and his tribe led some of the earliest Iraqi resistance to al-Qaeda in Iraq, in 2005, which is cited by some as one of the first organized "awakening" efforts.

Sheikh Sabah was interviewed by Colonel Gary W. Montgomery and Chief Warrant Officer-4 Timothy S. McWilliams on 25 February 2009 in Amman, Jordan.

Sheikh Sabah al-Sattam Effan Fahran al-Shurji al-Aziz: The western side of Iraq, as we say, is from Haditha to al-Qaim and al-Rutbah. In the beginning, it was invaded by British forces. After two or three months they changed—the American forces took over from the British forces. When they entered as invaders, for sure, it's the right of the people to resist invaders.

One of the biggest mistakes the Coalition forces made at the beginning was getting intelligence information from people that were not trustworthy. And when they got the information, they acted blindly. They started by humiliating the people, scaring children and women. This was the first mistake by the Coalition forces.

Two weeks after, I was detained by the British forces—having done nothing—they detained me on the 17th of April in 2003. It was for false information passed to them by a false man.

We are—we inherited this from our fathers, and grandfathers, and great-grandfathers—we are a brave and traditional tribe in al-Qaim. And we are brave and strong. Some of the tribes—and I say some of them—used to concern some of the smaller tribes, and they wanted to retaliate against us by using the Coalition forces. We, as a tribe, we did not want to create any conflicts among us, especially after the invasion of the Coalition forces. On the contrary, we wanted to keep stability with the Coalition forces and our tribe and other tribes, too, and our traditions.

When the American forces took over from the British forces, unfortunately, the mistakes started to increase. For history and for honesty, the British treatment of us was much better than by the Americans, as the British had more experience with Iraqi people, and in general with the Middle East as a whole. No assassinations were done by the British. It was much less than was done by the Americans, I can say about 70 to 80 percent less killing done by the Coalition than by the Americans.

Unfortunately, the Americans used to deal with violence and toughness. I'm talking about the first two years of the invasion. And they didn't listen to us at all when we told them that the tribes are the keys to solving Iraqis' problems. After the weakening of the tribes, terrorists started entering our province—not only the province, but the whole of Iraq.

We used to meet with the Americans, either through the governor's office or through the local mayor. And we used to tell them frankly in our meetings that the Americans will pay a high price for these mistakes.

It was a disaster when al-Qaeda entered our country, killing and executing Iraqis. Whatever the Tatars did against humanity, al-Qaeda did it worse, worse than anyone that you can think of.

The reason for our conflicts and disagreements with al-Qaeda, there are many points that we disagree on with al-Qaeda. The first thing was al-Qaeda tried to isolate and to humiliate the tribals in the areas. . . . The other thing they did was trying to stop the opinions of the tribal people, to stop the Iraqis themselves from having any opinions on the ground. The only people that we should listen to were them—to al-Qaeda—and these people were not even Iraqis. They were foreigners who entered from Yemen, Saudi Arabia, Syria, and they called themselves emirs. They wanted to have their word and their opinion over us.

In our personal experiences with them, they dealt violently and toughly with all Iraqi citizens. They accused every Iraqi of being a traitor or a spy for the Americans. And if you weren't a spy for the Americans, then you should listen to them and kill Iraqis, and execute them, and steal money from Iraqis, and then they can think you are better to them than to the Americans.

The other point is that they chose to have supporters in our areas. They entered from the gate of martyrdom. They said, "We came to help you fight the invaders who invaded Iraq." In this matter, they used two paths. The first path was by scaring people, and the other path was financial. The families were in financial difficulties. None of them had any finances left on them. They were spending huge amounts of money, giving to the people. So in this way, they gathered supporters around them. And if anyone in the area said that al-Qaeda were not Muslims, nobody supported him or believed what he said.

People like us, and others who were quite wise and educated and professional, started to realize who these people were. Some of them were from the former army. Some of them were notable people who had the wrong vision. They started to know that these came in, abusing the religion of Islam, and they were abusing their people by executing innocent people. People started to realize that they were blackening the word "Muslim," so they realized what their mission was.

Then, at the end of 2004, the conflicts between us and them started. And we continued these conflicts on a low level up to May 2005.

Colonel Gary W. Montgomery: That began in 2004?

Interpreter: That began in 2004, when the conflict started, the low-level conflicts, and then up to May 2005.

Sabah: When you start to find the bold lines among the lines, we realized what their mission was, we in al-Qaim, especially our tribe, the Albu Mahal—and the whole of Iraq. We started to understand their mission was to destroy our tribe.

The first thing they did, they assassinated the chief of police, who was a member of our tribe. And then I said, "That's it. Now the time has come." And we started fighting them, and we removed them from the center of al-Qaim.

Unfortunately, we didn't have the arms to fight them at that time because the Coalition forces were surrounding us. Despite the American forces around us, we managed to get rid of al-Qaeda inside our cities, our villages. But militarily, al-Qaeda was even more in control after we kicked them out, because they started to surround the area. They sent a representative to us to have a dialogue so they could reenter al-Qaim. We rejected that.

The big conflict was in August 2005 after they arrested the governor, who was one of our cousins. Unfortunately they assassinated him later. And then after they assassinated our cousin, we said, "That's it. We have to fight against them." I called the minister of interior, Mr. Sadoon al-Dulaimi, and he was here in Amman.

I want to go back to what I said. In August 2005 and the fighting with al-Qaeda, I wanted to mention to you that al-Qaeda won. They reentered al-Qaim, and we had to withdraw. I think the number who entered al-Qaim were about 4,000 to 5,000 al-Qaeda members. And this is where the Americans made a mistake again. These al-Qaeda members who came all this distance—they came from Bayji and Mosul all the way to al-Qaim, and the Americans couldn't even stop them. They used to see them, but the Coalition forces didn't do anything. I think this was a big mistake by the Coalition forces in the human rights of the women and children who lost their lives.

So what I did, we built a military division with the minister of interior, and we called it the Desert Protectors—less than 400 people, 98 percent of them from my tribe. With God's blessing and the support of a small number of the Iraqi army, we managed to prevent al-Qaeda from entering al-Qaim again. And thank God, things got better from that time until now. We cleaned it up.

And then after a year, a year and a few months, the Ramadi Awakening started. A number of people speak about the Awakening in Ramadi. I'm not a member of the Ramadi Awakening. And another Awakening started in Haditha prior to Ramadi. But there were only a small number in Haditha. And then the whole province united, and the Awakening started to move to Mosul and Salah ad-Din and Baghdad and Diyala. And Iraq, as you see it, has been stabilized, and we thank the Lord for his assistance and the tribal leaders. Just to emphasize without going back again, as I said earlier, the tribes are the key to stabilization and security in Iraq.

Montgomery: What role did the Americans play in the Awakening, if any?

Sabah: In the Ramadi Awakening, the Americans played a big role. It was the American support for the Awakening that made it really successful, because they are the main force on the ground. And then we felt that the Americans started to change their behavior, and they were working in the right way. But they did play a big role, I have to admit.

Chief Warrant Officer-4 Timothy S. McWilliams: What year did they change their behaviors?

Sabah: In 2006.

Montgomery: Which officers do you remember playing a role in the Awakening?

Sabah: I believe General [John R.] Allen.

Montgomery: What effect did the two battles in Fallujah have on Anbar Province as a whole?

Sabah: In the first conflict, there was support for the resistance. In the second Fallujah, it changed the balances. In the first, as I said, many people sympathized with the resistance, and the second one changed the view and the vision of the people against al-Qaeda, because they started to realize who al-Qaeda are. Al-Qaeda are people who kill, demolish houses, rape people, so the people started to change their view of the resistance.

Montgomery: Is that because of the behavior of al-Qaeda in Fallujah in between the battles?

Sabah: Yes. It was in the whole of the province, not just Fallujah.

Montgomery: Okay. Did the battle of Sufiyah have a larger effect on the rest of the province? Are you familiar with it?

Sabah: As you know, I'm far from Ramadi. I'm 300 kilometers away from Ramadi. The same thing that happened, the conflicts happened in al-Qaim, happened in Haditha and Ramadi.

Montgomery: Right. We've heard about al-Qaeda grabbing a woman by the hair and pulling her out of a car. Are you familiar with such an incident?

Sabah: They did worse things than that. I'll give you an example of one of the things they did. Four members of one family in the al-Qaim district—not from my tribe, from the Salman tribe—they were former soldiers. They brought them out and killed them in the middle of the street. They cut off their heads, and they put each head on the back of the body. This was in August of 2004. The family came to pick them up, to take them and bury them. Al-Qaeda stopped them. I contacted the director general for the phosphate factory to bring a shovel so he can just bury the bodies. It was starting to smell. They stopped them. After a week or 10 days, if a car wanted to pass through this area, he had to put a mask on his face from the smell. What they did, they came and put TNT on each body, and they called the family to come pick them up. When the family came at dawn, they exploded them. With these four people, they killed another eight, and they injured many others.

I will ask a question. If you are a Muslim, a Christian, Jewish, Buddhist, any religion, for what reason do you allow something like this to happen? "I am a martyr" is the excuse that al-Qaeda used. This is one of the hundreds of thousands of cases that happened. This is what alienated people from the real resistance. This is what I've seen from my own eyes. I've seen the bodies. And we tried to bury them, but we couldn't.

For example, I went to Baghdad. From al-Qaim to Baghdad is 400 kilometers. In these 400 kilometers, I would see about 10 to 20 bodies lying on the street beheaded. So for them to pull a woman's hair is nothing compared to what they did to the other bodies.

A man was accused of killing four Shi'as in the al-Qaim district. I said to him, "You are accused of killing these four people." His father was with him. He said, "No, I didn't kill anyone. But if the

Saudi emir tells me that I killed them, I will say 'Yes, I killed them.'" This is the mentality that I'm trying to explain to you, that al-Qaeda were brainwashing the people. The same man told me, "If the al-Qaeda emir told me to assassinate my father, I will assassinate him." They were brainwashed to that extent.

We went through hard times, very, very hard times.

Montgomery: Where do you think their funding came from? You said they spent a lot of money.

Sabah: Iran. Iran was the number one in supplying the financial aid. And I can say tens of millions of dollars were supporting al-Qaeda. Imagine a boy of 15 or 16 years old. Imagine he's got five or six cars outside his house. Where would he get this money?

Montgomery: How is it that if these men were from Yemen, Saudi Arabia, and other places, which is on the Sunni side of things. Why would they work with Iran?

Sabah: He came to assassinate the Sunnis because he's being paid to kill the Sunnis.

Montgomery: Even though he's from a Sunni country?

Sabah: Yes.

Montgomery: Would it be accurate to say that they could make that arrangement because religion was not involved?

Sabah: This is political and traditional in what they believe. They will agree to assassinate and kill anyone. He will change his religion and his tradition and his belief for the sake of money.

Montgomery: So this was really political and criminal.

Sabah: Yes, exactly. . . .

Of course after the Awakening formed, the most important thing is that the killing had stopped in the province. In one or two months, you see nobody has been killed, while prior to that, five people were being killed on a daily basis. That's why it goes back to what I'm saying, that the Americans put the tribes aside, and what the right thing is, is that the tribes did play a role. This is the most important thing, that civilians can walk on the street safely.

The mistake that has been made on the national level is that you brought people that are not Iraqis into the central government, and up to this minute, most of them are not loyal to Iraq. And this is the worst, if the Americans withdraw.

I think if the Americans withdraw, two things will happen. Iran will enter through the militias. That is one. This is a big danger to us. The second one, the Kurds will start all over again, the violence will start.

My advice to the Americans: we are not a democratic nation, and democracy does not suit us at present. It's going to take 10, 15 to 20 years for the people to understand the meaning of democracy. I tell you this as advice for history. The Sunnis have to play a role, their natural role, and all of these things about elections, and this and that, is all forgery. Take the election in Anbar two weeks ago, where most of them are Sunnis. There was forgery and corruption. So what I can advise is that we are not ready for democracy yet. People are not ready for it. We have to be fair with the Sunnis. And I believe that for the benefit of America that the one who rules Iraq should be Sunni, and he will protect Americans' interest.

We have a saying that "you cannot hold two pomegranates in one hand." One of the pomegranates is America, which is big. Just a little bit smaller than the other pomegranate is Iran. So any Shi'a rulers who come to Iraq—especially the Islamic ones—he is linked directly in his beliefs to Iran. He can never serve American and Iranian interests at the same time, which are in opposition to each other. So what we say, that a man who comes, it could be a secular gentleman, who could be a Sunni or a Shiite. This is an exit for the Iraqis' crisis. This is my opinion. We believe this is the right solution for Iraq.

Montgomery: This is for clarification. You said the Americans brought non-Iraqis into the government. Are you referring to Iraqi Shi'as and Kurds, or are you referring to Iraqis who are in the pay of Iran, or something else?

Sabah: Their loyalty. Their loyalty is not to their country. [Abdul Aziz] al-Hakim, in one of his speeches—and he was the head of the governing council—asked Iraq to pay compensation to Iran. At the same time, many of the international countries were writing off Iraqi debts. So his loyalty is not to Iraq. Look at their militias and the killing they've been doing. We, as the Sunnis, we fought al-Qaeda, and we eliminated al-Qaeda. As you know, at the Ministry of Interior, there are people who speak Iranian, and other locations, too. Iranian intelligence—I don't know what they call it—they are the ones who are ruling the country. The Iranian infiltration into Iraq is very strong.

So for the present government, preparing themselves for the new coming election, they are just speaking with the Sunnis for the time being, just wasting their time. And if this present government is reelected again, you will see for yourself that Iranian influence and Iranian power will increase more than it is now. Even the Sunnis who are in the government now do not represent all the Sunnis.

So my advice to the Americans: they should know how to deal with the Sunnis so they can gather maximum support from the Sunnis. And I hope many matters can be changed, because Iraq has sacrificed a lot, economically and in blood.

Look at Jordan. Jordan's a respectable country. Two days ago, I came from Egypt. It's a nice country. Why in Iraq, up to this moment, is there no development? We have no roads. People are talking about security, security, security. Why? It's been six years since Iraq was invaded. There's no electricity, no clean drinking water, and to my knowledge, Iraq is the richest country in the world. We have gas, oil, agriculture, and professional people with great minds. We know the answer. The answer is the people who are responsible for ruling the country are not Iraqis. We were wishing, with the oil prices going up so high, we were expecting some construction and infrastructure stuff to start to erupt. Billions of dollars have been spent from the American treasury and the Iraqi treasury. The money they spent could develop two countries, not one. Where is the development? Where is it? Nothing. You don't see anything.

*Political
Perspectives*

Interview 10

Governor Mamoun Sami Rashid al-Alwani

Governor
al-Anbar Province

Governor Mamoun Sami Rashid al-Alwani is a member of the Iraqi Islamic Party. Before the 2003 invasion of Iraq, he worked as an engineer in the housing and construction industry. In 2004, he ran for political office and was elected to the Anbar provincial council, which chose him as its chairman at the beginning of 2005. In June 2005, the provincial council selected him to serve as governor of the province.

In accepting the position, he would have been acutely aware that his predecessor, Governor Raja Nawaf Farhan Mahalawi, was kidnapped and killed. Also, he would have known that Governor Abdul Karim Burghis al-Rawi had resigned in 2004 after his sons were kidnapped and his house set ablaze.

Governor Mamoun was protected by Marines and his own personal security detail. Nevertheless, he was the target of 45 assassination attempts during his term as governor, and his 12-year-old son was kidnapped in September 2005. Governor Mamoun took an advance on his salary, paid a $6,000 ransom, and his son was returned the next day. He continued to work.

On 1 September 2008, he had the satisfaction of representing al-Anbar in the Provincial Iraqi Control ceremony, which transferred security responsibilities in al-Anbar province from American to Iraqi control.

Governor Mamoun was interviewed by Colonel Gary W. Montgomery, Lieutenant Colonel Bradley E. Weisz, and Chief Warrant Officer-4 Timothy S. McWilliams on 16 February 2009 at the Provincial Government Center in Ramadi.

Governor Mamoun Sami Rashid al-Alwani: The problem with Anbar is that it's a tribal-oriented society. The tribes are a bunch of groups that are attached to one entity, and these tribes are spread throughout the districts here in Anbar, which is made up of eight districts.

After the fall of the [Saddam Hussein] regime, there was a big vacuum government-wise. The province did not get into a struggle and did not play a role in the fall of the regime. The Coalition forces and the government that was in place here kept the government working normally, so to speak. The tribal leaders were very careful to ensure that they kept the province secure and stable and protected the people. The quiet period lasted until April 2004, maybe even until the end of 2004.

At that time, an ideology developed that went against the security of the province. That ideology included religious extremism, sectarianism, which was just being established. There were military operations, starting in Fallujah. In 2004, there were great battles that caused the destruction of the city and caused many people to leave the city. There were also, at the same time, people who were trying to establish security and establish the rule of law, to establish a mayor, a council, specifically in Fallujah.

Unfortunately—because we did not have conscientious people, and because of speeches given by imams that misled the people—they created an internal struggle. That caused attacks against the Coalition forces, and of course they started challenging the legal system. It required a lot of sacrifices from many, many people, but in the end, the biggest loss was the city itself. Terrorism found a door by taking advantage of uneducated people and implanting extremist religious ideology, supported by money.

There was also administrative or governmental breakdown. One of the biggest breakdowns was the open borders that we had with other countries, which gave access to people to come into Iraq. Many foreigners spread out in the province. We felt, as soon as that happened, that these people were not actually resisting the presence of the Americans inside the country, but they came to politicize their own agendas on the people. Many people were drawn into their ideology, and we felt it tangibly.

At the same time, the Coalition forces that were here did not know the makeup of the society and the people in this province, so they dealt with the people in a harsh way. Those two reasons—not having people that are conscientious about what was taking place here during the fall of the regime and not having the Coalition forces understand the society and the culture and the makeup of the tribes here—led to failures and disorganization. We did not expect that from a modern country such as the United States, where we are used to hearing about dialogue, human rights, freedom, and democracy. So the behavior of the Coalition forces and the mistakes that they committed accumulated. It fell right into the hands of the insurgents, and they took advantage of it.

Actually, the presence of some wise leaders and generals and representatives from the embassy, and when the troops abandoned their previous cruel behaviors, created new groups, which wanted to cooperate with Americans.

Interpreter: What behaviors?

Mamoun: Before, there were cruel actions that created negative reactions. When new generals and ambassadors, especially in 2005 and 2006—big generals like General [James L.] Williams and Mr. Smith from the embassy—were assigned, this created a transformation in relations with the Americans.

These actions created sympathy—

Interpreter: Sympathy?

Mamoun: Resistance. Resistance against the Americans, especially late in 2004. The beginning of 2004 was quiet, but when the attacks started in Fallujah in the middle of 2004, it created a totally new direction. But this changed in 2005 because we and the generals could—

Interpreter: Stop it?

Mamoun: More than that—we could win the support of the sheikhs. Although it was slow, this compelled the generals and sheikhs to reach this consensus.

There are three main elements in Anbar. The first element is the local government. It was a civilian government and basically had no power because nobody was actually coming forward and volunteering for the police and the army. The second element is the presence of the tribes, which did not want to work hand in hand with the government. One part of the tribes was working with the insurgents, and the other one wanted to be neutral. And the third element that played a role here is the Marines and the American Army.

I wanted to start a dialogue to bring everybody together—the three elements: the tribes, the local government, and the Coalition forces. The first people I was able to win over were the Coalition side. So I and the Americans were looking for the third missing element, which was the tribes. As I said, we were trying to hold conferences— meeting after meeting—in order to win over that third side, to be one hand, so to speak, one side, to try to face the insurgency.

But unfortunately, we were too slow to gather the support of the tribes, the third element, and meanwhile the insurgency events were rising so rapidly that it was hard for us to control. As soon as things got calm in Fallujah, things started getting worse in al-Qaim. Tribes started fighting. They wanted peace and stability in the country, and there were great battles taking place. There were some tribes that stood and fought for the whole country, and there were tribes that helped out the insurgents. Because of that struggle, and because of the open borders, the struggle continued until the situation calmed down in al-Qaim and then started rolling over to Haditha and Rawah. Some people were on the side of the law, the government, the Coalition forces, and some people were working for the insurgency, and the situation stabilized in Haditha. The same thing happened in Hit, and then it ended, too.

To be truthful, and to be fair to Hit, historically it was ahead of other districts, because there is a specific tribe whose name is Albu Nimr, together with many of the good people of Hit, who fought the insurgency and tried to stabilize their own city themselves. The same thing happened in Baghdadi.

After the insurgency left Fallujah, Hit, Baghdadi, and al-Qaim, the battle moved into Ramadi. At the time, new replacements took over. General [David G.] Reist was present at the time. We were looking for that same accord between the three elements: the local government, the tribes, and the Coalition forces. Thankfully, there was a tribe that specifically played a role in this great changeover. In the meantime, there was already peace in Fallujah, al-Qaim, and Haditha. We would sit, General Reist and I, to see how we could win those tribes.

In August 2006, Sheikh Khalid Araq was assassinated. He was one of the Albu Allehi tribal leaders. His body was thrown in the street for three days. He was beheaded, God rest his soul. That incident drove the people to vengeance for this person against the insurgents and the terrorists.

I sat down with General Reist, and I recommended the following: since there is a big tribal drive, let's establish police stations inside the tribes that were harmed. The idea succeeded. Four or five tribes were chosen, and many of the sons of the tribes volunteered for those specific police stations. My tribe, Albu Alwan, also established a police station inside Ramadi, and the rest were outside. They were south and north of the river. All we asked from them is to get rid of the insurgents—of the bad elements—from their own tribes. Some of the tribes took it upon themselves to do that, to take out all the bad elements within their tribes.

They announced the formation of the Awakening movement on September 14, 2006. The person who took over that conference was Sheikh Sattar Abu Risha, because he was a brave man, God rest his soul. He didn't want the insurgency and the terrorists to touch his own people. Sheikh Sattar's father and three of his brothers were killed just before the Awakening started. I mentioned before that the most injured tribes started the uprising, and his tribe was among the most injured by the insurgents. From there started the Awakening, so we are clear when the Awakening started. It started on that date in Ramadi, and the rest of the province was quiet and peaceful, thank God.

When the other tribes saw the great victories, these are the forces that stood up to the insurgency. It was having the local government, the tribes, and the Coalition forces. The tribes started recruiting their own people into the police force. That encouraged other tribes to follow in their footsteps, because it sparked the other tribes to do the same thing. And, truthfully, that was the spotlight in Ramadi at that time.

If we discuss generally how the province of Anbar became stable, and we start from eastern Anbar—starting from Fallujah—you will see that two tribes, Albu Issa and Albu Alwan, started to stabilize their own areas, and some of the allied tribes that worked in the Amariyah area in Fallujah, for example. The credit goes to the Albu Issa tribe, period. Albu Issa gets all the credit for having a stable area in Fallujah.

Unfortunately, Karma started late in the stability of Fallujah for one reason—a very important reason—because it's open to the borders of Baghdad and Samarra, so enemies come forth from two sides. Sometimes our police, and even sometimes Coalition forces, are helpless because their area of responsibility goes only so far. So that was the second calm state after Ramadi. The people who contributed to that were the following tribes: al-Jumali, al-Hallabsa, Albu Aefa. Albu Alwan also played a role in Karma, and other areas included the Zoba, and some of the Tamim tribes, and some of the other allied tribes with them.

I remember one of the historical stories that the Zoba tribe fought against each other. Half of them fought for the insurgency, half of them fought for the country. That's the way it was in Fallujah.

Al-Hamda takes credit for stabilizing the third area—in Saqlawiyah, in Fallujah—and together with some of the allied tribes with them. These are the tribes I mentioned that played a role in stabilizing the Khalidiyah area and the Habbaniyah area, coming toward Ramadi.

Same thing in Ramadi, there was the Albu Alwan tribe, together with Albu Assaf, Albu Soda, and Albu Jaber. One of the first tribes to stabilize the area of Sufiyah and Ramadi was the Albu Soda tribe. Albu Mahal, Albu Ranem, and Albu Fayed also allied with that tribe in order to conquer the insurgency.

And the same situation applies to Hit. At the forefront was the Albu Nimr tribe, as I mentioned earlier. In Baghdadi, it was the Albu

Abed tribe. In Haditha, it was the Jahaifa tribe. It was allied to the Mola tribe. It rolled over into Ana, Rawah. They also tried to stop the insurgency, going all the way to Rutbah. The same thing applies to al-Qaim, which was stabilized by Albu Mahal and its allies.

If you notice, the places where the three powers united stabilized first. That's how our story goes.

Colonel Gary W. Montgomery: What role did Coalition forces play in the Awakening?

Mamoun: They were supporting first the local government, whether it was the governor or provincial council. In addition, they were supporting us and starting dialogue with the tribes. So they will start the dialogue with the tribes in order to work together to stop the insurgency, together with the local government. Because the military force was in the hands of the Americans, that reinforced the position of the governor, helped the legislation and execution of the laws or orders issued from the provincial council. They were recruiting and establishing the police. They trained those people. They equipped them with weapons, vehicles, and fuel. Sometimes, the military relied on the Coalition forces to feed them They played the main role. I always called them the main referee, who refereed the whole game.

In the end, the mind, the dialogue, and the logic won over, and we were able to establish a government. We were able to establish local police throughout. Most of the government offices started operating again. Fortunately, the picture turned from black to white. That was finalized during the Provincial Iraqi Control ceremony, when authority was transferred to the local government of Anbar on September 1, 2008.

What I talked about previously was only the military side of the story. Aside from that, there was a great amount of money spent on reconstruction, reconstruction of simple things like removing litter from the streets, building light posts on the streets, schools, and medical units. They bought furniture for the schools. They bought furniture also for the local government offices, gifts for many of the local citizens.

There is one side I wanted to get involved in—the supervision of the management of those funds and the way they were spent. I was hoping that we would get involved with the expenditure that was taking place, but unfortunately, it went against the rules and regulations. They were partners in allocating some of the projects, but they did not partner with us during the execution and supervision of the projects. Sometimes you try to get into all the details, but unfortunately, you can't get into all the details. This is the story that we had with the Marines, and also together with the Army that was present here. We kept very good relationships until now, whether it's the military side or the civilian side. What else would you like to ask?

Montgomery: If I could back up a minute, you mentioned resistance against al-Qaeda in Haditha, I think. It was around the time of Fallujah, but I'm not sure if it was before or after the battles there.

Mamoun: Fallujah is where resistance started—the uprising against the Americans.

Montgomery: Oh, against the Americans. Okay.

Mamoun: Of course resistance started against the Americans. There is no country that doesn't want to rise up against the people who are occupying it, but there are different kinds of resistance. We actually made agreements with the Americans, that they would come into our city without even fighting. We spent eight months together with the Coalition forces without any incidents. When the resistance started against the Americans, it took another path. We wanted to work with the Americans, to start a dialogue based on logic and understanding.

Part of the Americans, unfortunately, made mistakes, and some of the resistance that was facing the Americans, they were looking at it as if there was no way but to use a weapon against the Americans—the only way to talk to them. Unfortunately, this manner was not taking the interest of the province into mind. For example, I was trying to build a dialogue, in order to rebuild my institutions here in the province; but instead, I was faced with people—my own people—fighting against me. There were numerous—45—assassination attempts, VBIEDs [vehicle-borne improvised explosive device] and so forth, against my life. Of course, when your only solution is fighting in order to win over your province, you have to, at the same time, think of the blood that you're going to give in return when you're fighting the Coalition. When I decided to go into the provincial council, I also wanted to start a dialogue and a relationship with the Coalition forces, and I succeeded because that's what I wanted. I wanted to establish a relationship through dialogue.

Chief Warrant Officer-4 Timothy S. McWilliams: I understand this compound, this building, was under attack by al-Qaeda in 2005 and 2006?

Mamoun: No, it wasn't under the control or the siege of al-Qaeda. This building here, nobody entered it whatsoever. Ever since I was here, nobody entered this compound, for two reasons. First, because there was a Marine force present here, in addition to my personal security detail, and I never left this desk or office whatsoever. I was hit three times [pointing to various places in his office], from here, from there, and from there. When that happened, I moved to the second room, but we used to get hit with mortar shells. I was also targeted on the way from my home to the provincial government center; and, when I was leaving the compound, I would also be targeted.

May 2nd, I think, 2007, when I was coming over, they blew up a VBIED, trying to target me right on Michigan Avenue [Main Supply Route Michigan] in front of the judicial center. Thankfully, I got out of the incident alive, so the Americans asked me, "Where do you want to go?" I told them I'm going to come here to the provincial government center. I just wanted to challenge al-Qaeda. I stayed here for two to three hours, and then I left and went back home. And the second day, I went back to work.

I don't want to mention the rest of the attacks, the regular attacks: PKC [machine gun], mortar shells on my home, blowing up my home, and so forth. I was hit with two VBIEDs. First, I lost some of my personal security detail. The second attack—and of course some of the houses were demolished. The second hit, two of my nephews were killed, not to mention some of my cousins who were beheaded, their heads thrown in the streets. They were 16 years old.

Thankfully, because I was trying to take the right path, I was trying to build a good relationship with the Coalition forces, and thanks, as you can see, to all my friends here [referring to photographs on the wall]. We were visited by President [George W.] Bush. I visited him back in 2007 in the White House. I visited him again in 2008. And President [Barak H.] Obama came here to visit me, and we were visited many times by Ambassador [Ryan C.] Crocker. I visited Mr. [Robert M.] Gates in his own office in 2008. General [David H.] Petraeus [USA]. That picture is in my office. This is his present to me. The relationships are good, thank God.

This is a very dear general to me, General [John R.] Allen. General [John F.] Kelly, who just left a few days ago. General Reist, General [Martin] Post, [Ambassador John D.] Negroponte. . . . These are friends.

Lieutenant Colonel Bradley E. Weisz: What type of actions did General Reist take that caused him to develop such a strong relationship?

Mamoun: It was a friendly relationship. The relationship that I led with the generals resulted in the great accomplishments that we made. For example, in 2005, we had General Williams. . . . We used to meet together with the tribes, numerous times, but the fruit of those meetings, the fruit of the labor, was gathered by General Reist. After him, we also started building more, planting. By the way, General Allen is now General [David H.] Petraeus's second, I think, his deputy. He came after General Reist, and we also reaped many of the fruits that he sowed. After him, General Post and General Kelly came.

As I know right now, and you know the area of Anbar is not small—there are organizations I don't want to leave out; for example, the United States Agency for International Development, International Relief and Development, and the Research Triangle Institute. They all played a big role in activating the province, whether it was with men or with women. In general, those organizations promoted projects, but there were some elements, some contractors, that did not execute their duties as they should have.

McWilliams: What is your outlook for al-Anbar?

Mamoun: First of all, it's the main security artery of Iraq. Second, it put an end to al-Qaeda in Iraq. Of course, al-Qaeda raises the Sunni flag. They're mostly Sunnis, and they were beaten by Sunnis. Anbar also proved that terrorism is a crime. If you ask anybody on the streets, "Those al-Qaeda terrorists, what are they?" They will answer you back that they're terrorists, they're criminals. We also defeated them politically, not just ideologically, but politically we defeated them—al-Qaeda—and religiously, because we proved to the people that they do not have religion. And it was the only province that liberated itself by itself, but with the help of our friends, the Coalition.

Our friends in other provinces—why didn't they free themselves? The Coalition forces helped to also free some of the other provinces. The province of Anbar helped liberate some of the—the army and the police—helped liberate some of the other provinces: Baghdad, Basrah, Maysan, Diyala, and Mosul. What do you expect? This is Anbar.

Interview 11

Mr. Kamis Ahmad Abban al-Alwani

Vice Chairman
Anbar Provincial Council

Mr. Kamis Ahmad Abban al-Alwani has a degree in management. He served in the old Iraqi army for nine years during the Iran-Iraq war and the Gulf War. He was elected to the al-Anbar Provincial Council in 2004 and has served two terms. He was interviewed by Colonel Gary W Montgomery and Chief Warrant Officer-4 Timothy S. McWilliams on 16 February 2009 at the Provincial Government Center in Ramadi.

Mr. Kamis Ahmad Abban al-Alwani: After the invasion of Iraq, Anbar had something special. Some sheikhs and some educated people at high levels in the province wanted to negotiate with the Coalition forces. There was a conference near al-Rutbah city. The deal was that the Coalition forces would not go inside the city (as a military, to be specific). It was very quiet, and there was a very good relationship between the Coalition forces, and sheikhs, and some of the educated people.

Then we started to build our institutions. One of them was the provincial council. From 2003 until 2004, they gathered the sheikhs, and they formed a city council in each area, and they had certificates from the Coalition forces about this issue. The year 2004 was very good stability-wise, and we held free elections for the provincial councils. The civilian from the Coalition forces was Mr. Keane,* who was responsible for doing this.

After that, the Coalition forces started going inside the cities, and they settled down in the government center. I don't mean the whole military of the Coalition forces, but the civilian side of the Coalition forces. They had posts for the military people in the palaces and in camps outside the city.

---

* Possibility Gen John M. Keane, USA (ret).

The first elected provincial council was established in 2004. People were elected according to their skills, meaning different social categories were represented, like engineers, doctors, educators, tribal sheikhs, etc. It had 49 members: 10 sheikhs, and the others. Some social categories had two representatives, and others had one representative.

First, they elected Amar Abdul Jabbar Sulayman the provincial council chairman. The deputy was Mr. Mamoun [Sami Rashid al-Alwani], who is now the governor. After that, we elected a governor.

The former governor was Raja Nawaf [Farhan al-Mahalawi], an engineer. He was a general director. Also, he was a provincial council member and one of the al-Qaim sheikhs. He was a cousin of Sheikh Sabah al-Sattam in al-Qaim. We saw he was qualified to be governor, but after he went to his house and came back, he was confronted by terrorists, and they kidnapped him and his son. His son was released by the terrorists. There are two stories about him. Some said there was random shooting on the house where he was being held, and he was killed. The other story says he was killed by the terrorists.

So there was a gap. There was no governor. So we decided to elect someone else, and we chose another engineer. We chose Mamoun Sami Rashid, who is the governor now, as the Anbar governor. This was between 2004 and 2005. We kept going, and there was an election for another council in 2005. We established a new provincial council, but there were very few candidates. So about three lists won at that time. There was the [Iraqi] Islamic Party; the Reconciliation and Liberation Party, which is led by Sheikh Mish'an al-Juburi; and another, smaller party, under the name of Falah al-Naqib. He was the former minister of interior.

Before Raja, the governor who was killed, there was a guy called Fasal [Raikan Majris al-Gaoud], when Ayad Allawi was the prime minister. He came to office by force. After them, Mamoun took over.

Until this time, the situation was good. After the 2005 election, especially after the election, the situation got worse, for many reasons. First is the location of al-Anbar Province. It borders with five other provinces in Iraq and has international borders with Syria, Jordan, and Saudi Arabia. With the provinces inside Iraq—Mosul, Salah ad-Din, Baghdad, Babil, and Karbala—these borders are open. The terrorist element started to be active in these areas, and they found people to accommodate them, especially in the countryside around outside the cities.

Then the situation started to get worse and worse. First they killed a former provincial council member named Khadher, and then they killed another provincial council member. They killed city council members of Fallujah and its provincial council members. They assassinated many people in the cities and districts, so these places were controlled by al-Qaeda. They started kidnapping and raping and stealing.

At that time, the police were very weak in al-Anbar, because the Coalition forces weren't satisfied with their qualifications or work. So the Coalition forces wouldn't give us good heavy weapons to fight the terrorists because they didn't trust the police not to sell or pass these weapons to the terrorists. The police saw that the terrorists had better weapons, and they couldn't even protect themselves. At the same time, the Coalition Forces wouldn't supply them with weapons for fear that they would sell or give them to the terrorists. The situation stayed like that, and the terrorists gained control of some of the main offices. The police broke up—dissolved—and the Coalition forces went inside the city and pushed away the police. Only some people were given salaries, and we do not know why. Maybe they were working at the south palaces or the north palaces for the Coalition forces.

After that, we were forced to bring in a director of police. His name was Chaaban. Chaaban started to work in the province. He's a resident of Fallujah, but he couldn't give us anything because there were no people volunteering to be policemen because the terrorists would kill them. They were pushing back. No one would volunteer for the police, or the army, or any security organization, because of the terrorists. So this is a major point, which made the province unstable, that people couldn't volunteer for these organizations for fear the terrorists would kill them.

The Iraqi police or Iraqi army that were present in the province were from outside the province, not sons of al-Anbar, and they were just on the major checkpoints. They were named the national guard.

At that time, we were looking to find men for the police, the army, and the government. We contacted many high-level people in Baghdad on this subject, and there were many suggestions that we put forward. One of these suggestions was to put 10 guards for each provincial council member, and between 20 and 50 for the sheikhs, to protect them. Our idea was that you are planting seeds, building policemen, so the sheikhs and these people will stay inside the country, and they can move and start to think about growing or building. This didn't happen.

We started with our personal connections to people in Baghdad. We started to build a council, called the rescue council. We visited Ibrahim al-Jaafari, the former prime minister. He issued some money for reconstruction, but the situation was very bad. Al-Anbar Province was considered a hot spot. They started killing many people, starting with the tribal sheikhs. They killed Sheikh Nasser. They killed some sheikhs from the Albu Risha tribe. Some others—I can't remember their names—they were killed because they had no weapons to protect themselves. So, because the Coalition forces—and we don't know; we call them Coalition forces whether they are Marines or Army—they were checking the houses, and they wouldn't let people have private weapons. They couldn't have weapons to save themselves, so they started killing all the sheikhs.

Colonel Gary W. Montgomery: What year are you talking about? What time period?

Kamis: It's between the end of 2005, beginning of 2006. There was a military tone, and the only ones who were controlling the area were Americans. The terrorists were very strong, and they were marching in the streets. It felt like they were controlling everything. Life just stopped, except for some departments like Health and Education. They kept working.

We were moving—me, as the provincial council deputy, or Mamoun, as governor—we moved with the convoys of Americans.

We stayed in this situation more than six months. In that time, they killed the deputy governor. They killed the private secretary for the governor. They threatened all the other government organizations not to work. They controlled the banks, and they stole some of the employees' salaries. They robbed the Rafidain Bank and al-Rasheed Bank. The situation got very bad. We had a very difficult time.

After that, I think some of the people from the Awakening started forming groups. They had weapons, I think with the agreement of the Coalition forces. They liberated areas district by district. They started with the Jazeera area. They liberated suburb by suburb.

People hated the names of the terrorists, because the terrorists were getting anyone. They had many excuses. They liked to kill. One of the excuses: "Maybe he belonged to the Islamic Party." "This one did contract work with the Americans." "This guy is an interpreter working for the Americans." Many excuses. "He works for the Americans." "This guy gives information to the Americans." So many excuses. They were false excuses, just to make the people believe in them. When they killed someone, they said, as an excuse, that he was a spy, but they were from the honest resistance.

At first there was a movement called "resistance." Some people were convinced that even President [George W.] Bush said, "If anybody invades my country, I will resist him." So some chose to take up arms like the military. Some worked as terrorists. Some just wanted to demolish and terrorize, and some did political work. Also, agendas came into Iraq from abroad. All this came into al-Anbar Province.

Since we don't have communications like TV, radio, electricity, and mail, or anything, you cannot tell people what is right and what is wrong, even simple things. There is no electricity, so there is no TV, no speakers. You cannot start anything. I think there are many things you can build up and make people believe through the media. But we didn't have a chance to explain to the people through the media what was right or wrong, except some sky channels* that are on the air. We didn't have power to put it on TV.

---

* Possibly satellite channels.

The first time they started killing the terrorists was in the al-Qaim area, in the Albu Mahal and Karabla tribes. These tribes resisted and killed the terrorists in that area only. They had support from the national guard and the army over there. So they started killing terrorists in al-Qaim, before the al-Anbar Awakening; also in the Kubaysah and Amariyah area, and also Khalidiyah. These areas started before the Anbar Awakening. But at that time, they couldn't use the media to declare themselves. The thing that was in the media was the Anbar Awakening, so it was distributed to what you see now.

I think the most important point is the Awakening—the first point to start awakening, the area where they could move—was the Jazeera area, and the support and help of the Coalition forces.

And the other point, which is a major one, is that the people didn't believe the terrorists anymore. This caused a reaction from the people. No one would accommodate them. Also, the people started to own weapons, so they defended themselves, and the situation continued until what we've got now.

After that, some of the Awakening council got into the provincial council, so there was coordination between them and us to build a good future for al-Anbar. We work together now, as a provincial council.

We have some problems, like the police, unemployment. Some unwanted elements got inside the police. Now the police are infiltrated. Some of them receive many salaries. Now we have unstable safety because many things interfere in the police. I think we need to empower and evaluate many elements in the police. We want to train and develop the police because we on the Anbar side, we want to achieve stability through construction and investment. Some people, when they speak in the media, they send a message to people outside that al-Anbar is unstable. We want to have a partnership with the U.S. government, and the countries that are in the Coalition with them, to build investments and shared organizations. This is one of our goals in the provincial council.

There were many excuses for the terrorists. They thought that the American forces were invasion forces. They didn't bring them electricity, or reconstruction, or anything good. That was the message that was being delivered to the poor people. Also, many of the government offices stopped working, and many people lost their salaries. There were many people who had no chance for work, so the terrorists used them, gave them some money to work for them.

There were many mistakes. We—the Americans and we—suffered for these mistakes. Many sacrifices were made by the Coalition forces; many sacrifices were made from al-Anbar Province especially. The random arrests on false information. There were 30,000 arrested just from al-Anbar Province, and this figure is from the Red Cross. Many mistakes happened in that time. They made terrorists sprout up because, as I said, the excuses were already there. When some of the family has been killed, like a husband or a son or a brother, and the other person was arrested, and a third guy is unemployed, this is one of the things that makes terrorists grow.

That's all I have. Do you have any questions?

Unknown: Did you see any difference between the Marine Corps forces in Ramadi and the U.S. Army forces in Ramadi? Was there any difference or distinguishing factors?

Kamis: At first, we couldn't distinguish. Anyone wearing a uniform was U.S. Army. All of them were U.S. Army. Later, we knew that this was a Marine uniform, and that was an Army uniform. We learned the difference. Most of people don't know how to recognize between the uniforms, except for those of us who work closely with them. At the end, we knew it. And this time the Army was coming, and they were very well behaved. Some of the units of the Marines were not good. At some specific time, some of them were not good, and you know they always change. Some here called them the "dirty division."

Interpreter: He said, are there any names under this one, "dirty division?" Is there something the Marines call the "dirty division?"

Unknown: "Dirty division?" No, you have 1st Marine Division, 2d Marine Division, 3d Marine Division.

Kamis: Maybe the terrorists called them that name. Or some of the works they did, the people called them by this name, because some of the units in other areas were very good. And it depends on the time, because sometimes they changed.

Montgomery: In this "dirty division," if you give us a location and time, then we can go back and look it up.

Kamis: I think in 2006—at the end of 2005, beginning of 2006. I heard it from people. . . . Maybe it's a small unit. You know, maybe it's a brigade or a company, but in Iraq, in the Islamic language, we call it "division." We make it something bigger, but it's maybe a small unit doing some jobs during that hard time, and they called them the "dirty division." Maybe they were just a company.

Montgomery: All of the battalions and some of the brigades have nicknames for themselves.

Kamis: We don't know, but the people were talking because maybe this company did something not good, and they started saying, "all the division is that." This is for history, as you say it.

I want to say something for history. Some of the units were very good. Some of the, particularly the officers who were working here, and especially those whose location was inside the cities. And the other point is the commander of the patrol. It depends on how personal he is. Also, the interpreter, sometimes he makes mistakes. Some interpreters, sometimes they harm U.S. forces. That's what we saw in our province. Most of the time, the interpreter changed the facts. This affects even the American side. Sometimes I say something, and the interpreter says it differently or from his point of view. It makes problems at a time we are hoping, and we need, to live together. We need to hear you and you need to hear us, but the only way between us is the interpreter. So if the interpreter was faithful, our point of view was delivered well. Sometimes, maybe he means to intentionally change the facts; sometimes maybe he doesn't have the qualifications or the ability to transfer the idea.

At that time, many of the Coalition forces came with reconstruction teams and gave contracts and projects and did good things. So they were giving contracts only to some limited number of people. Other people considered them as traitors. They gave contracts to some chosen people. Maybe they trusted them, or these were the only people that believed in them, or they had dealings with them, but they just chose people and gave them contracts when they started reconstruction.

Montgomery: They weren't put up for competitive bid? They'd just hand it out?

Kamis: No, there was no competitive bid. They just gave it directly to people. So people started to hate these people, the Coalition forces and the guy who took the contract. So to give people evidence that we had a good relationship and we were working for the city or the province, we asked the Coalition forces to help us get back power—to buy generators for the hospitals, for immediate services—but they didn't cooperate at that time by siding with us so we could make the people believe in us. For example, the way we sit, like we sit now, otherwise it's a military side or a civilian side in the Coalition forces.

Sometimes, they had some general request that was fair: when you are raiding a house in the middle of the night, if you want someone, you can get Iraqi policemen or somebody, and they can get the guy for you. And then after you investigate him, if you don't find anything, release him after two or three days.

But the raids in the middle of the night, making noise and scaring people, broken doors, forcing your way into houses, the snipers on the buildings around the area, sometimes random shooting—when people sometimes put an IED [improvised explosive device] for a convoy and a Hummer blew out, they started shooting randomly around everywhere and shooting anyone on the road.

I think they didn't plan how to stay in Iraq. They were planning to get inside Iraq, and they thought it was very difficult. But the reality is that it's very easy to get inside Iraq. When they had reasons for invading Iraq, one of these reasons was that we had nuclear weapons. Then destroy the dictator, and then distribute democracy.

So the terrorists used these reasons, which they thought were false, to make the people not believe the Coalition Forces. People on the street were confused, except for some people who benefit from stealing money from the central government or the government over here.

Montgomery: You just gave three reasons for the invasion of Iraq. Did you know those things before the invasion? What did you expect before the invasion?

Kamis: They started the 2003 war. It started in the media first. So the people start to believe, when the Americans come in, they will free us and kill this dictator. And we knew before that the Coalition frces had a good relationship with the neighbors around Iraq, like their relationship with Jordan, Saudi Arabia, and other countries around us. They also thought the same way, when you came inside Kuwait and reconstructed, the same way you were going to do it in Iraq. People believed that's what's going to happen when the Americans come in, but this didn't happen. . . .

The terrorists had reasons that convinced people. When people don't find work, there's no income, he's got no food, no health care, no power, no water. For all these reasons, it's going to make the terrorists exist. Let's talk about Europe, where they have a demonstration over there of unemployment or a decrease in their salaries. Iraqis didn't have anything. So what can he do?

Montgomery: I understand that they were desperate, and so they did whatever they had to do to get money. But do you think that they trusted the terrorists or had confidence in them? Did they buy into the program, so to speak, the philosophy?

Kamis: If we're going to explain it, we will do it according to different mentalities. There are simple people. They don't have much education. They don't think too much, and it depends on the agenda that the person has, and depending on how much he's going to pay him—the money, the amount. Add to that the things that these people are missing in their lives. He needs it. Second step, they will trust the terrorist. That's why you will see that Anbar people are not all terrorists. A small percentage—the terrorists are no more than 100 or 200 at best.

Montgomery: Would this be the criminal element, or these were more of the fanatic types?

Kamis: Until now. A few things. The leaders, we couldn't capture the leaders. Sometimes we couldn't get anything out of people. We arrest him. Maybe there are some people who said something about him, but he doesn't confess. Sometimes people use pills, and he's out of his senses, he doesn't know what he's saying. And it's different from area to area.

To answer this question, you have to study it and go inside it, and think about it more, about the reasons. Like the militias in Baghdad are totally different from the terrorists in Ramadi, but the goal is one, which is killing, demolishing, and terrorizing. For example, when Prime Minister [Nouri al-] Maliki visits Basrah in the south of Iraq, the militias and the terrorists are on the same side against the law. And some of them are just gangs of thieves. They have no religious beliefs; their only thoughts are just to kill and to steal. Also, there are many people who were released from Abu Ghraib prison who had criminal records. They are criminals, originally criminals. They had no means, so they were on the street. This is one part of terrorism.

Montgomery: You said they had a meeting and suggested, in Baghdad, that each provincial council member have 10 guards.

Kamis: Yes.

Montgomery: Did you have any guards before that at all?

Kamis: No, they didn't have any.

Montgomery: And so before that—so there was a time when there were terrorists, and the Coalition forces would not let them have weapons, and you were involved in government at that time. Is that correct?

Interpreter: He was on the provincial council.

Montgomery: How did he stay alive?

Kamis: Well, it's by the blessing of God. He wanted it this way. The last budget in al-Anbar, we have the projects in 2006. We were forced to go into Baghdad and work on it for six months, so we can finish the budget for the 2006, so they will take their work and start working over there. Many people left to Syria, Jordan, the north of Iraq. That's what happened.

Chief Warrant Officer-4 Timothy S. McWilliams: Sir, in 2004, Fallujah was the site of two key battles here. How did that affect this area?

Kamis: At that time, I was a provincial council member. The governor, now Mamoun, was the provincial council deputy chairman. The reason of the battles was to finish the terrorists in Fallujah. So the first battle of Fallujah, as they called it, after three days of battle, some people representing the embassy came, and we went to Fallujah. A big delegation from the imams and sheikhs went to Fallujah, also me and some of the local government. We met some of the imams and sheikhs over there in mosque al-Khafel, where they gave first aid. The negotiators for the government of Iraq in Baghdad was a guy called Hacham al-Hosseni, and the president of Iraq, Ghazi al-Yawar, was present. So that delegation came from Baghdad to meet some people in Fallujah, and we met them as the al-Anbar government in Fallujah, but the meeting was just for certain persons. It was not public. The deal was for a cease-fire in Fallujah. After a few days, they stopped firing.

McWilliams: After the second battle, did the second battle affect Ramadi and al-Anbar?

Kamis: Of course. It's a part of al-Anbar Province. The link between us to go to Baghdad is Fallujah. We have to pass through it. So when Fallujah was finished, we couldn't go in and out to Baghdad. So most of the patients, people were taking them into Salah ad Din, north of—it was best for them. If they could, they took them to Syria because it was safer and better than going to Baghdad. The militias were in Baghdad. They were killing by identification card and by name. The name is Sunni or Shi'a—they followed the name.

McWilliams: You mentioned a delegation that went out to meet Coalition forces. When was that, and were you actually part of that delegation?

Kamis: No, I wasn't part of them. There was Sheikh Amer, Sheikh Albu Chillet, one of the Abu Risha, some of them, I don't know them. You can ask Sheikh Amer about it, he can give you the right names.

Iraqi Perspectives

Perspectives of the
New Security Forces

Interview 12

Major General Tariq Yusif Mohammad al-Thiyabi

Provincial Director of Police
Al-Anbar Province

Major General Tariq Yusif Mohammad al-Thiyabi was born in Ramadi in 1964. He graduated from the police college and worked on the borders of Iraq in the 1980s and into the 1990s. During the war with Iran, he worked with the Iraqi army, which guarded the borders jointly with the border police. When the war ended, the border police took over again. In 1992, General Tariq was court-martialed in absentia and sentenced to death. (He stated that his offense was helping Marsh Arab fishermen in southern Iraq, but he did not go into the details.) He evaded arrest until the Ba'ath regime fell 11 years later.

General Tariq was interviewed by Colonel Gary W. Montgomery and Chief Warrant Officer-4 Timothy S. McWilliams on 17 February 2009 at the Provincial Government Center in Ramadi.

Major General Tariq Yusif Mohammad al-Thiyabi: Saddam Hussein's regime fell, and the Coalition forces entered Iraq. I came back and worked the borders. We established—myself together with the Marines—the borders along the Syrian and Jordanian side. Things were going very well. Things were looking bright, because it was a new country. There was no resistance, no terrorism, none of that at all, all the way from 2003 to the beginning of 2004.

Then the operations in Fallujah started. The Americans started getting attacked, and they called that resistance. Former Ba'ath Party members were involved in that resistance, along with other people, and sometimes they referred to them as mujahideen—strugglers for a religious cause. That's not our subject to explain why the resistance started, why the uprising started, but you came here to know about the history of the Awakening.

Colonel Gary W. Montgomery: I think how the insurgency developed and the rise of al-Qaeda may give a little background for how the Awakening came about, but you can describe this in as much or as little detail as you want to. It's whatever you want to say, however you want to do it.

Tariq: The people were making excuses as to why they were attacking the Coalition forces. The entry of American forces into Iraq scared some of the neighboring countries, specifically Syria and Iran. As you know, Syria has a Ba'athist regime. So did Iraq. The Ba'athist regime members from Syria used to roam the streets of Iraq normally. They used to call them the "Syrian mujahideen." Saddam Hussein personally received those Syrian mujahideen before the American forces entered Iraq. This was a historical event for Syria to get rid of those mujahideen and throw them onto the Iraqis. Certainly wherever those people go, they will influence the place that they enter, so they were more than happy to get rid of them.

Initially, the American forces were liberators. Then they became invaders, so to speak. When the terminology changed to invader or occupier, it gave people an excuse to attack. When you classify American forces as occupiers, psychologically it's not acceptable. Syria and Iran took advantage of that to back the resistance fighters here in Iraq. The media also took advantage of the opportunity.

The American force's misunderstanding of Iraqi culture also contributed to this. For example, the way they conducted searches and raids created friction between them and the local people. Iraqis have learned modern ways of searching people. In the beginning, when an Iraqi was being searched, he looked upon it as an assault. The way the American forces searched a person, they stopped him, made him turn around, raise his hands, and they searched his body. That sort of posture is insulting for Iraqis. It's even insulting for me to speak about it in front of people.*. . . That's why friction started, and other people who were against the American forces took advantage of the opportunity and used it for themselves, such as the media and the resistance forces.

---

* In an omitted portion of the interview, Gen Tariq explained that Western frisking techniques had homosexual connotations for Iraqi males. The cultural differences were exacerbated by a shortage of interpreters.

And so the problems arose in Fallujah for the first time, and then the second time. That contributed to the disbanding of the police force in al-Anbar. Criminals infiltrated the police force at that time, also. Major General Ja'adan [Muhammad al-Alwani], when he sat at this desk, he supported those organizations. That's why the police failed and were disbanded. That's why terrorist organizations generally controlled society here in Anbar.

To exercise control even further, they started beheading and slaughtering and killing people. For them, to kill a person with a pistol is normal. But to slaughter someone, to behead someone in front of other people—it's a monstrous scene that is supposed to terrorize people. They used to slaughter people just like they slaughter sheep. They would take advantage of any opportunity to kill people.

If we had an American convoy roll down the street, and one of the people happened to wave to them, that person could consider himself dead. Terrorist organizations started killing people just on suspicion. They did not need absolute proof—or any proof—in order to kill a person. They just acted on suspicion alone. This is the way the ideology works: if we kill him, and he's made a mistake, then he deserved what he got; but if we kill him by mistake, then God will forgive us for what we have done. They act as if they are sent from God—lawyers from God. That's radical ideological thinking. That's why they terrorized people with their ideology and were able to control the province.

They started killing officers—high-level officers, tribal leaders, former police officers. Any person that was part of establishing the police again was killed. If they didn't find a police officer, they killed his relative—his father, or his brother, or his next of kin. That's why they were able to control all the areas. It reached a level where they were able to walk down the streets in the neighborhoods without even being armed.

You're going to ask me, "Who were those terrorist organizations?" In mid-2004, 2005, all the way to the beginning of 2006, the emirs were foreign Arabs. They were Lebanese, Algerian, Saudi Arabian—they were foreign Arabs. As far as why foreign Arabs were in charge instead of Iraqis, I'm not sure why. I think it was because they wanted to bring financial means to support the organization. That's why they didn't use the lowlife people that they used to work here.

The prince could not be talked to or discussed. Nobody could talk to the prince at all. No one in his organization was authorized to look him in the eye. He was authorized to give a sentence over his people, or over anyone else. Each emir was given control over a certain area. For example, al-Jazeera had an emir. Ramadi, there was an emir in charge of that area.

Every emir had a group of people working under his control. Every group was independent of the other. They did not know what was happening in other areas where other emirs were operating. Inside, the groups were subdivided into subgroups. There were people called security. They were the strongest people within the group. They were responsible for gathering information and executing people. There were groups within the cells that were administration, or management. They prepared the place and took care of the location. And there were people within the group that they called "the eyes." Their function was just to bring information. Even these subgroups working within the cell were working independently. There was no connection between them. And each group within that cell had a leader, and not all of them met the emir. The emir had a wide span of authority. Nobody in the world had such a wide span of authority as this emir.

Iraqis were working with them, of course. I can't say whether the Saudis and Yemenis working here were dirty, but I can tell you about the Iraqi people, because I know them. The lowlife elements, the criminals, the basest of the base, were the only ones working with these terrorist organizations. This lowlife person hated all the legal elements in society: the police, the [government] employees. He did not respect them, because he lacked respect himself. Society did not respect this person to begin with, because they were dirty, and they were lowlifes. You can imagine those criminal, lowlife people rising up and terrorizing people. Some of those people would slaughter in the middle of the street. He would order as he wished. He would kill as he wished. He would go into any shop, as he wished. And so, sure, he's going to have blind authority over other people. That's why they started killing all the high-level people within society, the tribal leaders, former officers, and so forth.

The destruction in Anbar got to the state where in some areas you'd think that a tsunami went through. That's how bad the destruction was. They would fire against the Coalition forces, and the Coalition forces would fire back, and—destruction. The areas were destroyed. Work completely stopped in the province. The life cycle basically stopped here in Anbar.

The teacher was killed right in front of his students, and the student was killed in front of his friends. They reached a level of criminality—monstrosity. They would behead a person, and they would bring his head to his mother and say, "Here's your son's head." They overstepped all the red lines. There was a sense of revolt, but because of fear, people could not revolt. It got to the point where three or four or five people could not gather together and talk against these so-called mujahideen, because you're exposing yourself to death if you do that. There were some people who were aggressive, and they talked, but they were killed. They were able to control all the areas. Nobody could open his mouth.

On the Ramadi level, there were two areas they weren't able to control, though: the area where the deceased Sheikh Sattar Abu Risha and his family lived, and the area where I used to live. In 2005, I was in a confrontation with them. I was injured as a result. I was able to kill two of them. They killed several of my men in return. I left my position as a border policeman and came back. I declared in public that I was going to fight al-Qaeda. At the end of 2005, beginning of 2006, I declared war on al-Qaeda. The only people who were fighting al-Qaeda at the time were Sheikh Sattar Abu Risha and me. I don't mean myself alone, but the people in my area.

Then we started to reestablish the police. I tried to meet with one of the American officers at the time, but it was really dangerous for us to meet any of the Americans. You were basically putting your life in danger. When we stopped the Americans and told them that we wanted to establish the police again, they would laugh at us, and they would say, "What are you talking about? Are you serious? You must be dreaming." The terrorists used to kill people on the slightest suspicion that they worked with the police. If they couldn't kill him, they'd kill his father. So everyone that was associated with the police ended up killed.

On the personal level, I was cooperative with the Americans from 2003 until now. But the relationship strengthened at the end of 2005, all the way to the beginning of the Awakening movement, because we fought together even before the police was established. We used to go on missions. We used to go out and fight. We did not have much to fight with, but the Coalition forces did. So we used to show the Coalition forces where the terrorists were hiding so they could attack them and kill them.

Then the Americans were convinced that there was a need to reestablish the police again at the beginning of 2006. We were able to convince them all the way to the end of March 2006. I was one of the people who was most insistent on reestablishing the police. I was a colonel at the time. And so they asked me if it were possible to get volunteers. We had guards working in our area. I was able to gather 60 people. We took them directly to Camp Blue Diamond. They put them in vehicles, rolled them up all the way to the airport, and flew them to Amman, Jordan, for the academy.

I waited for two months for these recruits to come back again. I went through many sleepless nights because when I sent those 60 men to Amman, Jordan, while only 13 people remained here with me. My area consisted of a five-kilometer square stretch, surrounded by al-Qaeda from all over. Sheikh Sattar's area is right after the river. Below him is Shamiyah, and above him is Jazeera. We did not have that in-depth of an area to fight in. The mortar shells were raining down on my area all the time. I had 13 men to fight with, some number of rifles, and one PKC [machine gun]. I started fighting with them, of course. We would raid them, and they would raid us.

Then I started a media war, so to speak. I was able to get some radios from the Ministry of Interior and get the message out with these Motorolas. I could contact the Americans. I could contact air support if I wanted to. I was using scare tactics, spreading the message.

Sometimes I sent these 13 men away from my house to do patrols or to go on missions. The only people that remained with me were my two young sons. Now they're a little taller, but back then they were very small. They didn't know how to use a weapon. They couldn't even carry a rifle. I was so tired; I hungered for just a half hour's sleep. So it got to the point where I would load my rifle with a bullet and have it ready for my son to fire. And I would instruct him, "As soon as you hear any strange noise, just fire the round." And that would give me a signal to wake up again. I was sleeping right beside him.

We were going through a tragic time, where your son would look at you in strange ways and wonder whether we're going to win this fight or not. And you would have questions and concerns from your wife, too, looking at you and saying, "Are you sure you're up to this challenge?" Keeping in mind all the mortar fire that was raining on our area.

The United States, as powerful as it is, couldn't control al-Qaeda. You wanted to control al-Qaeda? I think President [George W.] Bush concurred with me. I think he declared that al-Qaeda was out of control. He was almost declaring that Anbar was out of control in 2005, if it wasn't for the Awakening. At any rate, I stayed as I was. I did not compromise at all. The 13 men used to be employees, working with me previously on the borders. They know my history. They know the challenges that we faced. They know that I challenged Saddam Hussein for 11 years, being an escapee from his regime. We are challenging al-Qaeda right now. There will come a day when al-Qaeda will come and bend and kneel right in front of us.

One of the men used to criticize me. He said, "We're only 13 men. Counting yourself and your two sons, that's 15 people. You think al-Qaeda is going to come and kneel in front of 15 people?"

I said, "Just wait until those 60 men come back from Amman, and you'll see how al-Qaeda will kneel right in front of you." Right after that, the 60 men came back.

Waiting for those 60 men to come back—I might have gone through that period too quickly and didn't explain it in detail—but you can imagine yourself with 13 men, trying to defend yourself with al-Qaeda all around you. It was a very difficult period we went through. This was a historical challenge for us, especially living right among our families: our wives, our mothers, our children, our families. So I said that was a historical challenge for us to make against al-Qaeda. We were encouraged even by our children. Even my mother said, "Well, you've taken this route. We're with you until the end." My wife and my men's wives, they all stood with us.

Then the 60 men came back, and we were able to open up the first police station in Anbar—al-Jazeera Police Station. We opened al-Jazeera Police Station with 60 men and two vehicles. There was a Coalition team with them, and then the two vehicles became four with the support of the Americans. They patrolled the area, about a kilometer or two kilometers around the station. Of course they were targeted by mortar shells and fire.

I received information right after we opened that al-Qaeda was really shaken by the news of a police station opening. This was going to be either the end of our beginning or the end of their beginning. They hit that police station with a VBIED [vehicle borne improvised explosive device] carrying, I think, a ton of explosives with gasoline and so forth. We opened that police station in May 2006. It was attacked the same month. I don't remember what date, but it was attacked the same month. Many policemen were burned. The Coalition forces rescued as many people as they could. Many of them were burned alive at the station. That was a very big blow against us, because that was our only police station.

Fortunately, we had a couple of vehicles in the back of the police station that were not damaged. We were able to turn them on and use them again. I asked Colonel Adnan, the police station chief at the time—even with the damage the vehicles had: the windows were broken, but the lights still worked—and I asked the colonel if we could still go and patrol the area, a kilometer or two kilometers around. He agreed, and we went and patrolled. Keep in mind there were injured. Some of them were partially burned. They were greatly shaken by the attack, but they were still defiant. We went and patrolled the area.

Montgomery: This was the same day of the attack, right? They went right out and patrolled?

Tariq: That was about an hour after the attack. We went out to patrol, knowing that there were bodies that were basically coal black. We couldn't even identify them. So I told my men to leave them aside. We needed to go out in patrol vehicles and show these people that we were still here, because I was challenged.

At the same time, we were planning to gather more men from the tribes around the area to send them to Amman. We had only a roster of their names. Many sheikhs would come in and simply give us the names of volunteers to join the police force, and we were able to gather about 200 names for the next run to Amman. Because of the attack, we were afraid that we might not get those volunteers to go to Jordan. We encouraged them to go, and in fact they did go.

Our popularity started going up, and al-Qaeda's popularity started going down. Other areas started looking at our area, and they were encouraged by our standing up the police station and wanted to do the same thing. So al-Qaeda started getting shaken up by the fact that people were rising up against them. It got to the point where al-Qaeda couldn't roam the streets as they wished. It got to the point where the martyr, Sheikh Sattar Abu Risha, and I were able to keep in touch with cell phones that were given to us by the Coalition forces. We maintained communications among myself, Sheikh Sattar, and the Coalition forces. So our communications were very fast.

The sheikhs were a little more liberal than they used to be, movement-wise. The tribal leaders started gathering courage more than before and weren't as afraid of al-Qaeda as they had been. The roads were liberated. They were not under the control of al-Qaeda anymore. They used to set up checkpoints along the routes all the time, and they couldn't do that anymore. The Coalition forces supported the Iraqis with about 12 vehicles, and they patrolled the roads and kept al-Qaeda off them. You could tell the area was secure because the police sirens and the police lights were roaming that area.

There were Coalition forces and Iraqi army forces, but they couldn't do anything because people were afraid to approach them. They were afraid that as soon as they got in touch with them, they would end up dead, so these forces lacked information.

The tribes started working again, and we could feel the movement coming back again. Who could gather all these people so that we could have one voice? We had to hold a conference. Sheikh Sattar was the only person capable of doing that because he was the sheikh who openly declared against al-Qaeda. He was a descendent of a great family and a big tribe. His house was adjacent to the Coalition camp, and that gave easy access for the Coalition forces to visit Sheikh Sattar. Also, he was very rich. Because of his status, he was able to secure barracks for these sheikhs—food, transportation, whatever they needed in order to stand up against al-Qaeda. Many sheikhs were suffering financially, and he helped them so that they could manage their affairs properly to encourage their own people to rise up against al-Qaeda.

The conference was held at the home of Sheikh Sattar. That was the first meeting in two years where the tribal leaders were able to gather at Sheikh Sattar's house and declare openly to the people that they were going to fight al-Qaeda. That first meeting, they called it the Awakening council, and to this date, even the political party name is the Awakening council. And so the sheikhs met. He declared in that conference, in front of the media, the TV, that he was going to fight al-Qaeda. That was right in the open, in front of everybody. We refused any armed militia or organization. We did not accept any so-called "honorable resistance." We considered all of those to be terrorist organizations. We declared that publicly, and it was announced on TV.

The person in charge of Ramadi at the time was Colonel [Sean B.] MacFarland. He was from the Army, but his higher up was a Marine officer. We opened more police stations as more recruits came back from Jordan. Albu Risha Police Station opened, Albu Faraj, Albu Hajasa, Albu Hassaf. And then we entered al-Tamim neighborhood. Most of the police stations were established in the villages on the Jazeera side. That was our first step inside the city.

The police were involved in great battles against al-Qaeda. We suffered the deaths of many policemen.

We were careful that this would be a legal revolution, not a tribal revolution. As soon as we appeared on TV, the government wanted to meet us. Of course, going to Baghdad was very difficult at that time. Sectarianism was at its maximum level. But when we came out on TV and declared a fight against al-Qaeda, and declared that there is no difference between Sunnis and Shiites, we won over many of the Shiites from the south as friends. Nevertheless, going to Baghdad was like going to an unknown fate. We did not want to go in a convoy escorted by the Coalition forces. We wanted to go alone to show that we were a nationalist movement. In fact, we did. We went in a convoy by ourselves, protected by patrol vehicles from the police stations that we opened. We were received very strongly by the prime minister.

The local government here did not accept our behavior at the time. They were very upset at our movement, knowing that we were protected by the Americans. They were upset when they heard us declaring that there was no resistance, that all resistance groups were classified as terrorists. They were indicating that there is honorable resistance and there is dishonorable resistance. What they meant by honorable resistance is that people were allowed to kill Americans and not kill Iraqis. How can a governor protected by the Americans declare that there is honorable resistance? Why am I being protected by these people then? Where is the honor in that? There is a person protecting me—the Coalition forces. By the same token, I am saying, "There is honorable resistance. It's okay to kill the person who is protecting me." So the local government stood against us from the first day. But we did not care too much about that matter.

The Coalition forces tried to get us closer together. We held a conference: the governor, the sheikhs, the provincial director of police, and the Coalition forces. At that time, I was not the police chief. I was a military planner, working along with the Americans. I was in charge of planning the battles against al-Qaeda with the Americans. All the battles that were fought by the police were planned by the Coalition forces and me.

Governor Mamoun [Sami Rashid al-Alwani] did attend that meeting. This is history. History is not merciful to anyone. I am not in a position to be complimentary to anyone. History has to be told truthfully. We asked the governor to appear on TV and to say, just as we said, "We are against al-Qaeda. We will fight al-Qaeda." But he refused. He did not want to appear on TV and publicly announce that he was fighting al-Qaeda. He refused to do that. He couldn't ask the citizens to fight al-Qaeda. Because he was the governor, we wanted him to clarify that there is no honorable and dishonorable resistance. We didn't want him to differentiate between types of resistance. We wanted him to classify them all as terrorists, and for the citizens to rise up and fight them, but he refused. He refused completely.

So we went and met with the government. We met with the prime minister, Nouri al-Maliki, and the minister of the interior. We were able to get hiring orders for thousands of police recruits throughout the province. The federal government asked us to establish emergency battalions throughout the province. I was personally in charge of those battalions. We successfully formed three battalions. We established them very quickly, and the Coalition forces supported us with vehicles, weapons, ammo, and training. We abandoned sending people to Jordan. We were incapable of sending them to Jordan because there were thousands. Instead, the Coalition forces were put in charge of training them, and they would sometimes jointly go out on operations.

The local government, who are part of the Islamic Party, objected to the support given by Nouri Maliki, the prime minister, to—as they were labeled by the Islamic Party—"the villagers" who led this movement because they were seeking more support for the governor because his position was weak at the time. The prime minister started calling Sheikh Sattar, started calling the police chief, instead of calling the governor, because the governor did not follow up. He did not even follow up with the central government.

The prime minister said that the situation in Anbar was so bad from 2005 until now, but he never approached us in order to help him out. Why did he not come forward and ask for help from us?

The Islamic political parties in the parliament, which the governor is part of, started working against us. This is the truth. You can ask more than one source about it, because all of the Islamic political parties stood against us, and they were openly talking against us in public. They were pressuring the prime minister to stop supporting us, but the prime minister insisted. We told him to look at our accomplishments, look at our security, how it's improving day after day. And look at these people, and all he can hear is them objecting and talking in the parliament against us. So all he heard was talk from one side, but look at our accomplishments on the other side.

So security moved forward in Anbar. We entered Ramadi then. The first forces that moved into Ramadi were Sheikh Sattar's and mine. The first people who were able to appear right here in front of this building were Sheikh Sattar and me, in front of the governor's building. There were so many weeds in front of the governor's building that they went all the way to the roof of the gate. They were so high you couldn't see the gates.

We were attacked by terrorists here. Fortunately, we were able to protect ourselves behind the concrete barriers. As a military person, I took cover behind the concrete barriers. I have to declare for history's sake that Sheikh Sattar did not want to hide. Knowing that he was wearing a white robe, and it made him conspicuous from a long distance, I told him to take cover behind the concrete barrier. He said, "No." He remained standing. He said, "I will stand and fight." Colonel [Thaddeus] McWhorter [USA] contacted me. He was pleading with me to pull Sheikh Sattar out because the danger was escalating and Sheikh Sattar had become a symbol for all of Anbar. They were afraid that something would happen to him, and it would cause a great downfall to Anbar. I used all my means to pull Sheikh Sattar out of danger so he wouldn't get hurt.

And then we liberated Ramadi. We were pleading with the provincial council, which was meeting in Baghdad at the time, to come and work here. But they refused because they said it was still unsafe. We told them that we knew there were dangers here and there—IEDs, VBIEDs—but it was safer than it used to be. And we told them, "Come over here. You're a provincial council. You're supposed to come here and perform your duty from your city." Finally they agreed to meet here in Ramadi, but they were brought here by Coalition forces, by General [John R.] Allen, by helicopter from Baghdad to Camp Blue Diamond. They considered that an accomplishment—a miracle—to meet here in Ramadi, even though it was at Blue Diamond, and even though it was under the protection of the Coalition forces. As soon as the meeting was over, they went back to Baghdad. I attended that meeting. They were proud to tell themselves that they met in Ramadi, but in actuality, we didn't feel that we were meeting in Ramadi, because this is Ramadi, here, not Blue Diamond. When you are meeting in a fortified camp such as Blue Diamond, it's not really a brave thing. It's not bravery. Bravery is coming here, right in the middle of the city, and walking freely. When it was 100 percent clear, they came and met at the provincial council building, right here.

And then they started interfering in police business. They brought a police chief affiliated with the Islamic Party and put him in charge. He was scared. He couldn't patrol the streets. He couldn't know how his police were working. He was working out of Blue Diamond. We were forced to go to the government and tell them that the police chief was a failure. It's no good. The prime minister told me, "There is no other way but to appoint you as the police chief." I didn't want to be a police chief, but I became a police chief. The Islamic Party objected to that decision, and to this date they're still objecting. I was the one who established the police.

Nobody could come and say, "We fought al-Qaeda." Sheikh Sattar and I were the first people to fight al-Qaeda. You will hear a lot of people saying that they were the first, but the truth is right here. The first people to fight al-Qaeda were Sheikh Sattar and me, but unfortunately, Sheikh Sattar died ahead of me.

And now the Islamic Party is coming here and telling us to our face that the police basically are not that good, not fit to be police, or "You are a failed police chief." I am the failed police chief who started with 30 fighters, and now I have 28,000 police. I know the areas one by one. I know where the fights took place. I know all the hot zones, all the dangerous areas, one by one. When I give a brief in a conference or in a meeting, I don't need to rely on notes because I can speak freely off the top of my head. The map is right in my head. And I think the Coalition forces were present throughout those meetings, and they were with us, and I was also present. Now the Islamic Party comes and evaluates me, and they tell me that I am not fit to be a police chief.

Al-Qaeda was able to infiltrate some of Sheikh Sattar's personal security detail, and he was killed as a result. It was a great blow to us, but we are used to challenge. I am a person who challenges all the time. I challenge mistakes, and I challenge danger, since I have faith that what I am doing is right, and I'm working to better my country.

The relationship that developed here between the American forces and the Iraqis was unlike any other relationship in the world. During meals, we offered the Americans spoons to eat with, but they refused. They ate just like Middle Easterners, with their own hands. Everybody supported our movement. The Army and the Marines—I can't say one supported us more than the other. Even the local international police advisors supported us.

And of course, it's an ongoing movement. The Awakening movement developed into a political entity. They had good presence in the election, if it wasn't for the counterfeiting and forgery.

There are many points in history that we are proud of, and there are also many tragedies that we remember. I lost many friends from 2005 until now. But the road to freedom is filled with good. If we read the history of nations that fought for freedom, we see that they offered many sacrifices.

Interview 13

Staff Brigadier General (Pilot) Nuri al-Din Abd al-Karim Mukhlif al-Fahadawi

Head
Directorate General of Intelligence and Security
Al-Anbar Province

Colonel Said Muhammed Muad al-Fahadawi

Director General
Iraqi Special Weapons and Tactics

Staff Brigadier General Nuri al-Din Abd al-Karim Mukhlif al-Fahadawi entered his current position on 21 May 2007; prior to that, he served in the Directorate General of Planning in the Ministry of Defense. Also, he occasionally worked in the office of the Ministry of Defense for Planning on operations to rescue al-Anbar.

Colonel Said Muhammed Muad al-Fahadawi is a graduate of the National Security College with a degree in military science. He is the founder, as well as the current director general, of Iraqi Special Weapons and Tactics.

General Nuri al-Din and Colonel Said were interviewed by Colonel Gary W. Montgomery and Chief Warrant Officer-4 Timothy S. McWilliams on 12 February 2009 at Camp Ramadi.

Staff Brigadier General Nuri al-Din Abd al-Karim Mukhlif al-Fahadawi: When the Coalition forces entered Iraq, the headquarters for the Coalition force was at K-17 [kilometer marker 17 on the highway]. This was in April 2003. The security situation was good at the time. The sheikhs of the tribes agreed to send a delegation to the headquarters of the Coalition force to negotiate with them to go into the cities without forces and without any fighting so we could avoid destroying the buildings and the infrastructure. One of the delegates was Staff Brigadier General

Mohammed Thumay [al-Jarawi], who was later killed by the insurgents. When they actually got inside the cities, it was very quiet, very normal. Even the government officials were in their offices in Ramadi. There was no looting like in Baghdad. They were being protected by the tribes, and there were police in the province.

The rise of the mujahideen and some military action began in 2004 with some armed groups operating in the name of jihad. They started easy at the beginning of 2004 and increased to the end of 2005. They were being called by the imams of the mosques. As you know, in our religious tradition, they say jihad is one of the main pillars Islam when they are attacked by an occupier. Speaking outside this subject, jihad law states that there should be equivalence in the fighting forces so that it abides by Sharia law. If the forces are not proportionate, it is forbidden in Islam to resist. So this is the rule of jihad.

Many people sympathized with this invocation from the imams because they believed the calling was a religious one. People started to support the mujahideen with ammunition and weapons, housing and accommodations—everything. There were too many armed groups around. Al-Qaeda was one of these groups. In time, al-Qaeda rose up and controlled everything. They had a lot of support from outside the border, and they started to attract people with money, because they had a lot of support and a lot of supplies. They had millions of dollars from outside Iraq. When they became stronger, they started negotiating with the other groups: "If you are with us, okay. If you are not with us, you are our enemy, and we're going to kill you." And honestly, they killed a lot of other groups because they didn't want to be with them. Most of them joined al-Qaeda under threat.

The American forces started to arrest and detain a lot of people. The Coalition forces couldn't identify, through the people, who wanted peace and who was a terrorist, so there were a lot of arrests—and tending not just to arrest, but also to beat. Whoever passed along the main road, the snipers might kill him, or he might be arrested, or they might do anything to him. They didn't let him move. The problem we had was that even an innocent person who was arrested during that time, he went to jail, and after a year they released him. His mind was changed to be with al-Qaeda.

Then al-Qaeda started to work against the Americans and the Iraqi forces, and even the common people. And the public started to have the feeling that al-Qaeda had a connection with the Americans through some indicators. The terrorists had the same handcuffs that were used by the Americans. They had American weapons. People started to wonder, "The Americans took innocent people, and the insurgent is free to go in and out—they don't even come close to him."

The terrorists started killing many, many, many people. Every day there were killings. They killed sheikhs, officers, pilots, engineers, doctors—in public—many people. And there were many excuses. They killed him, cut off his head, and put a paper on his body: "He is an agent of the Americans."

So what do you do? We started talking with people: "These terrorists are not working with the Americans. But the Americans don't know the good guys from the bad guys. They are confused." People thought, "No, the Americans have two armies: this army with the tanks and the Marines and everybody, and the other army is the militias and the terrorists."

We started to work, and we started forming groups, and started working against al-Qaeda. We made connections with people that worked with the American Department of Defense, Iraqi intelligence, and the American embassy. We provided them with information about who's a terrorist, who's an insurgent, and where they're working—locations, any location that was available. That's the foreign terrorists, because most of the terrorists were foreign. The leaders were foreigners—not Iraqis. Some Iraqis worked under them. We started to give them information on where they were. We gave it to intelligence, intelligence passed it to the Americans, and the Americans started attacking them from the air and killing them.

We started to form groups for the tribal sons, and they were civilians. We started to work against the terrorists. One of the groups was commanded by Colonel Said, and he passed us information through the Internet. We didn't have any other communication system except the Internet. He was passing information about the locations of the terrorists. We started to collect intelligence elements and people in the areas around us.

The terrorists, when they wanted to do an IED [improvised explosive device], every three days they came back to maintain it. Our elements started putting an IED next to their IED, and when they came back to maintain their own, they blew up. The terrorists thought their own IEDs blew up. These are just introductions to what we did before we grew.

This was before we announced the Awakening under the name of Sheikh Abdul Sattar Abu Risha. We started working like this in March 2006, and the Awakening was announced publicly in September 2006, so we started working before we announced the Awakening. After we announced the Awakening, a delegation came from Baghdad, from the Ministry of Defense and others, to meet Sheikh Abdul Sattar Abu Risha. I couldn't communicate with them, but they were told through friends that I was working on this side and taking care of it. They gave them my mobile number. They called me, so I met them at the Mansour Hotel in Baghdad. They asked for my support. I answered that I was working in the same direction for the last six or eight months, so we were one team, and we had one aim.

I was able to get a large quantity of weapons from the government: exactly 100 PKCs [machine guns]—it's a medium weapon, not a big one—500 Kalashnikovs [assault rifles], and thousands of rounds of ammunition; also 25 vehicles.

I called Sheikh Abdul Sattar to say: "You control your place. Also, go to the media and make an announcement and talk on TV. Leave the rest to me. I will go down to the street."

I gave the minister a plan. He said to let the headquarters leadership of the [inaudible] and Lieutenant General Ali Ghaidan was working [conversation with interpreter]. I explained my plan on the maps. And so the minister asked me how much time I needed to implement it. I told him 45 days. He laughed at me. He didn't believe it. He said, "The American forces and Iraqi forces have been three, four years—and they can't achieve anything that you're saying you can do in 45 days." I told them the story is very simple, but there is a problem. The American forces are confused. They don't know who's good and who's bad. And they depend on reports, half of them wrong. And the Iraqi army just started. They are weak. They have more training to do. They're too weak to do something like this.

So he asked me, "What are you going to fight with?" I told him, "I have groups of the tribal sons. I have reports. I have been working with these people for 10 months. I have accurate reports about the terrorists, where they are, how they work, what they wear, their cars' numbers, their IDs, and even their crimes—sometimes specifically which month, which day, and which hour."

We called these groups the Anbar Revolutions. We gave them Thuraya phones, and each one had a recharge card. We bought them from the local shops in Baghdad. The money was, honestly, my brothers gave it to me—Sheikh Hamis and Sheikh Hamater. They gave me money to buy these things, and I gave my people salaries. It was a simple one, but at least it enabled them to live.

People came for me in Habbaniyah. I met the 1st Division leader, Brigadier General Bada al-Azawi, in Habbaniyah. I didn't know him before, but I handed him a letter from the Ministry of Defense. He said, "We need to help you." I only needed weapons and food for my people. The man cooperated and helped me a lot.

We started doing jobs. We started from inside Ramadi to inside Fallujah city, and up around the left and right shoulders of the river. The Coalition forces and the Iraqis secured the area around us, but the actual job was done by Anbaris, because they knew their targets exactly. They didn't ask for IDs to know the terrorists. They could identify their faces not just their names because these people were from the area. They knew the people. We continued doing operations for 45 days. We went out at sunset, and we came back at sunrise.

I forgot to say something. There is an idea about these terrorists that people started identifying, which is wrong. Ninety-five percent of the people were against the terrorists, but they couldn't do anything because they were afraid they would be killed. You can tell people, "Come on, stand up and help me." But he won't unless he sees the results himself. So I was very keen to take action and go to the streets so the people would see me. I'm moving; I'm there to protect them—so they can help me.

I remember one night I brought in 77 terrorists. Lieutenant Colonel [James F.] McGrath came to me and said, "General, you're going to make a problem for me. In one night, you brought in 77 terrorists." I'll tell you something, all these 77 were real terrorists. I don't move randomly; I plan and then move accordingly. I know my target; I know what their crimes are; then I arrest them. And I went to arrest them every night. He said, "Now society will be upset that we captured all these people." I told him he was wrong: "Society will be happy because they know all these men are real terrorists. Let's go among the people, and you will see the happiness in their eyes." I rode with him in the Humvees. We had our security, and we went in the suburbs and in the city. The people were waiting for us, and they were happy. He said, "Look at the happiness in their eyes. You're right."

And we continued our jobs. We brought in hundreds in 45 days. We had some fighting, where we killed many very dangerous terrorists. Some of our people were killed during the fighting. After that, I publicly introduced myself, and I told them, "I am Brigadier General Nuri al-Din." They started to celebrate and clapped for me, and they were happy to see me. They got on the loudspeaker and said, "General Nuri al-Din came here. Maybe he will be the leader of the army. He is definitely a good guy."

We started establishing police stations and centers for the army volunteers. The people were happy, and they cooperated with security, but only when they saw something real. If you just keep talking, they won't answer you. When they saw us, and they saw our weapons and our fighting, and we told them, "We're going to protect you," the people came out and helped us.

We established police stations. We supported them with weapons and vehicles, but there was still one problem—salaries. For eight months, the minister of interior didn't issue salaries for them. During this eight months, Sheikh Ratta, my brother, was helping with some money. He gave some furniture for the offices and some communications devices. After eight months of going in and out of the minister of interior's office and the prime minister's office to get the employment order so they could issue salaries, they finally had salaries.

I started to get former military officers back on duty—about 400 from the army, about 10,000 soldiers, and the situation continues as you see now. And the police—I brought back policemen from eastern Ramadi down to Fallujah, about 5,000 to 6,000 policemen. This is the general idea.

Lieutenant McGrath, the battalion commander, came to my office one night very upset. I asked him, "What's wrong?" He said, "General, I finished my duty here, and I'm going back to America, and I don't know what's going to happen." He said, "Where there were mortars and IEDs all the time, suddenly the people just come up, and they are happy, and they say 'It's secure. We need the rule of law. We need everything.' So I don't know what's happening. I will be embarrassed when I go back to America, and they ask me, 'What's happening? Why are things changed like that?' I don't know how to answer them."

So I will tell you briefly what happened. When the terrorists came into Anbar, and the people felt that the terrorists worked with the Americans, we went inside and told them, "No, the terrorists are not with the Americans, and the Americans have a real desire to get rid of the terrorists." So we put this idea on the people's minds: "The Americans want security and peace." We placed some people secretly, and we started working with them, and we worked with the cooperation of the Coalition forces and the Iraqi forces. The people needed it. That's it. That's the whole story.

It started with a few people, and the people cooperated [inaudible]. West of Ramadi, Sheikh Sattar Abu Risha started to work. And from east Ramadi down to Fallujah, Colonel Said, General Khadim Muhammad Faris, and I worked. We volunteered, and many hundreds of Anbaris volunteered to work with us. We worked seriously and with a lot of courage because inside we really wanted to get rid of these killers and keep them away. Thank God, we achieved something good and successful. I don't think it was just the people who worked with me, the sons of the tribes; there was also a really big effort from the ranks of the Iraqi army, which was represented by the 1st Division.

That's the general idea. If you don't have any questions, I will turn it over to Colonel Said.

Colonel Said Muhammed Muad al-Fahadawi: Before I start, I want to follow up on some of the points that General Nuri al-Din mentioned. The delegation that went to negotiate with the Coalition forces in 2003—the staff general, Mohammad, was my brother-in-law. The delegation was three persons. The first one was Mohammad Thumay al-Jarawi, and he was chosen by the tribes because he was the commander of the army in al-Anbar. The second one was Brigadier General Ahmed Sadak al-Zebawi. Before 2003, he was the leader of the Saddam Fedayeen. The third one was called Faris Hamid Sadak. He was the cousin of Ahmed and the driver who took them over there.

They said they went and negotiated with the Coalition forces. They wished them well and everything and said that we're going to cooperate. But in reality, Mohammad told me—he told me the truth, because we are brothers—they felt very sorry because of the way they needed them and why they needed them. My brother said, "We volunteered to go over there to negotiate with them, so that we could give them al-Anbar Province without any fighting. What happened? They put us in a very small room, like a jail, for three days. There wasn't even a pillow to sleep on. We took our shoes and used them as pillows." This was a very big insult.

In 2003, there was Iraqi army inside al-Anbar before the fall of Baghdad.

My brother continued, "After three days, and after this insult, the Americans said, 'We want you to go with us to prove your story. Get in a helicopter with us and show us where those Iraqi army units were.' So we got in a helicopter, and I started pointing to false areas. And because of this insult, I wished that we would get shot down and everybody would get killed."

After that he came back, they told him, "We will call you back." And until 2006, the year he was killed by terrorists, no one called him from the American side. This is the first comment.

The second comment is in regard to the feeling people had that the terrorists were being helped by the Coalition forces. We have a good connection now, and the relationship with the Americans is strong, but we still have to know why that feeling existed. I spoke with leaders of the Coalition forces about this subject. I related that on the American side there is a judge, there is a law, there is a court, and there are human rights. Many people were arrested by the American forces. There were no witnesses, so they said, "He's innocent," and they released him.

Interpreter: You understand what he means, sir? The Americans arrested people, but no one from the public would be a witness, because he would be killed. The Americans had no witnesses that he is a terrorist. So they released him. So the people started feeling the Americans were working with the terrorists. That's what he means.

Said: Well, I tell you, they still have the same regulations. Three months ago, Mohammed Dohatch Lobom, the leader of al-Fatihin Army, was released from Bucca. Now they ask us to go find him again so we can arrest him. People start to wonder why they would release him and then come back and want to arrest him. But I know that, according to American law, he was punished, and they couldn't extend his time in jail. They had to release him.

The third comment is regarding the Coalition forces in al-Anbar. Honestly, they made a very courageous decision. The central government does not support the idea of establishing a strong police and Iraqi army in the province. But on this occasion, I want to be clear about something. I want to extend my appreciation and thanks to Colonel [John W.] Charlton [USA]. . . And the second guy is Lieutenant Colonel [Charles] Ferry [USA]. He was the commander of the battalion east of Ramadi. What they did, these brave people—they were Army, not Marines—in the beginning of establishing the police, they made a brave decision. They took all the police and took care of them, gave them weapons, trained them, and gave them uniforms. And they gave them help, monthly—$200, $300. They gave them weapons, HESCO barriers to protect their offices, and furniture.

I attended a meeting between Colonel Charlton, Lieutenant Colonel Ferry, and the police in Ramadi. We made the police a reality and forced the government center to deal with that reality. They couldn't say no. And that's what happened.

About Brigadier General Nuri al-Din, he has the right military rank, and he's the sheikh of a tribe. His tribe is the biggest tribe in Anbar by area and by population. His brother was Sheikh Massab Abdul Karim, the paramount sheikh. He had a PhD and gave lectures in al-Anbar University. He was killed by terrorists. The other tribes awakened because the Albu Fahd tribe awakened, so it goes with them. That's what I have here.

Going back to the Awakening—to be honest and for history—the Awakening started in al-Qaim in the middle of 2005. The Albu Mahal tribe revolted and started to awaken. They're on the border with Syria. After the Islamic State in Iraq, which is terrorist, announced that they're in al-Qaim, these tribes rose up. And to be honest, these were the first people to awaken. They established police, and they are still there.

The second announced Awakening, Abu Risha, happened in September 2006 in the Jazeera area. From Sheikh Abdul Sattar's announcement in September until the 5th of February 2007, when the Albu Fahd tribe came out, there was only Sheikh Abdul Sattar. It was confined to the Jazeera area. Some Awakening councils were established, but they couldn't establish any government until the Albu Fahd tribe came out. Then everything started to return to normal.

About the Albu Fahd tribe, their location is from the center of Ramadi city to Fallujah. Also, they are with the [Dubad], and across the river in the Jazeera area.

As for me, personally, the terrorists killed my sister's husband, Staff General (Pilot)—he was the commander of the air base in

Nasiriyah; Ali Air Base, which is now Tallil. This was requested very strongly by the Iranians because he was involved in the Iran-Iraq War. The terrorists killed him in Haditha City.

Colonel Gary W. Montgomery: The terrorists killed him because he was involved in the Iran war?

Said: We think that al-Qaeda was supported by the Iranians, so we guess it was revenge. Pilots were killed by al-Qaeda. General Mohammed, whom we talked about, was killed by al-Qaeda. Too many officers were killed by al-Qaeda. My house was blown up by al-Qaeda, and I was not involved with the police or anything.

The 1st of April 2006, General Nuri al-Din was in Baghdad. He sent someone to tell me that he wanted to see me. After he found out what happened to me and who al-Qaeda had killed from my family, we met in Baghdad. He also sent for Staff General Khadim Mohammad Faris. And he was talking about what we have to do to face al-Qaeda after they killed our sheikhs, and our officers, and our families. The Americans and the Iraqi army couldn't do anything.

The terrorists were getting stronger with the presence of the Coalition forces. They enforced some habits which we didn't have before. Females shouldn't work. Schools for girls were not allowed. They changed the way we pray. They changed the call to prayer in the mosques. They controlled all the resources of the province. They controlled some of the government offices: the Department of Education, the Health Department, the Facilities Protection Service. Each director general had someone sitting beside him from al-Qaeda.

After they controlled the people by terrorism, by killing, they went back to the groups that were working with them, the jihad or mujahideen groups like the Islamic Army, the 20th Revolution Brigades, the Islamic Movement, the Mujahideen Army, and other groups, and told them, "Either you give us your weapons and your vehicles, and you work under our control, or you will not be allowed to shoot a single bullet, even if you are shooting at the Americans." According the information we have, about 60 percent of these groups cooperated with them. The 40 percent who were against them were either killed or fled abroad, mostly to Syria. And the rest, some people just sat at home and did nothing. They stopped their activities.

Going back to the meeting in Baghdad between me and General Nuri al-Din and General Khadim, we met in an apartment, and we talked together and discussed our thoughts. One idea was to buy some sniper rifles and go hide somewhere and start shooting them like snipers. But then we remembered what happened to a guy called Sheikh Rijad. He resisted them. They killed him, and they killed his family, even the women. So General Nuri al-Din said the best thing is to work with the government of Iraq and with the help of the Coalition forces. So the suggestion was that he should stay in his area and continue working with the Iraqi Army.

I met with Iraqi intelligence, and there were also some people from the American CIA [Central Intelligence Agency] there. The suggestion in this meeting was that we establish a directorate general of the Office for Iraqi Intelligence inside al-Anbar.

We had seen how communication would be—it was very hard for me to physically go in and out of Baghdad. So we started exchanging information through the Internet. Thuraya phones were very hard to deliver into al-Anbar because there were terrorist checkpoints. If they checked us and found them, they might kill us. So General Nuri al-Din took care of it, and he delivered it to al-Anbar for us.

I started collecting people who were very close to me, starting with my family, my close friends whom I trust, and we established a group of about 15 people. They covered the whole of al-Anbar in person. Each city had two or three people.

After that, they gave us some GPS [global positioning system] devices. The only way of communicating with Baghdad was through the Internet. Al-Qaeda had some very good technicians. They usually watched the Internet cafes and monitored information on the Internet, so they gave me a laptop that was encoded so they couldn't hack it. The targets were documented with grids and pictures on the Internet, and we pushed them to

American and Iraqi intelligence. Also, I cc'ed General Nuri al-Din. I documented everything, and I kept copies for myself.

In one of the reports that I saved from before Sheikh Sattar's Awakening was announced, I told them there would be an uprising in western Ramadi. It would control only the Jazeera area and the highway. But the center of Ramadi and eastward to Fallujah would not be controlled. I mention these documents because I want you to understand that there were people fighting al-Qaeda secretly. For us, in reality and as something for history, the Awakening started in February 2006, but it was announced to the people in September 2006. This is documented. I have it as a person who was responsible for the intelligence office in al-Anbar. Also General Nuri al-Din has the same documents, as does the Iraqi army.

As General Nuri al-Din said, we started working with the Sons of al-Anbar. So the decision was to go and become known to the people and not remain secret.

Nuri al-Din: Some comments. The real work was between 15 December 2006 and 1 February 2007. This 45 days was hard and real and a very brave job. There was work before that in February 2006 in the east of Ramadi. But the real work, in which we achieved everything, was from 15 December 2006 until 1 February 2007. This period of time was secret, and we worked just at night. After 1 February 2007, we appeared to the people. Before, we were top secret; and now the people are with us, and we went public.

Said: On 5 February 2007, only four days after going public, we established the first police station, so the people could believe in us. In addition to my job as the director of the intelligence office in al-Anbar, I was the commander of this police station, so that the people will believe in us. During this time, I was the commander of the al-Shibadah police station in the eastern Ramadi area and also the intelligence director of al-Anbar.

I was going in and out to the offices of the government of Iraq in Baghdad, so I asked to open a real office of intelligence in al-Anbar, so we would be known and available to assist the army with information. The Coalition forces and the Iraqi army agreed, and they supported me. But the CIA people and Iraqi intelligence wanted to wait six or seven months. They didn't believe it could be settled down in just two or three months, because we did it before—opening some offices for intelligence and information in Salah ad Din Province, and also in Kirkuk Province, and the terrorists killed them.

I resigned and came back. I got Colonel Charlton and Lieutenant Colonel Ferry to agree to establish an intelligence office for the police. It was established and became an office for fighting terrorists. We started with 50 employees in Ramadi city. They were very brave. They supplied me with weapons, with vehicles and furniture, and buildings. After that we developed our office and the Coalition forces helped us and supported us. One of them was Lieutenant Colonel [Bolin?]. We worked with the Navy. We kept going. There were weekly meetings. I established branches of our office in the whole of al-Anbar. And we changed the name to Iraqi Special Weapons and Tactics.

In my office, I have documents about al-Qaeda, and the targets we did, and the jobs we did. We had the honor of liberating two very hot areas in al-Anbar Province, which are the [inaudible] area and also [Ali Bahi?] area. These are north of Baghdad. We have many documents from the Coalition forces and the Navy.

I have some small comments. One time Sheikh Hamis, General Nuri al-Din's brother, met us in Baghdad. He was a teacher, and he read history. He knew about our work against the terrorists. He told me, "You know how all the revolutions happened in the world? They were planned and executed by a small number of people." I feel very honored, very proud, that I was one of the persons who helped do this one and rescue al-Anbar from the terrorists.

Nuri al-Din: For history, military action started because of mistakes the Coalition forces made. One of the reasons behind it was the dissolution of the army. [L. Paul] Bremer's dissolving the army was a very big mistake. It was a direct reason for the rise of military action. Some of the behavior of the Coalition forces was a mistake. I remember one of these situations. The public was protesting for some reason. There were no essential services, so they started protesting until the American forces shot them. The reaction against these people, it made them angry.

The second thing was the Americans were taking advice from only one side. If we want to be precise, they took advice from Shiites. They described Anbaris as Saddam's people, as Ba'ath Party people. This is not true. It is unjust to describe them like that. It's not good for the Anbaris. Because of this, the Americans didn't trust these people and didn't support them. In time, the situation started to be clear to them, and they understood it.

Interview 14

Staff Major General Abdullah Mohammad Badir al-Jaburi

Commanding General
7th Iraqi Army Division

Staff Major General Abdullah Mohammad Badir al-Jaburi joined the new Iraqi Army in 2004. He served in the 1st Iraqi Army Division as a battalion commander, the division operations officer, the chief of staff, and as a brigade commander. He subsequently commanded the 2d Division, and then the 7th Division. He served mainly in Taji, Habbaniyah, and Ramadi.

Staff Major General Abdullah was interviewed by Colonel Gary W. Montgomery and Chief Warrant Officer-4 Timothy S. McWilliams on 22 February 2009 at Camp Mesi, al-Asad, Iraq. An unknown officer who was present also asked a couple of questions.

Staff Major General Abdullah Mohammad Badir al-Jaburi: During this last five years, we have been in different phases working against the terrorists. The terrorist activities have changed during the time from 2004 until today. The main highlight of terrorist activities is just to terrify people—the civilians, the Iraqi army, and the police—in order to accomplish their agenda. They do this, they try to attain their goal with a different type of technique.

In the beginning, we were Iraqi security forces. We were in the defense, and they are attacking, especially during 2004 and 2005. And after the Iraqi people understood the goal of the terrorist cells and organization, our work entered different phases.

In the beginning, facing a very critical situation at the time, the people didn't want to cooperate with the Iraqi security forces for two reasons: either they were terrified of the terrorists, or they were cooperating with them. Then, when the terrorists conducted criminal activities in the area, when they destroyed our infrastructure, people understood that they had to work against the terrorist organizations, and that's when we started the Awakening.

This was the Awakening: when the people started working against al-Qaeda.

And the other point, U.S. forces weren't proficient in dealing with the Iraqi population in the beginning, or they didn't understand how to treat Iraqis at that time. So many Iraqis turned against U.S. forces because of their behavior during raids. They didn't treat family members in a good way. Consequently, most Iraqis did not accept the U.S. presence in their areas. If the U.S. forces want to treat the Iraqi people in a better way, they shouldn't treat them the same way that they treat the British or Americans. They have to understand Iraqi culture. That's going to help them do their job. But this wasn't there.

At the same time, the Iraqi people looked on the Iraqi security forces as traitors or collaborators to the U.S. forces, so they didn't accept them, either, in the beginning. But later on, when they worked in their areas, they treated the people better than the U.S. forces did, and we became closer to Iraqi society.

We had three points: what we call the igniting of the Awakenings, when the U.S. forces became culturally advised regarding Iraqis; when the people understood that the Iraqi security forces were willing to work for them, not against them; and when the people understood that the terrorist organizations were working against the Iraqi people willingly. All these things together ignited what we call the Awakening groups. Also, the people started understanding that the new government was willing to work for them.

At the beginning, the Awakening group didn't have their weapons with them. They were just participating and helping Iraqi security and the U.S. Marines with intelligence information about any terrorist activities in their area. They identified them for us: "He is the emir of a group. That one is a cell leader. This one is a member in the organization." This kind of information. We call this the beginning phase of the Awakening. Even now, we expect that, just theoretically, if there were a new terrorist organization coming to their area, as soon as the Iraqi people know, they will provide us with the information, and we could deal with them, and we could defeat them. But without any intelligence information, it's going to be hard for us to identify the target and deal with it.

I will be frank with you. We still have terrorist activities to this day. There are many IEDs [improvised explosive devices] that are planted in our area every day, but the good thing is that we get information from the public. They tell us where the IED is, and we can deal with it right away. This is the benefit of the people, when they cooperate with us. This is a simple explanation for the Awakening: when a common man comes to the Iraqi security forces and tells them where an IED was planted. This is the good result of our success. This kind of cooperation between the Iraqi people and the security forces indicates that the Iraqi security forces have to improve their technique during searches in a way that adheres to Iraqi culture. Nowadays, we are maintaining this kind of cultural awareness with the Iraqi people, which induces them to provide more information to us.

For the last few years, we worked with the Marines, and during this time our friendship and cooperation got to the level where we could deal with any situation, under any circumstances. That brings us to the way the Marines understand Iraqi culture more than they previously did. Also, civil affairs operations have been maintained by the Marines, bringing the people in the area to a better level of cooperation with the Iraqi security forces.

Interpreter: He's covered everything on the Awakening, sir. He wanted to know if you had any specific questions, or what you might want him to cover next.

Chief Warrant Officer-4 Timothy S. McWilliams: I do, sir. You described the Awakening, but I'm curious, what did Coalition forces do before the Awakening to help gain the trust and turn the people?

[The question was translated into Arabic as, "How did American forces help in the Awakening?"]

Abdullah: I think that there are many elements here that prepared the ground for the Awakening. There are al-Qaeda mistakes, like when they attacked civilians. U.S. cultural awareness improved. Iraqi security's dealing with the civilians—these three elements help together. There is not just one side here.

Colonel Gary W. Montgomery: Did you see U.S. cultural awareness, did it change quickly or very slowly over a long time? Was there any time where you could say, "This is when it changed?"

Abdullah: I think that during 2003 and '04, the U.S. forces committed lots of mistakes regarding cultural awareness, but after that, they came to the conclusion that they had to change their technique in how to deal with Iraqi civilians. Plus, they started to cooperate more with Iraqi security. Joint operations—that helped the situation.

Unknown: What would he also recommend to win the hearts and minds of the folks? As far as from his perspective, what are the things the Americans can do better, could have done better, as well as what we could do in the future to make sure that we're winning the hearts and minds of the folks. . . .

Abdullah: Good treatment for the Iraqi civilians will bring better cooperation and better information providers. The U.S. forces changed their technique. In the beginning, everybody was afraid of their convoys. I have an example from my village. All the kids, when they saw a U.S. convoy, they ran away. But day by day, we're getting to better cultural awareness. People, day by day, don't become afraid of U.S. convoys. I believe it's a good accomplishment. I think that, for an answer to your question, more involvement with Iraqi culture and society, and they will be more cooperative.

Montgomery: During the actual Awakening, or once the fighting began clearing al-Qaeda, was there a lot of coordination and a strategy, or was it more of a psychological thing, that everyone just rose up at about the same time?

Abdullah: In the beginning, Sheikh Sattar Abu Risha awakened for revenge for his family members who had been assassinated by the terrorists. Then it became larger when he started coordinating some of the tribe members with him to start this Awakening, and then the government of Iraq started helping him, and the U.S. forces also started helping him. That all improved the Awakening.

Interpreter: General Abdullah said he was there since day one, and he had many meetings with the Awakening group at that time.

Unknown: When they started beginning the Awakening, we had heard through previous interviews that they initiated it in the al-Qaim area, although it stayed out there, and then it slowly made its way east. I just want to know how he thought about that, if that was the initial "Awakening."

Abdullah: That's right. The Awakening started, but it did not extend all the way. It started there and stopped there. All the tribal leaders in that area supported the 1st Iraqi Brigade from the 1st Division. I wasn't there. All the area of al-Karablah, al-Qaim, and al-Ubaidi was surrounded by two or three layers of [inaudible], but when the army started showing progress, when people were very much suffering from terrorism, they directly cooperated. So in al-Qaim, the Awakening started there and stopped there. But in 2006, they resumed in Ramadi. It stopped before Haditha's borders; it didn't extend, but it emerged again in west Ramadi.

Unknown: Were there other locations? Were there other cities out here in the al-Anbar area that it was possibly some sort of initial beginning as well?

Abdullah: It wasn't immediately after the Awakening stopped in al-Qaim. It wasn't ignited again in another area for six months, when we had it in Ramadi under the leadership of Abdul Sattar Abu Risha.

Interpreter: The commanding general had many meetings with the Awakening groups, and we had a lot of cooperation at that time. And Sheikh Sattar Abu Risha got lots of support from the U.S. side to enable him to stand up and be a good leader.

Montgomery: In 2003, do you think, was it possible to avoid an insurgency of some type?

Abdullah: At that time, there was no coordination. There was no Iraqi police, no Iraqi army. There was no coordination between the U.S. and Iraqi security forces. Since there was no coordination between all these elements, I don't believe we could stop any kind of insurgency at that time.

Montgomery: My impression is that the Iraqi security forces and the American security forces, neither one could defeat the insurgency alone, and even together, they could not defeat the insurgency without the support of the populace. Is that accurate?

Abdullah: Definitely. I will give you an example of this. In the beginning, when we arrested any terrorist suspect, he had a fake ID [identification]. When we asked him about his name, he would say he was someone else and present a fake ID. We didn't know. But later, when we had cooperation with the people, they said, "Don't worry, this is a fake ID. He is the real guy. He is the terrorist." Since the Iraqi people started cooperating with us and identifying the real terrorists, we get them in their homes. Even if we don't ask him about his ID, it doesn't matter. If they tell us he is there, we grab him, and he starts to confess whatever he's done in the past.

Unknown: He spoke very highly of the military transition teams [MTTs], that they worked well with the Iraqi security forces. As we continue to go forward with the Awakening, is there anything else that he would recommend that would continue the progress or allow us to even go to a next level, to continue the improvement between the American forces and the ISF?

Abdullah: The relationship between the MTT team and the Iraqi army is based on a good foundation. It can improve, but what we have now is not bad. . . . In the beginning, the American supervisor would listen but would not take anything we said seriously. But later they started taking the information we passed to him seriously. When we ask, they go to their higher, and they discuss it, and they bring us the answer we need to improve ourselves.

Most of the Iraqi security forces get their logistical support these days from the Ministry of Defense, and in many occasions the MTT team is working hard to push our higher to support us better that way. That's the better way to deal. The MTT team has reached a level where they can understand the details inside our units. Every time, when we discuss any matter, he knows. He has the response: what to answer, how to answer.

Unknown: Could you give us a quick comparison between the Awakening in al-Anbar Province as compared to possibly Ninawa, Diyala, some of the other provinces? Were there some similarities, differences, that kind of thing?

Abdullah: The difference between the Awakening group in Anbar and in other provinces, the Awakening group in Anbar was established in the beginning. So they had the opportunity to join the Iraqi security forces as policemen or soldiers. But what happened in Diyala or Ninawa, they were late in awakening. They don't have any place for them to join. The Iraqi organizations have been completed. So they are like militias now. They are civilians. They were getting paid by the U.S. Now they're getting paid by the Iraqi government, but there is no explanation for them. There is no name for them. Are they Iraqi army, or police? Or are they some other organization? This is the problem of the Awakening groups in Diyala, and Salah ad Din, and in Ninawa.

Montgomery: Al-Qaeda tried to start sectarian warfare, tried to start a civil war, but it didn't work. Why is that? I think that's something we don't understand very well as Americans.

Abdullah: Al-Qaeda is continuing to do this. Al-Qaeda continued to have this technique. They started last week when there was a pilgrimage in south Iraq. They attacked the pilgrimage in order to have sectarian violence. They continue to do this because if we have a civil war, the U.S. can't intervene. They can't identify who is who. And they would let the Iraqi security forces deal with this sectarian violence. We'll be busy with it, and they will have enough time to bring people who support them from abroad and come in and control the country. This is their goal, to let Iraqis live in chaos. When Iraqis live in chaos, they can control the country easily by their ideology. They succeeded, at certain times, at igniting civil war. But, thank God, people understood the reason for this, and they stopped it, and we defeated that ideology.

Montgomery: So the Iraqi people saw through that tactic?

Abdullah: Yes. There is no difference between the Iraqi people. On April 9th, 2003, when the regime fell, at that time there was no police, no army, and there was no law, but we didn't have civil war. There was no difference between Iraqis. But later on, the interests of foreign countries led to helping these terrorist organizations, feeding them with money, and letting them start with their civil war.

Montgomery: During the Iran-Iraq War, the Iraqi Shi'a fought with the Iraqi Sunni against the Iranians, even though they are Shi'a, so I'm wondering if perhaps the Sunni-Shi'a thing is exaggerated in the West.

Abdullah: As I mentioned from my example, in 2003 when the regime had fallen, there was no law, no Iraqi forces, and we didn't have a civil war. I have to say that this kind of hatred, we don't have it inside our hearts and minds. But interference from foreign countries helped these organizations to develop in that direction. Iraq is not just Shi'a and Sunni. There are Kurds, there are Yazidis, there are Assyrians. There is a mixture here. We don't have that difference unless someone has intervened, and he has his special interest.

McWilliams: I'd be curious if there are any other significant events or successes against al-Qaeda that you led or witnessed that you would like to tell us about.

Abdullah: I think that all Iraqis now understand that the Awakening was the best thing for them. They had to "wake up," and the ideology of al-Qaeda has to stop. This is the way they are. In the future, when any kind of such ideology appears on the ground, I think there is no way for them to succeed.

Montgomery: So the Awakening is permanent?

Abdullah: Yes. Definitely, the Awakening will be permanent, because the people experienced when they were sleeping what kind of danger happened to them. Now there is no way for them to go back to those dark days.

Iraqi Perspectives

Interview 15

Staff Brigadier General Haqi Isma'eel Ali Hameed

Commander
2d Region Directorate of Border Enforcement

Staff Brigadier General Haqi Isma'eel Ali Hameed was born in 1958 and graduated from military college as a lieutenant in 1979. He served in the air force and the Ministry of Defense. He finished in the top of his class at the staff college, and was subsequently retained as a lecturer there. He holds a PhD in military science. He left military service in 1995, but after the fall of Saddam Hussein, he returned to take command of the 2d Region Directorate of Border Enforcement.

General Haqi was interviewed by Colonel Gary W. Montgomery and Chief Warrant Officer-4 Timothy S. McWilliams on 19 February 2009 in Ramadi.

Staff Brigadier General Haqi Isma'eel Ali Hameed: Before the invasion, when we listened to the news—at that time, we didn't have the satellite channels. It was forbidden. The people of Iraq expected something different than what they actually saw after the operation. Everyone thought there would be democracy and an improvement in the scientific and technological fields, and the quality of life would improve. They thought that all of this would happen after the operation.

Everybody wanted to change the previous regime, but no one wanted it in this way. We really hoped that we could change the regime from inside Iraq, but it was too hard. No one could do it. Even all the other countries around the world accepted the idea that it wasn't going to happen from inside Iraq.

After the invasion of Iraq by the Coalition forces, and after they were inside all the cities and towns, we saw some really strange and weird behavior by the Coalition forces, especially what they did with honest Iraqis who were unarmed. It's because the Coalition forces were relying on information from people who came with them from outside Iraq. The information that the Coalition forces received from them was 100 percent wrong. We saw some really weird behavior from them toward Iraqis. We were shamed to the point where there was no trust toward the Coalition forces, and the Coalition forces didn't trust any Iraqis. It created a very bad impression among Iraqis toward the Marines, and the Coalition forces in general.

Some honest Iraqis were killed for no reason. For example, some people were walking in their usual way, and there was a snap checkpoint. They walked by and got killed. They didn't know that they shouldn't go that way because the checkpoint wasn't there before. Several people didn't do anything to deserve to get killed, but they were killed for no reason.

People didn't know how to act with the Marines, how to communicate with them. This lack of information caused them to make mistakes that cost them their lives. And if they didn't get killed, they would be arrested and spend several years in jail for nothing. All these behaviors from the Coalition forces made the Iraqis feel that they had to fight.

On the other hand, I can say that I talked with some American generals and officers in the Marines. I told them there is a distinctiveness to each town, and city, and area in Iraq, and they should treat people in one area differently from people in another area of Iraq. They shouldn't just treat all Iraqis same because we have different communities inside these towns. In the countryside, where you have tribes and sheikhs, you have to deal with them differently than people living in Baghdad or in the cities. People living in the south of Iraq should be treated totally different from people in the north of Iraq.

But the problem was that they didn't listen. They didn't believe what I said. They didn't accept what I said because they didn't trust us. We were giving all this advice because we wanted to reduce the casualties and to stop the fighting before it begins. But they didn't listen to us; they listened to the people who came with them from outside Iraq. The people who came with them don't know anything. They continued listening to them until we came to a deadlock, to a point where there's no way forward and no way to go back. They were in a position to maintain good relationships with Iraqis, but they didn't use it. They didn't invest in a good relationship. I hoped they would listen to the good people of Iraq, who really wanted to improve the situation at that time and to stop all the casualties and all the fighting, but they didn't do that. They listened to the people who came with them.

As an example, in the countryside, in the tribal areas, they have a tradition of getting revenge when someone kills one of them. So when one of them—just one individual of that tribe—gets caught by the Coalition forces, they do everything they can to take revenge on the Coalition forces.

In addition to that, resistance to invasion is the right of all Iraqis. They have the right to fight back and to protect themselves. It's a right. They don't have to ask for it. It's the right of anyone who gets invaded and occupied by another country's forces. And since we are an Islamic country, meaning a majority of Iraqis are Muslims, it made people feel that they needed to fight back and to protect themselves.

That's what led the people of Iraq to start fighting the Coalition forces, in three different ways. There was a strong feeling among the national, or the good Iraqis that they had to fight back. They had to get their country back from another people. They wanted an independent country. On the other hand, there was that religious desire to fight back, because that's what their religion told them— that you have to fight back, and get your freedom back, and to protect yourself. And the third way was the Iraqi response to the bad treatment that they received from the Coalition forces. This point includes the main tradition that I talked about—that the tribe has to take revenge on people who kill one of them.

That's why they started to form small groups of insurgents. Some were religious groups, and others were nationalist groups, and some were military groups. Some of them were from the previous army, and some of them were from the previous security forces. Some groups were Ba'ath Party members and people who were close to the previous regime. At that time, we thought that they had the right and the privilege to fight back and to protect themselves. So that's why they received wide support from the Iraqi people, especially in the middle area, like Baghdad, Diyala, Salah ad Din, and at the top of the list, al-Anbar. And also Ninawa and Mosul. These groups started by attacking the occupation forces. They depended on light weapons. They were funded by people who believed in their cause, or maybe they donated their own money.

That leads us to the emergence of the al-Tawhid wal-Jihad groups, who were linked to al-Qaeda. They worked tirelessly against the Coalition, but we found out that they had a hidden agenda. Their agenda was to destroy Iraq. Especially in 2005 and 2006, they had many excuses and tried to confuse the issues. At that point, people weren't able to recognize which of these operations was resisting and which one was against both the Coalition forces and the Iraqis, too. They were targeting the Iraqi vehicles that were in Coalition force convoys, even if it was Iraqi police or Iraqi army, but not the American vehicles in those convoys. They attacked some of the American vehicles, but only to give them a cover story or to give them something for the news. Then they went and killed honest Iraqi people who had nothing to do with this.

They had huge financial support and huge resources of weapons. We—the Iraqi people, the civilians—we were forbidden from even having a stick inside our cars to protect ourselves. We were forbidden from having any kind of weapons with us. But we could see that all these groups of al-Qaeda, and some other groups, had weapons in their cars and on their persons. We were surprised. We thought that they were cooperating and working together with the Coalition forces because they controlled everything in al-Anbar Province. People would address them as al-Qaeda and members of al-Tawhid. It was easy to address them. They controlled all the government buildings and facilities, and they controlled all the roads. They were charging fees for people to use these facilities and to use the roads.

In the last days of their era, they tried to fund their operations by abducting people and holding them for ransom. They proclaimed fatwas that this thing is forbidden, and that thing is approved and accepted in Islam—according to what was useful to them. They didn't believe in the development of the scientific and technological fields. They didn't believe in technology at all, and they didn't accept it. They didn't think about or improve the quality of life for Iraqis. They really wanted to keep all the people in a very bad situation.

They were evil to a point that they didn't want anyone to be better than them. They killed the best people in Anbar. They killed some of the distinguished officers in Anbar, some of the distinguished sheikhs in Anbar, some of the distinguished, well-educated people in Anbar. They were killing anyone who was in charge during the Iran-Iraq War. They killed the most distinguished of Iraqi military officers who fought in the Iran-Iraq War and stopped Iran from invading Iraq. They killed the best, the most distinguished pilots, who fought against Iran in that war. By killing those people, they made the people of Iraq start to think. It made Iraqis understand that these groups were not working for the benefit of Iraq. They were just trying to destroy Iraq.

But we have to be honest and say that they were planning, in a smart way, since they could scam the Iraqis and make them think that they were working for the benefit of Iraq and according to the Islamic religion. They got support from foreign intelligence services and foreign media support, which enabled them to do all that. Without foreign support, they would never be able to get above all those people.

During that time, some of the most important tenders for rebuilding projects had been given to some Western and some Iraqi construction companies. But they were given to bad people. The implementation of these construction projects was really poor, and it wasn't according to engineering standards. Supervision by the Marine Corps wasn't good. It was really weak. Large amounts of money were spent, and a lot of bad people benefitted from it. A lot of construction companies benefitted, but project implementation was poor.

In my personal opinion, I think that these tenders were given to people who had a special relationship with the Marine Corps. Some of these construction projects and tenders were given to some distinguished sheikhs and to some other people that must have a special relationship with the Marine Corps. My personal opinion is that it was done to support certain people financially and to get them to side with the Marine Corps. Some of those people were really bad. Before the operation, they were considered bad by the people in this area. Then, after the operation, when the Marine Corps gave them all these tenders and all that money, they became distinguished and considered good. Of course they're regarded as good guys by the Marine Corps, and that creates negative feelings among the Iraqi people in this area, and they don't accept it. And a lot of money was stolen, and many projects would not get completed and many would be partially completed.

We are an oriental culture. Giving financial support to people who are disreputable inside the community makes the rest of the community feel uncomfortable with contacting the Marine Corps and working with them. People here thought the tenders were distributed dishonestly, and that everyone should benefit from the financial support. So the Marine Corps wasn't successful in establishing a good relationship with the Iraqi people, and they weren't as successful in making the Iraqi people like them. If they did it a better way, they would be able to have that good relationship, and then the Iraqis would love them. We know that the Marine Corps spent a lot of money, but it was not well spent.

Now I'm going to talk about the Awakening at the end of 2006, specifically in September. Because of the criminal activities of the al-Tawhid wal-Jihad groups—the al-Qaeda groups—and because of the fighting they did, all the people here had the feeling that these groups were bad for Iraq. They were trying to destroy Iraq, except for a small portion of people who were benefitting from them and being protected by them. The people got involved with these groups because they thought that they were good people who were doing something good for Iraq. They were just a small number of people. Most of the people who were involved with them didn't believe in their ideology. I guess they were only working with them because they needed the money, the big financial support that these groups got from other countries.

Because these groups were targeting the good people—the distinguished officers and tribal sheikhs, and all the well-educated people here—it made people change their minds. They changed their minds 180 degrees, and everyone here started to believe that these groups didn't want anything good for Iraq. They were destroying bridges, schools, clinics, hospitals and police stations, all the military facilities, all the government facilities. They prevented people from going to their jobs.

Because of all that, and because we got to a point where we couldn't talk with those people—we couldn't do anything with them—because of all that, a small, limited-attendance meeting was held in Sheikh Abdul Sattar Abu Risha's house. It was 14 September 2006. All the people who attended the meeting believed that we must start to fight the terrorists by using anyone we had to fight. At that meeting, they decided which side they're going to work with and who is going to support us. And at that meeting, we decided who would provide financial support, who would provide weapons and ammunition, who be on our side, and who would be on the opposite side—from the Iraqi people, the Iraqi government, and the Americans.

After asking for God's blessing, and after we talked with the Americans and the Iraqi government, we got approval to start this project—but in a formal way, according to Iraqi law and human rights, with all the judgments in an official court, according to Iraqi law. That's why the tribal sons started enlisting in the police forces. The Iraqi government approved the establishment of the police in al-Anbar Province, and they were going to support us with weapons and salaries. Thousands of tribal sons enlisted, and they were inducted immediately into the police forces. Then we got training support from the Americans and from the Iraqi army. And the Americans gave us very good intelligence support, and we got very good support for the prime minister, the minister of internal affairs, and the minister of defense. And that was an official announcement to start fighting back against the insurgents, according to Iraqi law.

After starting all that, which was just limited to a small area where there was popular support, all the people throughout the whole of al-Anbar started to support this operation. We opened official offices for the Awakening in all al-Anbar towns and cities. And people started enlisting in the police forces by visiting the Awakening offices directly.

We got very good support from the Iraqi army. The 12th Division and the 7th Division came to Anbar and provided good support. And the support that we got from the Iraqi prime minister, by visiting the sheikhs in Anbar, and the Awakening leaders, and other people who were involved in this operation—it was a very good thing from him, and he really encouraged us and made it better.

All Anbaris were together in support of the Awakening. We held a lot of big conferences that were open to all Anbaris to attend, and we described and explained this big project, the Awakening. I personally attended more than 10 conferences to explain and describe this subject, and to tell all the people about the Awakening, and to encourage them to enlist in the army and police, and to fight the terrorists according to Iraqi laws and regulations, and to tell them that we won't accept any arresting without a warrant from a judge. When we arrested people to put them in jail, we were informing them that they can [inaudible].

At that time, we had very good intelligence cooperation and intelligence support from the Americans. We worked together and informed each other about people we arrested and jailed. And we continued that cooperation with the Marine Corps until we destroyed al-Qaeda in Anbar Province in about the middle of 2007.

Al-Qaeda members really got the point that Anbaris didn't like them. They didn't want them—except for just a few, who were gaining financially from al-Qaeda. And that's why they escaped to other provinces, like Ninawa, Salah ad Din, and Diyala. We followed them, and we fought them there, and we arrested most of them.

In our security assessments now, we think that there are some sleeper cells, and we think that there are some people who might support the terrorists again, later on. The majority of the people don't want to work with al-Qaeda or support them anymore. We believe that they are the kind of people who cannot fight face to face.

If the Marine Corps had accepted the idea of giving weapons to the regular individuals, to the people in al-Anbar, there would never have been that kind of fighting at that time. But the terrorists knew that the normal people—who had civilian cars or were walking to schools and offices—they didn't have weapons. That's why they were easy targets. That's why they started to kill a lot of people—a lot of people.

Now we believe that al-Qaeda will not come back as they were before, and they're going to escape to another country. We will have a very good security situation in Iraq when we finish building our security forces—the police, the army, all of them. And also because I believe that the Iraqi people really, really understand that these groups from al-Qaeda are bad for Iraq. They are trying to destroy Iraq. People won't support them again or give them any place to stay.

We will enjoy peace and security after founding a strong army, and police, and border guards. Those forces will be the key to stopping the terrorists from coming back. The thing that we really hate about al-Qaeda is that they targeted the good people—the distinguished officers, the distinguished, well-educated people, the distinguished sheikhs—and all the good people in Iraq. Their ideology is not logical. It's not something that we can accept. These ideas that they have don't work, and they aren't compatible with the development of the country, and the developed world, and how the conditions of life should be for the Iraqi people.

Without the Awakening and the sons of the tribes who enlisted in the police and the army, we couldn't stop the terrorists in al-Anbar, and we couldn't have this good security situation in al-Anbar.

So from this stage, I want to send my greetings and my support to the Awakening—all of them. I pray to God to bless Sheikh Abdul Sattar Abu Risha. I worked with him very closely until he was killed by those evil people. And I am going to send a greeting and a prayer for his brother, Sheikh Ahmad Abu Risha. I want to express my support and my appreciation for all those people who laid the cornerstone for the Awakening in September 2006. And I want to express my thanks and appreciation for all the Anbar sons who enlisted in the police and the army, and who fought al-Qaeda and did their jobs to make Anbar secure.

Also I want to thank the Iraqi government, and especially Prime Minister Nouri al-Maliki, because he supported all the security forces in Anbar. His first visit to al-Anbar, when the security situation was bad, was very supportive. It was a very good thing that he started talking with the sheikhs here in Anbar, and they felt good when they found that the prime minister was here with them. I also want to thank the minister of interior affairs, Jawad al-Bulani, and the minister of defense, Hamid Abdel Qadir.

And also I want to send my thanks to all the Albu Fahd tribal sheikhs, who were responsible for east al-Anbar on the right and on the left of the river. That's all that I have, and if you want to ask me for anything more, I am ready.

Colonel Gary W. Montgomery: In the months before the conference in September, were there small groups of Iraqis starting to resist al-Qaeda?

Haqi: Yes. We called them al-Anbar Revolutionaries. Some of them were cooperating and coordinating with the Marine Corps in al-Habbaniyah, and some of them were supported by the Iraqi army. This group of Anbar Revolutionaries that was working with the Marine Corps went out with them on missions to arrest the terrorists in their areas, because they lived in the same areas where the terrorists were living and making hits. So they already knew where to find them, and they told the Marines how to catch them. So they were working together. I recall that there were 22 individuals working with that group. They were going on missions at night, almost every night, with the Marine Corps and with the Iraqi army. The Marines supported them by surrounding the area where they thought the insurgents were, and this group of Iraqis went inside the houses and arrested them by themselves, and then they gave them to the Marine Corps. And that was the most important, and the best, thing that happened in the story of al-Qaeda.

Montgomery: What is that "thing?"

Interpreter: It was that this group of people was working together with the Marine Corps to arrest those insurgents. That was the most important weapon against al-Qaeda.

Haqi: At that time, this group with the Marines, they arrested most of the insurgents and terrorists. Just a few of them were outside the houses at that time. It was just a timing issue that they couldn't arrest all of them; but they worked hard, and they did their best to arrest them later, and they did it.

Montgomery: You mentioned getting intelligence from the Americans. I would think that the Americans would want intelligence from you. Without getting too specific, because things like that should not be talked about openly, what was the nature of the intelligence that they needed from the Americans that was useful to them? Was it signals intelligence—intercepted radio signals, or something like that?

Haqi: The Marine Corps had very accurate—not semi-accurate, but very accurate—intelligence about the terrorists and insurgents in these areas with the help of the Iraqi people who were living there. They were coming to the Marines and telling them about all that was going on there and where the insurgents were living. So they already had very accurate information about these things.

When I talked about the cooperation and intelligence support that the Awakening received from the Marines, I wasn't talking about very specific details and deep professional intelligence work. I just wanted to say that the Marine Corps got some good, accurate information from the Iraqi people in these areas; and they invested that information by sharing it with the Awakening so they could go on missions together.

Montgomery: So the great value was that they were sharing that information? It was the cooperation that mattered?

Haqi: I can talk from personal experience on this subject, and I'm going to give you an example. I attended some meetings with Sheikh Abu Risha in his house, with Marine officers there in the meeting. They were telling us about some intelligence they got from some Iraqi people about the insurgents in their area. Sometimes we corrected them and told them it wasn't accurate. You've got to be accurate. In other cases, at other times, we offered intelligence to the Marine officers, which we thought was really accurate. But the Marine officers corrected us and told us something totally different, which made us change the mission.

So in general, we were correcting each other, working together, trying to support each other for a common goal—to destroy the insurgents and al-Qaeda. The most important thing was that the goal was the same for the Marine Corps, for the Iraqi government, and for the Awakening—to destroy the terrorists, to keep the security situation in good condition, to stop these groups from targeting honest people, and to stop these groups from targeting the Coalition forces.

So that's why we cooperated very well in everything, and we supported each other, and provided each other with whatever we had. And because we were working in a good way, all the people in al-Anbar supported us and supported the Awakening. And after that, we got to a point where it became normal to have meetings with the Marine officers and with people who provided us with information attending these meetings. So at that time, the Marine officers were visiting the tribal sheikhs' houses, and they were eating lunch with them, and it was something normal to be together as friends.

Before the Awakening, it was strange to have an American inside the house of a sheikh, and you didn't want anyone to know about it. When American forces came to Iraq at the beginning of 2003, we had hoped that it would work this way. We hope that the Iraqis from 2003 to 2007—we hope that Iraqis truly believed that the Americans came to Iraq to maintain an independent Iraq, and just to change the regime and support the Iraqi people in developing their country. But the bad things that happened during these years made the Iraqis feel something different.

We'd really love to develop the Iraqi country through cooperation with the Americans—to improve the scientific fields, the technological fields, health, and all of the other areas. We really need that, and we would really love to have that.

From my point of view, the reason that all of these bad things happened during the first years was because of your relationship with those people who came with you from outside of Iraq and provided you with inaccurate information about Iraqi culture and about the country. You should listen to people who were living inside Iraq at that time, because they know everything about this country. You shouldn't listen to people that left 20 years ago.

Montgomery: Can I ask one more question? The Awakening conference was in September 2006. Approximately one month later there was a battle at Sufiyah.

Haqi: Yes.

Montgomery: Was that a local event, or did it have an effect on the entire province? What was the effect of that battle?

Haqi: The battle at that location was between al-Tawhid wal-Jihad groups and Sheikh Jassim [Muhammad Saleh al-Suwadawi] and the Albu Soda tribe. Do you mean the battle when they even killed some of the women, and some of the houses were burned down?

Montgomery: Yes, he had 17 men.

Haqi: Seventeen, yes. Yes, I know about this event. I know about it.

Montgomery: What effect did it have on the province as a whole, or did it?

Haqi: Two points on this. The first point is al-Tawhid wal-Jihad got the idea that there was going to be a police station in this area. And before this event, some people from al-Tawhid wal-Jihad were killed, and they thought that the people responsible for the killings were living in this area. They thought that Sheikh Jassim was in charge and leading his tribe against them. They thought he was a member of the Awakening, and his brother was the commander of the police station. That's why al-Tawhid wal-Jihad attacked the families. They burned down some of the houses. They killed 17 people—some of them were women, some of them were children.

This was one of the events that made us believe that they really wanted to destroy us. After that, everyone started working against these groups. It was really revolting. People hated to hear what happened there. It was like the first part of the whole operation against these groups. And also the killing of General Khalid Araq al-Ataymi. And Sheikh Jassim from the [Abu Ali] tribe. Killing him also made people really hate those people. He was a good person. I knew him personally. He was a friend of mine. They killed him when he was coming back from visiting a sick person. They killed his son and his nephew, too. His family wanted to take his body for burial, and they couldn't. They had to leave the body there for several days. They cut off his head. His family was begging and pushing for all the tribal sheikhs to get approval from al-Qaeda to take his body back.

These evil groups did hundreds of repugnant things in Anbar. That's why the people started a revolution against them, because from our point of view, people who do such loathsome things don't deserve live. It's not acceptable in any religion that an honest person gets cut up in this appalling way.

I want to tell them, these criminals, that from this moment, we will never allow them back unless they're going to walk over our dead bodies. It's us or them. We cannot work together. We will never accept them back in Iraq. Even a little child will not accept them. Many children have seen their fathers and their brothers killed in hideous ways, right in front of them. They watched that, and they will never forget it. After they killed someone, they cut off his head, and they cut off his hands and his arms and his legs. That's not acceptable. That's truly unacceptable.

Interview 16

Staff Colonel Abbas Ayed Radad

Commanding Officer
3d Battalion, 29th Brigade
7th Division, Iraqi Army

Staff Colonel Abbas Ayed Radad was born in 1967. He served in mortar and tank units in the old Iraqi army, in which he attained the rank of lieutenant colonel in 2002. On 24 March 2004, he joined the new Iraqi army. After three months of training in Jordan, he was assigned to the infantry and participated in establishing Battalion 21 of the 8th Brigade, 3d Iraqi Army Division. He served in Kirkuk and al-Taji, then Mosul, followed by Rabiah, near the Syrian border.

In 2005, Colonel Abbas assisted the election process, participated in combined U.S.-Iraqi clearing operations in the Tal Afar area, and then entered staff college in August. After graduating the following year, he was assigned to the 7th Iraqi Army Division as deputy G-3. He subsequently served in the G-1 and G-5 sections before being promoted to the rank of colonel in July 2007. In February 2008, he took command of 3rd Battalion, 29th Brigade in the 7th Division of the new Iraqi army.

Colonel Abbas was interviewed by Colonel Gary W. Montgomery and Chief Warrant Officer-4 Timothy S. McWilliams on 23 February 2009 at Camp Korean Village, near ar-Rutbah, Iraq.

Colonel Gary W. Montgomery: Could you go back and tell us how things were after the invasion, after Baghdad fell and as the insurgency developed, what was it like?

Staff Colonel Abbas Ayed Radad: I expected a lot of the Arab countries to support us because we had been imprisoned, but the opposite happened. A lot of Arab countries, and terrorists, and money, took over this country.

Montgomery: Could you describe, as the insurgency started to develop, what you think caused it and what you remember from that time?

Abbas: There were so many different causes, both internal and external. First, the internal causes—the spread of weapons. The armories were not secured, so the weapons fell into the hands of insurgents. That affected us in a bad way, and the Coalition forces, too.

And secondly, the government—the army, the police, everything—didn't work anymore. If they had left some units, at least to secure the armories, they would have been able to control the insurgency.

On the external side, the neighboring countries did not want a democratic system in Iraq because their systems are not democratic. Excluding Turkey, the rest of the neighboring countries are not democratic. Jordan has a more democratic system, so those two countries do not support terrorism.

Political conflict between the different sects was one of the factors that created insurgency. Money from abroad was also a contributing factor.

Montgomery: I understand that there were a lot of militias and a lot of different groups at the time. Did you ever see them start to consolidate into one large group, or was it all largely separate?

Abbas: They were always in separate groups, except in the first battle of Fallujah, where they formed one group. The commanders were led by external forces.

Interpreter: They controlled them, and they called them emirs.

Chief Warrant Officer-4 Timothy S. McWilliams: Who were these emirs?

Abbas: There were some emirs from outside, like [Abu] Musab [al-] Zarqawi, and another guy called Shami.

Interpreter: He's from the capital of Syria, Damascus.

Abbas: And he got killed, this guy, Shami. He died in Fallujah. [inaudible] There were small groups, and big groups like the Mahdi army.

Montgomery: What's it like being in the new Iraqi army?

Abbas: The new army is getting better each day. There is the level that governs the country, and we have the army, which protects the country. We are trying to build the national institutions of Iraq, institutions that don't allow the military to get involved in the political system. What I mean is, the constitution doesn't allow the army or anyone else, such as the Iraqi police, to get involved in the political system. And now the army is respected by all the people of Iraq, whatever their religion, whatever their tribe. We don't have enough equipment and logistical support, but we are getting there. And all the people—like the Kurds, the Sunni, the Shi'a, the Bedouin, the big tribes—they all respect us, and they trust us, too, especially after the operations in al-Basrah.

McWilliams: Were you down there in Basrah?

Abbas: There was an organization interfering in civilian life there. They controlled the port and some government buildings. So our law wasn't working there. Nothing worked well, and they were taking government funds for themselves. They enforced their own rules. I know that they killed more than 75 women in Basrah at that time.

So our mission was a success. We returned the honor of the country, and we gained the trust of the people, and we took democracy back.

Montgomery: What other operations have you been in? Which unit were you with at that time?

Abbas: In 2005 we were in Tal Afar. We used to work with the American armored cavalry regiment. We had a really bad situation there, and it was hard on us. Every day there were people dying, and a lot of bad things happening. A lot of the civilian population of Tal Afar left. There was no government there, and the terrorists controlled that area. They used to come from Syria to Ba'aj, and then to Tal Afar. They moved one by one.

We made a plan with the Americans. We divided the city into small parts, and the mission lasted 30 days. We brought in concrete barriers and set up checkpoints everywhere, and we cleared a section and moved to another one. A lot of terrorists were killed. Most of them were from Saudi Arabia and Syria. The hospital started working again. The government started operating again. We returned the mayor to work. So it was an excellent operation. Afterward, there were no more VBIEDs [vehicle-borne improvised explosive devices]. But the situation was not really that good. They still have some issues.

McWilliams: In 2003 and 2004, what were your impressions of the U.S. military, and how have those changed to the present?

Abbas: Actually, the Americans were welcome, and we all expected you to rebuild the country faster than it was. We thought that the economy here was going to be really good after that. And the dollars used . . .

Interpreter: Like, if you want to buy Iraqi dinars, one dollar can buy 150 dinars, but after you came, guys, you can buy 135 dinars. In the beginning, it was like 75 dinars for the one dollar.

Abbas: We got a lot of new equipment, new vehicles, new cars, universal phones. And we got the satellite, because we weren't allowed to use it in the past.

Montgomery: How has the satellite changed Iraq?

Abbas: We were surrounded, and the borders were blocked. So after satellite came, we started looking at the world, turning to the people around us and the people abroad, and satellite brought that. We have a totally different picture than before about the outside world.

Montgomery: Can you tell us about your experiences during the Awakening?

Abbas: The organizational base for the terrorists pressured the civilian population and created a dictatorship. People started forming groups to rebuild themselves, and they called themselves the Awakening. And the army really helped them a lot, helped to build the Awakening. And the friendly forces helped them.

Now we want the Awakening to melt into one pot in the national map. But now they trust it, and they did well in the election. As Iraqis, we want each force to put Iraq first. The government has tried to pull the Awakening people into the army and the police.

It's pretty hard. The hard times are not over. But time and wise political men will solve this problem. We want their loyalty to be to Iraq, not to their tribes.

McWilliams: You said that the army helped the Awakening. In what ways?

Abbas: I'm just speaking from my experience in al-Anbar. We were with the friendly forces, giving them some light trucks—just normal vehicles. We helped them by taking some of them to join the police, and we built some police stations for them, and we helped them in training with the friendly forces.

Montgomery: What was the training like in Jordan?

Abbas: Our training was in the military college. For two weeks, we learned only military subjects. And then there were civilian subjects. We learned about the Geneva Conventions, human rights, international law, civil-military relations, and peace operations. So those two weeks were new for us. I had some training on the M16, the M4, the 81mm mortar, and some western weapons, and the AK [assault rifle], PKM [machine gun], and RPG [rocket-propelled grenade]. . . .

Montgomery: What was the training like under the Saddam [Hussein] regime?

Abbas: It was just military. All the training in the military college, we just talked about military topics, nothing else.

Montgomery: During the insurgency and the rise of al-Qaeda, what did you think about the insurgents' training? Could you see differences from one group to the next? Were the insurgents well trained? I guess that's the question.

Abbas: Some of them came from abroad and some from inside of Iraq. Those from the inside, most of them used the same techniques as the old Iraqi army. The VBIEDs came from outside of Iraq. We wouldn't know what a VBIED is. Only the military engineers knew about this.

There are some really horrific ways of slaughtering people. They used to kidnap people and cut off their heads. That stuff we never had that before. They came from abroad.

There was a group that was controlled by the Iranians, which used IEDs [improvised explosive devices] made with uranium. We don't know those things. We heard that those IEDs came from Iran. I think they're high-quality. I think they're made in Russia and pass through Iran. I don't know exactly where they came from. I think it's just going through Iran. They used it for a while, and now it's not here anymore. So this is an enemy technique.

We saw some other techniques in Tal Afar. There were abandoned houses there. They emplaced explosives all around those houses, and when Americans or Iraqis get inside, they detonate the explosives, and the roof falls on them.

Montgomery: What do you think caused the Awakening?

Abbas: It's because the religious edicts and the self-appointed dictatorship were too hard. So they gathered themselves and formed groups. Most people couldn't leave their homes. People who left their homes and went to the city were captured and accused of being an agent and passing information to the Americans. They just killed anyone who went outside. Some of them they captured and killed in front of their families. And they caught members of the army and the police and killed them, too.

Then the Awakening began, and they saw the noose getting tighter every day. They saw that they were not really human beings anymore. It's not worth prolonging [inaudible]. So they sat down with the army and the police, and they asked for law.

At the beginning they were with the Americans, so the Americans helped them at first. After that, with the Iraqi government, with the police and the army, so the experience in al-Anbar was successful. In some places in Baghdad, it was successful, too. And now they've succeeded in [Tarmiya]. But I don't know about the other provinces.

McWilliams: You said that in 2003, the people expected the United States and the Coalition to rebuild Iraq, and that didn't happen fast enough.

Abbas: Yes, we expected to get electricity at least.

McWilliams: Do you feel that we're helping rebuild Iraq now?

Abbas: The American Marines and the American government still did a lot of things to rebuild Iraq, especially in building democracy and the political system. The results showed in the election in each state, and we expect the next election at the end of 2009 to be more successful than this one. And the Americans have been rebuilding the army and the police, too. And now America looks to be building a new banking system. They are building new universities, like the American University in Sulaimaniyah. And now they are trying to fix electricity and fuel. In 2004, 2005, it was really hard to get fuel. Now whenever you stop at a station, you can get fuel. . . .

There is not enough time to fix all the problems in Iraq, but we can do some things. What the common people have a problem with now is electricity. Electricity can solve unemployment by 75 percent. Restaurants, factories, people working as engineers, even farming—all these need electrical power. From the people who have small ice cream shops or small juice shops to the big factories, all those people need electricity. So electricity helped a lot by helping people who are not working and giving them jobs. We saw progress in the oil department, but electricity is not yet solved. It might even have gotten worse. And the reason for that, some of the insurgency groups destroyed the electrical towers. And if we insist on electricity, I think it's going to get better.

So Iraq's like, you know, we put our money into communications, cell phones, and now we have weak communication between each other. Now we need to put our money into electricity, because even communication needs electricity, the fuel sector needs electricity, too—manufacturing and farming—everything. . . .

If I want to say anything else, it's just about the army getting better all the time by working with you guys. It's just a matter of the time is kind of good now, so we will be done on time. We need some equipment and some training. Especially the border vehicles, they need radar so they can figure out who's flying over the country. It's really hard to cover all of the border in vehicles on the ground.

McWilliams: A lot of people are very curious about Iraq because we didn't know very much about Iraq before we came here, and we're learning. What would you like to tell us about Iraq that you think the rest of the world needs to know?

Abbas: Iraq used to be called a black-earth place. Black earth means agriculture, and a lot of people lived this way. And it's really a cultured place. It's cultured, and in the past there used to be so many people who came from abroad to trade. There were four civilizations here: Babylon, Asshur, Akkad, and Sumer. Those four civilizations were here. It's the grant for the prophets [discussion with interpreter regarding whether "prophet" or "messenger" is the correct term in English] like the messenger Abraham, Jonah, Elisha, David, Noah. Those are the names of messengers. All of them were born in Iraq.

Iraq is better now than in the old years. Even though we went through a lot for it, even though there were wars and fighting and blood around, we know we are better off. We have our freedom now. We make our decisions by ourselves, and we decide who is going to be in political office through our elections. And now we know where we spend our money. We're looking forward to working with all the world outside.

In Pakistan, there was earthquake. Among the first companies to go over there to help Pakistan and to build their tents was an Iraqi company. This was the first humanitarian assistance mission for us outside the country....

McWilliams: How is Anbar different from the rest of Iraq, or is Anbar different from the rest of Iraq?

Abbas: It's different—the tribes and culture. These people are kind of Bedouin, but they have their own traditions and their culture. You can say that they're beautiful and truthful, generous, honest.

McWilliams: How is security out there in this part of Anbar?

Abbas: The Coalition forces, and the border forces, the army, Iraqi highway patrol, need some work to improve their working together, but they're doing a good job. Now, the ways to Syria and Jordan work. So this helps our economy. Everything Iraqis need—like big generators—goes through this way. And everything else, like chlorine, too.

McWilliams: What are some of the challenges or problems you have out here?

Abbas: For the Iraqi army, it's logistical support. For me, the same thing, logistical support. We're missing fuel. We need more spare tires and some equipment. We don't have all of those.

McWilliams: Do you still have foreign fighters or terrorists coming across the border?

Abbas: Jordan is helpful all the time. The way from Jordan, Iraqis control the road, and they're doing a good job.

And Syria, I guess they still bring some terrorists over, especially through Mosul, al-Qaim, and Rabiah.

There are some people who are wanted. They are outside the country, and they come back. One of them was in Fallujah. We captured him, and he had committed a lot of crimes.

McWilliams: Who are they?

Abbas: He was originally from Iraq, but he left while security was bad. He ran away to Syria. Maybe he expected his situation was going to be more normal, but the police captured him—a terrorist. They investigated him, and they took him to every place he committed crimes. He showed them exactly what he did, and we learned from this guy. . . .

But one of the big challenges for Iraq now is to bridge the gap between people, to build trust.

Perspective of Former Regime Elements

Interview 17

Staff Major General Jasim Muhammad Salih Habib

Chairman of Research Center comprised of former Iraqi General Officers

Former Director General of Inventory, old Iraqi Army

Former Commander, 38th Division, old Iraqi Army

General Jasim Muhammad Salih Habib fought in Iran-Iraq War and commanded a battalion in the invasion of Kuwait and the Gulf War. He lived in the Soviet Union for two years, and he was a high-ranking member of the Ba'ath Party.

General Jasim was interviewed by Colonel Gary W. Montgomery, Lieutenant Colonel Bradley E. Weisz, and Chief Warrant Officer-4 Timothy S. McWilliams on 14 February 2009 at Camp Ramadi.

General Jasim Muhammad Salih Habib: After the first battle of Fallujah, Mohammed Abdullah al-Shahwani, the intelligence director in Baghdad, called me. I met with him and General [James T.] Conway, and we agreed to establish an army in Fallujah to control the city and let the American forces leave. I established the first battalion in Fallujah, and after the city settled down, I left because I was a division commander. It's not good to go back to a lower level. I remained available as an advisor, and I met frequently with General [John F.] Kelly and the leaders of the Marines in al-Anbar.

We established a research center to provide advice on how to establish the Iraqi army. We presented a lot of studies on how to reestablish the Iraqi army and put them back in active service in al-Anbar. We conducted many studies on the interference of the Iranians and other countries, and how to make al-Anbar more secure, and many other things. Six months ago [mid-2008], we started to write—other former officers and I—started to do many studies on these subjects. . . . And we, as the former leaders of the Iraqi army, conducted many studies on how to build the new Iraqi army, and how to train them, and how to establish a system to sustain them. I am the chairman of the center, and I have about 40 generals with me. We conducted research on the Gulf threats, and the Kurdish subject, and other things.

One of the important studies I did was on how even the oldest armies are victims of their countries' policies. I researched from the time of [Adolf] Hitler until now. The army is a tool in the hands of the politician. Sometimes we execute orders that we are not satisfied with. When we invaded Kuwait [in 1990], I was a battalion commander. I executed the orders, but I wasn't happy, and I didn't think what we did was good or right. We did our jobs over there, but we kept our dissent inside.

Through these studies, we keep current, and we exercise our minds, and we stay in touch in our lives, and we preserve our experience. This experience will be for our sons—a history, after we pass away.

The Marines over here support us financially to cover the costs of writing and printing these studies. And I suggest that this support continue in order to maintain the relationship.

To be honest with you, there is strong enmity between us and Iran. They killed many officers from the former army. Some of us left Iraq for a time. Now it's safer, so we came back. And I'm certain that one day you will fight Iran, if only to drive them out of Iraq. And if you do that, I will be the first to volunteer to fight with you, because this country has settled down, and it is known throughout history that the Iranians are the enemies of the Iraqis, and now is their opportunity to fight us. We know the land, and we know what's on the land. We know the ways—how to progress. We know their locations and their cities on the border. If we were blind, we would still know how to go over there.

And you have a responsibility: don't leave Iraq without driving the Iranians out of Iraq. I'm not talking for myself; I'm speaking on behalf of the officers I work with. All these leaders have very great experience, and recent experience. All of them will support you very well if you throw these people out. So we give you our experience, our lives, what we know, so make it useful for you before you leave.

We, friends, we didn't do anything wrong. We just defended our country. Every one of us is proud of himself and his country. We don't make problems; we obey orders and defend our country.

You fought the British when they occupied your lands. You fought them, and you had the honor to liberate your country. The British left, and now you are friends with them. We are the same. We could be your dear friends, and we could take care of your national interests and our own. We don't hate Americans as a people, or anything related to America. As a former leader in the Iraqi army, it's been very useful to have experience from the Western countries. We used to have French systems, the Super Étendard aircraft, and we used German technicals. During the Iran-Iraq War, we learned a lot from Western experience and, but for the mistakes of our political people, we should have continued working with them. This was a big mistake by Iraq's political leaders. We know that the West helped us to destroy the Iranian army. But politicians don't do what the army likes.

Now you, as leaders, have to be here because of your orders. You cannot stand up in front of political leaders and tell them, "I won't go." So it's not right that the Iranians and the Shi'a parties that are with the Iranians want revenge against the entire old Iraqi army. This is not logical. One day you will leave Iraq. No one will have the right to ask you why you invaded Iraq, because you are respected soldiers, and you obey orders. That's your job. . . .

Colonel Gary W. Montgomery: To cover how we got to where we are, could you back up a little bit and describe how the insurgency came about?

Jasim: In the beginning, when the Americans were threatening to invade Iraq, Saddam [Hussein] called for foreign fighters. Under the circumstances, they came as Arabs to fight with their brothers against the Americans, and most of them came through Syria. After the invasion and occupation of Iraq, most of them left. A few remained, but they started to increase again, especially in 2004.

The Syrians and the Iranians felt that the Americans were going to invade them, so the Syrians started to push a lot of people into Iraq.

The Iranians did the same thing. The purpose for this was to keep the Americans busy inside Iraq so the U.S. Army couldn't go into Iran or Syria. The political leaders in Iran and Syria expected to face the same thing that Saddam faced. So Syria welcomed all the international volunteers, and Iran secured ways from Afghanistan and Pakistan through to Iraq. They distributed their people throughout all the provinces to keep the Americans busy fighting them.

They formed cells and used religious cover to gain the sympathies of some of the groups that were already fighting. Some people believed this deception, and they gained the support of many Iraqis under the excuses of resistance and jihad.

Then they started slaughtering Iraqis. They killed former army officers, and they killed the sheikhs, and the imams, and the university professors. People saw it very clearly and started to realize that these people didn't come to fight Americans. They came to loot and steal, and to execute Iranian and Syrian policy.

As you know, deceit cannot last long. Consequently, their excuses [inaudible] hundreds of thousands of people that had helped them, especially in al-Anbar Province, Salah ad-Din Province, Baghdad, and Mosul Province. Diyala Province still has problems because it is very close to the border with Iran, and it's a transit area for these groups.

And I will tell you something: looking carefully, 75 percent of the resistance is connected to Iran, and about 10 percent from al-Qaeda, which is connected to the Kurds. They want to make a weak Iraq, a very weak army, and a weak administration, so that the Kurds can take half of Iraq, and Iranians can take the south, and Syria can take some of the lands in the west. But the good people of Iraq and their efforts [inaudible].

Al-Qaeda works for whoever pays. The Iranians pay. The Kurds pay. Syria pays. And Syria pays through the Iranians.

And now, with your efforts and the good Iraqis, we broke al-Qaeda's back. Maybe we're going to have some small groups in the future, because there is a difference between quiet and safe. It may be quiet for a week, a month, a year, but security is still not 100 percent. But there is a percentage, and there is a percentage of quietness. If you want complete security, and almost all the time, I advise you to bring back the Iraqi army—not me, but those who have been with me. I am ready, but don't send for me. I can give you the best leaders in the former Iraqi army, and this is in your interest and in ours. We respect your interests, and we care about our own. We believe in God. The way you respect our people, we respect yours. We are military leaders, we know how to behave, and how to be riflemen, and we don't lie. Just the opposite—we sacrifice ourselves, and this is the highest level of generosity.

Now for the future: bring back the former Iraqi army, make a balance between the Shi'a and Sunni, make a force against the Iranians, make the Kurds behave, and keep Syria and Hezbollah and their problems away. Iraq is a store of resources, but this treasury needs a force to protect it.

All the people in government, the politicians, they do not offer protection. They don't protect the people, and they don't protect the resources, and they don't protect the borders. They just protect themselves. We can't trust them to keep a country. We are pleading, and we trust you. You are honest people who make an honest effort. We met with you more than 20 times, but there is something missing. We need you to force the government of Iraq to protect the country. A long time has passed, and we haven't seen any strength.

The Shi'a parties, which came from Iran, don't like the army. The Kurds don't like the former Iraqi army. The Kuwaitis don't like the Iraqi army. Syria doesn't like the former Iraqi army. Even the Saudis don't like the former Iraqi army, which was creating [inaudible] from their countries. But what did we do wrong? We have resources, and there was always an army preserving these resources.

And honestly, I will tell you. We didn't follow Saddam and his politics. Saddam's terrible mistakes brought us into this bad situation. I have researched it, and historically, good armies are victims of bad policies.

We need a leader, a very honest leader, who will look out for all Iraqis, who will lead all Iraqis—Shi'a, Sunni, Arabs, Kurds—and keep a good relationship with the whole world, someone faithful and honest in protecting Iraqi resources and putting the country on the right path. Please, you and President [Barak H.] Obama, look for this person. Among Iraqis, there are thousands of such people, just as there are thousands of leaders in America. At least in Iraq, there are hundreds of leaders. Thank you.

Montgomery: Can you tell us how the Awakening came about? Or maybe I should say Awakenings, plural.

Jasim: As I told you, al-Qaeda started to humiliate people, and they started smuggling on the highway. Most of them were criminals and prison convicts. So when they started attacking our elite people—the scientists or imams or other leaders—people turned against them.

And when the Americans were fighting them with helicopters, or in other ways, a lot of houses were destroyed by the shooting. For example, if they are at this point [pointing to top of table], when the Americans attack them, many of the surrounding houses will be damaged [gestures to surrounding area].

Then they, themselves, when they detonated IEDs [improvised explosive devices], thousands of innocent people were victims. Because of that, the Iraqi people hated for them to be here.

They kept going back into the area until they lost the trust of the people. As you know, to survive, a resistance movement needs an atmosphere where people will accommodate them when they need help—help with fuel, with weapons, with whatever. But the people didn't want them. After a number of sheikhs were killed, the tribes started talking. Groups of tribesmen started working together, and the people took an oath to not just drive them out, but to follow them and kill them.

In the first phase, many of the sons joined the police or the army. These new volunteers were targeted by al-Qaeda. So there was direct fighting between them, and the police and army were supported by the tribes.

They lost the atmosphere of trust. They couldn't move freely. They could only move on the highways. And so the areas where they were concentrated became dangerous, and people started killing them. The sheikhs started fighting al-Qaeda in al-Qaim near the Syrian border, and it went down to the Abu Risha area, and went down to Baghdad.

And there is another point I would like to bring to your attention. The transgressions of the militias in Baghdad gave the Awakening the opportunity to appear in Baghdad. The Awakening in al-Anbar fought al-Qaeda. In Baghdad, in Diyala, they fought the militias. So the Awakening had two responsibilities: fighting al-Qaeda and fighting the militias. It's my opinion that the awakenings in the east and south of Baghdad stopped the militias.

But don't believe that the government of Iraq is finished with militias. The government of Iraq made the militias. What killed the militias was the Awakening. Consequently, the aovernment of Iraq now blocks the Awakening from joining the army and the police. Without your forces, they wouldn't have accepted any of them.

The Awakening in Baghdad was responsible for three things. They increased the military. They made a balance inside the army between Shi'a and Sunni. And they fought the militias very bravely and killed them—in the Karkh area, the Adhamiyah area, in the al-Jamia district, in al-Doura district. These Awakenings, you just give them the green light and they stop the militias permanently. Now, if we don't have the Awakening in Baghdad, the militias will come back again.

Could any part of the Shi'a parties be from Iran? All of them have their own militias. Therefore, they don't want the Iraqi army to come back because the appearance of the former Iraqi army will kill them.

So I'm telling you, take it from us, we don't need a personal advantage, because these people are your responsibility. The military is supposed to protect people. You are defending the American population, which is thousands of kilometers away. When we volunteer, we swear to defend the country and protect the people. You and us, we create a force that respects the people, creates stability, and defends resources, protects the borders, and maintains a good relationship with the world.

Now we have to make a stand. The stars of the political coalition are falling one by one, and I will tell you something. As I said before, I am a very analytical officer. After this election, former members of the provincial council intend to flee abroad. Some people have called for their passports to be taken to prevent them from leaving, because they are thieves, and they took the national treasure. They have no vested interests here, so they can take their passports and just run away. And the people in parliament now, after this year ends, and they can feel that no one is going to deal with them—they're going to run away too—after Iraq is destroyed.

Therefore we want to cooperate and have a human relationship and have the military honored. This is a matter of human responsibility. We need to put the right person in the right place. I was very honest with you—90 percent of the current Ministry of Defense was among the worst in the Iraqi army. I can give you the history of each one. They are very bad people, and they are very poor soldiers. And they have the highest ranks. Honestly, you have to take care of them. This is totally honest. If there was a guy selling something on the street, you would make him a general. . . .

Lieutenant Colonel Bradley E. Weisz: As we get ready to possibly downsize here in Iraq, what forces or capability do you think needs to stay behind?

Jasim: This is a very good question. The nature of the force is more important than the size. You have to choose a force that can move fast, that has helicopters. Also, they should have good information resources. And, in my opinion, don't work too hard on training. The former Iraqi army is full of instructors. You go for operations. If you put a division in Mosul, and one division in Baghdad, and one division in Diwaniyah or Nasiriyah, that is more than enough. . . .

Three divisions in our system is a corps. The number would be about—with administration, with service people, logistics, medical, everything—50,000 people is more than enough, if concentrated on these points. Make a good, active border force. Give the tanks and weapons to the Iraqi army, because I know if you transport them back to America, it will cost you more than leaving them over here.

You have high-technology weapons, and it takes a long time to train on them. But if we go to the main problem, if we bring back the Iraqi army, we could relieve you of this responsibility. You would have the main force and take care of the strategic things. But leave the technical things to Iraqis.

Don't depend on this army and leave a small force here, because you're going to be in trouble. Make a national, faithful army. Don't believe in the Iranians, and don't believe in the Kurds, and don't even believe in the Sunnis. We don't care. Iraq has Shi'as, Sunnis, and Kurds, et cetera. Bring back some military leaders. They didn't listen to them, and there are a lot.

Also, you've got to institute human rights. You will respect that army. It will be like your army. History will mention you in good ways if you leave this country, but not if it is demolished and fighting continues in a civil war. The consequences of that would be your responsibility.

If I were an American leader, I could withdraw all of my forces and not keep anyone here. But the results? Not good. It's not just your army. I could keep a personnel chart and make the numbers go down day by day, until I put the last ones on an airplane and took them away. But this is not in your behavior. It's not good. It is not the job you came here to do, and it's not good for your efforts in relations with Iraq or for American global relations.

In the meantime, I think 50,000 in three divisions, with firepower, mobility, and very good intelligence systems. Don't worry about training and everything. That's not going to get you anywhere.

You can't achieve quietness and security just by force, by reconstruction, and by good relationships. The government of Iraq must be forced to respect the people and to obey the rule of law. The other day, Mr. [Joseph R.] Biden [Jr., U.S. vice president] came. He forced the government of Iraq to follow a rule and stay together, and the government of Iraq was upset by this. And [Nouri Kamil Mohammed Hasan al-] Maliki, the prime minister, says "The days of American controls on the Iraqi are gone." If I were in your place, I would clip his wings and keep him on a perch, because the

Americans take better care of the people than he does. So suppose there were a declaration that told him, "Behave or we're going to throw you out."

What we have, your forces are a reality for us here and now. So make stability in the meantime. Sometimes political action is more effective than force. Maybe General [Raymond T.] Odierno [USA]—and my regards to him—can tell the government of Iraq that if they don't have a deadline for getting the politicians on board, then we, the Americans, have the force to throw you out and force you to do it in a way that gives us a limited time. Make them.

Six months ago, a delegation came from the Ministry of Defense in Baghdad and collected all the former military leaders here, and they interviewed us. I was there, and they talked nicely with us. "We are brothers. You are my friend. We are under your request. Who wants to go back?"

All of us said, "Yes, we'd like to go back and serve our country."

But in fact, they didn't return anyone. They lie on you; they lie to the American administration. They passed the election the way they wanted, and they didn't bring back the service. And they do it repeatedly. They go to Syria, Jordan, the Emirates, everywhere the former leaders are, and try to get them to come back—and they are lying. They won't do it. They are liars. But the former Iraqi army is sleeping now. But if they are still having unfair [inaudible], otherwise he's going to go up and kill himself. That's what I have.

After that, I will make sure we are friends. You and us, we have responsibility. Please correct the mistake that was made by [Ambassador L. Paul] Bremer. I believe it's not his fault. There was something—foreign reasons, and there were internal reasons. But, please, as long as you know that dissolving the former Iraqi army was a mistake, correct it before you leave. Thank you.

Interview 18

Staff Major General Khadim Muhammad Faris al-Fahadawi al-Dulaymi

Former Deputy Commander,
al-Anbar Operations Center

Former Staff Major General under the Ba'ath regime

Former 60th Iraqi National Guard Commander

Staff Major General Khadim Muhammad Faris al-Fahadawi al-Dulaymi was born in 1952. Following graduation from military college in 1977, he was stationed in the Kirkuk area, where he commanded a company in the 31st Special Forces Brigade. During the Iran-Iraq War, his unit moved to a sector east of Amarah and worked with the 9th Division, conducting direct action and surveillance and reconnaissance missions. In 1984 he attended a special operations course in Egypt. Immediately upon his return, he conducted a successful operation behind Iranian lines, for which he was highly decorated and tasked with establishing Unit 999, based on the Egyptian curriculum and his own experiences.

From 1984 to 1986 he earned a master's degree in military science and staff rank. Upon graduation, he was selected to create a special forces capability within the Republican Guard. He commanded the 16th Special Forces Brigade during the1990 invasion of Kuwait and the 1991 suppression of the Shi'a uprising in the south. About 1995, he was transferred to the Fedayeen Saddam, where he remained until assuming command of the 15th Division from 2000 until 2003. Little is known about his activities in 2003 to 2004; however, he became part of the Iraqi Civil Defense Corps in 2004 and then the Iraqi National Guard in 2005 when the Civil Defense Corps was disbanded. He left military service in 2005.

General Khadim was interviewed by Colonel Gary W. Montgomery and Chief Warrant Officer-4 Timothy S. McWilliams on 15 February 2009 at Camp Ramadi.

Staff Major General Khadim Muhammad Faris al-Fahadawi al-Dulaymi: If we start with al-Anbar as it was before 2003, it was a normal province, like other provinces in Iraq. There was a security organization—Iraqi police, and other security. They worked as Iraqis under the laws of Iraq. But it was also different from the other provinces in that there was a tribal culture here. The tribes had their own traditional laws, and they didn't interfere with the security systems of the central government.

When the Americans entered Iraq, and the country collapsed—the whole organization—al-Anbar was one of these. Before the American forces entered the province, the sons of al-Anbar went out to the street and protected the government offices and kept the province secure. The tribes worked together to keep the province settled down, and there was good coordination between the army and other forces and the tribes and the sheikhs.

When the American forces arrived at K-70 [kilometer marker 70 on the highway], some of the leaders and the sheikhs went out to meet the American forces. There was rumored to be a deal: the sheikhs and the tribes would remain in control of the situation inside the cities, and the American military forces would stay outside of the cities. The sheikhs and the tribes were going to take over administration and security in the cities, and the American forces were going to open an office, which was, maybe, under the name of reconstruction.

It was about April 2003, approximately between [inaudible] and K-70. I wasn't in the delegation, but I heard about it. One of the delegates was one of my friends, General Mohammad Jarawi, who has been killed, God bless him. He was the leader of the army responsible for protecting al-Anbar Province under the previous government.

A local government was established. The sheikhs and the Coalition forces had a deal and brought a governor and put him in as governor of al-Anbar. He was former Iraqi police officer. There was also a general called Ja'adan who took care of the police. And all the government offices kept working.

When the American forces went inside the city, they demolished the deal. It was quite secure for about six months. The reconstruction office was working, giving contracts to people. The government was working. The police were working. Everyone was working normally. And the Marines were walking around the streets. No one was attacking them or saying anything against them. Sometimes they were even buying from the stores, buying from the restaurants.

During this period of time, which was about six months, there were too many mistakes. The local government made mistakes, and some of the sheikhs who were very close to the Americans. There were some things done by the Americans that were wrong by the rights of the culture of al-Anbar. And there were other mistakes, which led to some small groups firing on the Americans. We heard and saw small groups hiding and shooting at American convoys when they passed by. They called themselves mujahideen. All the mistakes that I mentioned I detailed in a study. These small groups started getting support from both inside and outside of Anbar, and they started to grow and grow. As they grew, the mistakes of the other side—the Coalition, the sheikhs—became bigger and bigger. Many movements started to appear, like the Islamic Movement and the Army of Muhammad, and they were all fighting under jihad. And the people of al-Anbar sympathized with these groups.

Because of the mistakes, not for other reasons, until about the end of 2004 there was a new movement infiltrating these groups. They called themselves al-Tawhid wal-Jihad. They took all the kids and the people who lived in poverty or had low social standing, and they provided them with extraordinary support. Many people went for these things and said it was jihad, just like the other groups said. This movement got stronger very quickly and started to control the other groups of mujahideen. And they started to close in on the imams, the sheikhs, and the high-ranking officers of al-Anbar because they were dealing with the Americans.

Their leaders had a new name; they were called emirs. Each emir had too much authority—to kill, to steal, to do anything he liked. He had the authority, and people obeyed him. The people working with him adhered to his ideas on killing or stealing or anything. People began to recognize that this was not jihad. These people came to kill. So people were alienated from them.

Colonel Gary W. Montgomery: Did this emir get his authority from someone else, or just from the barrel of a gun?

Khadim: No, from high-level people, from his leaders.

Montgomery: From inside Iraq, or outside Iraq?

Khadim: This title, emir, came from foreign Arabs. They brought this title from abroad. These emirs, almost all of them were foreign Arabs—not of Iraqi nationality.

Chief Warrant Officer-4 Timothy S. McWilliams: Are you talking about Abu Musab al-Zarqawi?

Khadim: He was the big guy. What I mentioned were the local emirs. I was talking about al-Anbar, not Iraq. Abu Musab al-Zarqawi was the emir of the Islamic Country in Iraq, but I was talking about the local leaders.

McWilliams: So they worked for him?

Khadim: These emirs were distributed in al-Anbar in sectors. Each sector had an emir to control it, and they all belonged to the big guy.

Anbar started to suffer from destruction and poverty. And the mistakes became bigger and bigger. I'll give you an example of how the Coalition forces behaved at the time. They would attack and search houses, and they searched the houses of innocent people. So people saw the Americans trash houses and arrest innocent people, while the insurgents—the bad guys—were moving about freely. No one even talked to them. That means, in my opinion, the Americans didn't have good advisors to tell them how to behave in such a situation. And the people who the Anbaris saw close to them were only interested in how to benefit and to profit. They didn't care about improving al-Anbar.

In 2004, a national guard brigade was established under the supervision of the Coalition forces and with the advice of the sheikhs and the local government. This brigade contained bad elements because it wasn't established skillfully. This was at the end of 2004. There were security forces, local government, and Coalition forces, but the situation was unbearable. Sheikh Ahmad Abu Risha came to me at the end of 2004. He told me about the brigade and said it was already established with all its people, supplies, and everything. He asked me to be the commander. I was interested in having security back in the province, so I accepted the position.

I met the American generals of that time. They gave me written orders to start my job. But I couldn't make it go in the right direction to achieve security and stability. I tried to make it work, to activate this brigade, but the brigade was compromised. Many of the people inside it were loyal to the jihad groups, and some of them were there for the personal benefit of some sheikhs. So the brigade failed.

In 2005, the situation was getting worse, and everyone left his job. The police left, the national guard left, the local government left. They were just cornered. They couldn't move. They couldn't do anything. The government offices shut down, and the insurgents completely controlled the province.

The first experiment in trying to destroy the terrorists was in 2005 in the al-Qaim area. There was a group of tribes cooperating with the Coalition forces in that area, and they started fighting al-Qaeda. But al-Qaeda was a strong force. They were very aggressive and very active against anyone even suspected of dealing with these sheikhs. Consequently, this experience was limited; it didn't go all over the province. It was just in and around al-Qaim, but there were a lot of big sacrifices.

The way it started, al-Qaeda was getting stronger, killing on the road every day, and getting bigger and bigger. So the good people started forming small, secret groups to fight al-Qaeda. Publicly, fighting al-Qaeda was like committing suicide, so they started secretly in small groups, cooperating with the Coalition forces, and working the same way that al-Qaeda worked.

Some of these groups—which they gave names like the Anbar Revolution, and the Secret Police, or the Karama Companies— they started working in secret, and they did a beautiful job. First, because they were working secretly, al-Qaeda couldn't identify the members. The emirs started losing confidence in the people who worked with them because they couldn't fight or identify these secret groups. They attacked most of al-Qaeda's central groups where they lived. This is when al-Qaeda started to crack.

By the way, I mentioned that al-Qaeda started controlling other groups. At this time, al-Qaeda already controlled the others, and those who didn't obey, they pushed away.

While these secret groups were working, some of the sheikhs had the idea to go back and fight al-Qaeda. Some of these sheikhs lost many, many members of their families. In September 2006, a group of sheikhs appeared publicly at a meeting in the Jazeera area with Sheikh Abdul Sattar Abu Risha. They announced, "We are a group of sheikhs, and we are going to fight al-Qaeda and clear them from our areas." That was good news. It was a very happy day for Anbaris when they knew that a group of sheikhs was starting to fight al-Qaeda.

Sheikh Abdul Sattar Abu Risha started fighting from west of Ramadi to the Jazeera area. In this area, the al-Qaeda groups were not very strong. There were people working under al-Qaeda, but they were not the main groups. The Coalition forces started moving out of the cities and started making their bases out of the cities, not just inside the cities, which gave people hope that the Coalition forces would protect them. So they started to be courageous and to help.

Al-Qaeda started collecting all its groups and increasing its strength in order to suppress Abdul Sattar's movement. They used very strong people, and they used all the support they had. But with the help—especially in the Albu Soda and Habbaniyah areas—but with the help of the central government, the Coalition forces, and the good people in al-Anbar, they couldn't face Abdul Sattar's movement.

At the same time, the secret groups were very active, which helped the situation, and they became bigger and bigger. Al-Qaeda was being tracked down and hit by these groups in areas where Abdul Sattar wasn't fighting; that is, in their main base areas. When the Coalition forces opened an area, it helped the Awakening to spread to other areas.

I remember in October of 2006, I was sitting in my home, and a force under Lieutenant Colonel [DeGrossi?] showed up. They came inside my house and arrested me. This was the second one, not the first one, and they took me to a place in Taqqadum. They said, "We want to finish al-Qaeda." I asked —as a civilian, not as a military man—I asked if they were serious. Because people thought that the Coalition forces were helping al-Qaeda. As I mentioned before, the criminals were moving about freely, and no one attacked them; but innocent people were attacked and arrested and humiliated, so people lost confidence in the Coalition forces.

They said, "Yes, we are serious about finishing al-Qaeda, but we need your help."

I said, "If you ask me, I can give you advice about my area, my thoughts about al-Qaeda, the locations where they work, and how you can finish them." So I mentioned many locations for weapons caches, and the places where they met and did their planning, and the roads they used.

We discussed making a plan for finishing al-Qaeda. During the discussion, I said, "Part of the plan is that you have to deliver a letter to the people saying that you're going to finish al-Qaeda. Part of the plan is to be open, put your soldiers in 11 locations in these areas. And part of the plan, too, is that when you're searching houses, you do it in a friendly way. Talk with them, help them. If they need something, give it to them. Have tea with them. Have food with them. Be a friend. Show them that you are here to help them, not to hurt them."

And honestly, this man implemented everything we agreed upon. From the second day after the discussion, he started putting checkpoints on the road to control the insurgents, and he attacked their centers, and he found the weapons caches. Every day he had a schedule to sit with people, with the sheikhs, with the officials. He discussed things like a friend. And in eastern Anbar, he opened 11 posts. People started to trust the Marines. People started contacting the Marines and giving them information about the caches, weapons, and people, so the Americans could attack them and arrest them. The Marines were going inside houses, and they started eating the food.

In November 2006, so I could serve my people and my country in an official capacity and not as a civilian, I went to the Ministry of Defense and volunteered to fight the terrorists. And I started giving people over there in the Ministry of Defense plans for how to fight terrorists and kill them. And we got some help from the Ministry of Defense for Sheikh Sattar, to help him fight, like weapons and supplies.

One of the officers in the Ministry of Defense was the brother of Sheikh Nasser. He is Staff Brigadier General Nouri Abdul Karim. We started working, he and I together, in the Ministry of Defense to support Abu Risha, and also to formulate plans for clearing the areas where Sheikh Abdul Sattar couldn't go. We succeeded in this, and we gave a plan to the Ministry of Defense. He agreed to execute it, and we went back to Taqqadum and established a new center there.

We asked all the people to cooperate and to work with us on the eastern Anbar area. They had a lot of information about the terrorists—where they were, their locations, their weapons. We got a lot of information from these people, and we executed this plan in January 2007 in the Juaiba area with a lieutenant colonel from the U.S. Army. I don't remember his name. After we discussed our plan with him, we divided the people who worked with us between us and the Marines, and they started implementing this plan in three directions. It took 12 days, and we arrested 47 terrorists. We found many stores of weapons and ammunition and a lot of vehicles that had been used by the terrorists, and the area settled down.

After that, we came to east Husaybah, which is in Khalidiyah. We worked with a lieutenant colonel from the Marines with the same plan, and we accomplished a lot. Then we went over the Khalidiyah and the Falahat area. After that, we went down, with our Iraqi vehicles and the people who were working with us, and went to these areas with the sheikhs, with the high-level people, and discussed how we would work in the future. We found all cooperation from them.

In Taqqadum—it's in Falahat and this area—the lieutenant colonel—I remember his name was [James F.] McGrath—we cleared these areas, and we established Iraqi police stations. We opened all the area Iraqi police stations, and many of our area's sons volunteered to work in them. They wore the uniform, and had weapons, and worked officially. Then they asked the government center for orders to keep working and to pay them. And we had orders for them. They worked officially and normally, and they are still working.

In the beginning of 2007, we had some areas, like Fallujah, the Albu Issa area, some of the western areas, that were still under terrorist control.

Montgomery: You said that in October 2006, you were sitting at home and Lieutenant [DeGrossi's] forces arrested you and took you to Taqaddum.

Khadim: Yes.

Montgomery: And you came up with a plan.

Khadim: Yes.

Montgomery: Did you make the plan with Lieutenant Colonel DeGrossi, or his boss? What I'm trying to figure out is whether you were working with Lieutenant Colonel DeGrossi, or if he just came to get you.

Khadim: When the lieutenant colonel took me to Taqqadum, I met many people higher than lieutenant colonel—his bosses. Then they released me, and I came back home. Lieutenant Colonel DeGrossi started negotiating the plan with me in my house.

Montgomery: Right, and then you went to the Marine battalion's area of operations?

Khadim: Yes. [DeGrossi's] bosses, when we met in Habbaniyah, they told me, the situation is like this and this and this. So we discussed the situation, and they asked me if I could help them. I said, "Yes, and this is my plan."

About March 2007, after we had the security and stability situation in the east of al-Anbar, Lieutenant Colonel McGrath came to me. He was the commander of the Marines that had been in this area, and he moved to the Fallujah area where the Albu Issa tribe was.

He told me he contacted one of the sheikhs in the area, Sheikh Aifan Sadun al-Issawi. And he asked me to be a liaison between the sheikhs and the Marines in this area, because I had experience.

So we met with the Marines near the Fallujah bridge where Sheikh Aifan was located. We went over the highlights of the plan, how we're going to work to finish the terrorists. And we did another couple of things. We met in Sheikh Aifan's guesthouse with a group of the area sheikhs, and some of the official security officers, and the army that worked in this area. Some of the sheikhs were afraid to work because of the aggressiveness and killing of al-Qaeda. And we started working the Albu Issa area, and they used the cooperation of the people who helped them in this area, supported by the Marines, and they cleared the area of terrorists.

Many things happened over there. They tried to kill Sheikh Aifan. Many things happened. This work gave hope to the Anbaris. Some of the sheikhs came by themselves—without help from the Marines or Abu Risha or Aifan or the central government—and took control of the area and cleared it of al-Qaeda people. For example, Iraqi police followed the army, which was the Iraqi army in Fallujah. They worked together to clear the center of the city of al-Qaeda people. After that, we moved on to the western Jazeera area, the Albu Bali and over there, which was the headquarters of al-Qaeda there. And the same way we used the cooperation at the meetings, and with the sheikhs, with the Marines and the U.S. Army, the adviser asked them to fight and to clear the area, to move on in the areas of the Albu Bali, the Albu Issa, the Albu Hazil, and so on and so on.

The areas up to the west of al-Anbar, they cleared of al-Qaeda terrorists the same way, with the help of the sheikh, by the support of the Marines and the U.S. Army. They cleared it, and it settled down, and there was security over there.

After that, we worked in the Karma area and al-Tharthar. We cooperated with Sheikh Mishtem, and some of his tribe, and some of the Iraqi army. They cleared the area of terrorists. The last location, the Tharthar area, we brought some people to cooperate with us. They gave us a lot of information about the terrorists: their people, their locations, their weapons, and their weapons caches. Units from the Iraqi army and the police established posts in these areas. Also, the Marines and Army put some units in these areas. The area was cleared, and we opened the Tharthar road.

About June or July 2007, we can say we cleared the province of terrorists, and the police and the Iraqi army were officially working and performing their duties.

There's one thing I'd like to mention before I finish. The Awakening was not a military leader's movement, where you move from area to area to clear it. It was a psychological movement. They could rise, the people hoped, and many of the good people rose up—sheikhs, officers, good people. They all worked together to clear the area, whether they worked with the Marines, or with the Iraqi army, or by themselves. No one held favor above the other, but they all cooperated and worked together to clear al-Anbar. The people who now say they were the leaders of the Awakening, they were not leaders.

The Awakening was not a military thing; it was a movement. It was a psychological movement. They say, "We cleared al-Anbar." There was no one person who cleared al-Anbar. There were experiments and work in areas. This area is different from that area. But the public announcement of the Awakening gave people hope to come on board. Fear and hope. There were civilians who sacrificed more than these people who now say, "We are the leaders of the Awakening." But they're not on the political stage.

I will add something. The people didn't understand the letter from the Marines. They couldn't do anything. When the convoys of Marines were moving in the streets, the children threw rocks at them. They opened up to the people and made the people understand what they wanted to achieve. Then the children clapped for them and were happy with them, and talked with them, and respected them, and invited them to their houses. Also, the other good people, the sheikhs, started to work with them.

While you are writing history, here is something for history: they didn't finish the job. In my opinion as a military man, they quit while the job was half finished. The size of the sacrifice by the

Marines and other people was big, and the accomplishment was big—indeed, it affected the whole country—but did we achieve permanent stability and peace? I say "No." Because we built in a very critical and a very difficult time and gave everything to build this one. The government of Iraq didn't help us with anything. They knew the Coalition forces were paying the salaries of the police, but they will need maintenance afterward. So they didn't cooperate in this. Now our building is not on a good foundation for the long term, and it needs a good foundation so it can grow. That's briefly what I told you.

Iraqi Perspectives

Interview 19

Major General Ghazi Khudrilyas
Ambassador Sa'doon J. al-Zubaydi
Lieutenant General Raad al-Hamdani
Lieutenant General Abdul Aziz Abdul Rahman
Brigadier General Muhammed al-Azzawi

Lieutenant General Ra'ad al-Hamdani
Lieutenant General Abdul Aziz Abdul Rahman
Major General Ghazi Khudrilyas
Brigadier General Muhammed al-Azzawi
Ambassador Sa'doon J. al-Zubaydi

Lieutenant General Ra'ad al-Hamdani was the final commander of the 2d Republican Guard Corps, and he is the founder and chairman of the Association of Former Officers of the Iraqi Armed Forces. Lieutenant General Abdul Aziz Abdul Rahman is former chairman of the Scientific Board at Al-Bakr University for Higher Military Studies in Baghdad and a former commander of the 4th Division of the new Iraqi army. Major General Ghazi Khudrilyas was wounded and left disabled in the Iran-Iraq War. He was a military advisor to the Minister of Interior (1986-89) and served as the director of the National Joint Operations Center (July 2004-July 2006) under the new regime. Brigadier General Muhammed al-Azzawi was a special forces officer in the Republican Guard, and he commanded a Ministry of Interior Special Police Commando under the new regime. Ambassador Sa'doon J. al-Zubaydi was educated in Great Britain initially worked as a professor of English Literature. Under the Ba'ath Party regime, he served as Iraqi ambassador to Indonesia and Singapore, director general of research and data analysis for the Ministry of Foreign Affairs, and political advisor to the president of Iraq. They were interviewed by Colonel Gary W. Montgomery and Chief Warrant Officer-4 Timothy S. McWilliams on 24 February 2009 in Amman, Jordan.

Lieutenant General Ra'ad al-Hamdani: I tried to warn the politicians, in one way or another, during the period between 1991 and 2003—as a commanding officer in the war and a commander in the Republican Guard—that the danger of the American strategic objectives was the fall of the regime in Baghdad. But what do you expect? Many of them misunderstood, which enabled American decision-makers to achieve it after weakening Iraq for 15 years with the sanctions and the air war that continued during that time.

I warned President Saddam Hussein precisely on this subject in September 1994, in November 1995, and at a meeting with the generals in June 2002. I explained myself before President Saddam Hussein for a period of 45 minutes in a meeting at the Republican Palace next to the international airport. I asked to change the method of our thinking and to prevent our losses in the decisive coming war for the Iraqi state because we were a weakened army, and a weakened country, and a weakened people. As a military, we didn't have any air force protection. We didn't have one jet that could fight any of the Coalition air forces. Our anti-air weapons were so weak that I can say we didn't have any. We had only a little artillery that we could defend ourselves with. And in the area of rockets, we hardly had any.

But despite it all, Saddam Hussein listened to us and did not agree with my suggestions. We can not blame Saddam Hussein himself only, but the people at that meeting and his advisers, too. And this conflict between the commanders and me continued up to 18 December 2002, when we were called to present our defense plan to the leadership. I was responsible for it because we were the biggest division at the time. There was a contest between us, with my vision and my thought, and with the military commanders, and with the politicians, too, regarding my plan.

The main point of contention was that I didn't want the conflict to be inside Baghdad. It wasn't the same circumstances as it was in the battle of Stalingrad. It wasn't like war in the Middle Ages. . . . My decision was that when the war started with the Coalition forces, we would attack them with small groups of soldiers and not in large formations, which would cause us more casualties.

We knew for sure what air power the enemy had. Personally, I joined the wars against Israel in Jordan and Syria, and in 1991 against the Americans and the Coalition. We knew for sure what superpower air forces mean. Our weapons would be like bows and arrows if we fought as an organized army without air force cover. And I explained that precisely to Saddam Hussein since 1994. . . .

There was a huge misgiving in me that these big American forces, this great army, this civilized army, this great country—I felt the sorrow of our nation that our future depended on them. I knew that the fighting in Baghdad would not take but a few days. I said to myself at that time, "This is our fate. We lost the war." Despite the stupidity of the political leadership, this complaint was something that was just as bad. I would rather have this civilized, strong, brave army coming in better than an Iranian invasion.

I continued from 9 April 2003 until I handed myself over to the American forces on 11 June 2003. I was observing the way that the American Army surrounded Baghdad, and this is where the big warning bell started to ring. This is where I discovered the strategic mistake of the Americans after the liberation of Baghdad. They left the borders open, and I saw Iranian trucks with Iranian plates entering the country. There were two types. One type was transporting personnel. The other was the big kind, and they were stealing our military industries and transporting them into Iran.

The decision to dissolve the Iraqi army came on 23 May 2003. Then I had a meeting with seven commanding generals on one of the farms south of Baghdad. I told them that the Americans were starting to make their biggest mistakes, and all of their sacrifices of lives and their gains would be handed over to the Iranians as a free gift. In summarizing my stand at the time, I suggested that I would hand myself over to the American forces. Maybe then I could warn the Americans that they were making many mistakes that they might regret in the future. But to us, it was decimating the area.

There is a fact that I noticed when I was watching the American Army movements at the time. We have to say it before the historians leave us, and I mentioned it in my book, that the American soldiers were highly polite. They are well-trained and qualified soldiers. We used to think that the Israeli soldier was exemplary, but when compared with the American soldier, the Israeli soldier is Middle Eastern. With respect to all the armed forces, there is a big gap with the professionalism of the American and British soldiers. Despite the conflicts and wars between us and the Iranians and Israel, I have to make the point—the bad points and the good points—and this is to respect the military forces, whoever they are. . . .

Lieutenant General Abdul Aziz Abdul Rahman: After the fall of Baghdad, when the Kurdish leadership came into Baghdad, I met the president of Iraq, Mr. Jalal Talabani, and there were a number of people with him. And what they were talking about—what I understood from that meeting—was that all the former military should be either sacked or killed. Mr. Talabani's answer was, "You are mistaken. A lot of these soldiers are linked to us, to the Kurds." And he turned around to me and asked, "What are you going to answer them?"

I didn't know who the attendees were. I introduced myself, "I'm General Abdul Aziz of the Iraqi army. I continue to serve, and I'm not a Ba'athist. I'm an independent gentleman. I'm Kurdish. With my relations with my old friends in here, I'll give you a guarantee, and I tell you that 80 percent of the Iraqi officers are not supporters of Saddam Hussein. And members of the Republican Guard— they're the elite of the Iraqi army. I can say [inaudible] they are professional people. They chose professional and qualified soldiers to join the Republican Guard. So all these units don't belong to Saddam Hussein or to anyone else. They are units of the national Iraqi army. There is a small percentage somewhere in the hierarchy, maybe some of them are related to Saddam Hussein."

A few days after that—after they found out some people are still with the Iraqi army and still not Ba'athists—they contacted me at the Rashid Hotel. I attended a meeting at the Rashid Hotel with many of my American friends, and they asked many questions.

At that time, the Iraqi people were clapping for the American soldiers and giving them roses and flowers. I saw it with my own eyes. In the Ameriya district, I saw an American soldier eating at a restaurant, and his weapon was over by his tank. He felt safe there. The people supported him. During that time, I informed my

American brothers that the day will come when it will be hard for an American soldier to walk in Iraq's streets. That is because of the mistakes that occurred by soldiers or junior officers behaving badly to the Iraqi people. That is what got us to that stage. The resistance started and terrorism against the situation that we were in. These matters could be solved by several meetings with some well-known leaders of the Iraqi army. They were known even to the Americans, too. These meetings did not happen. And this is why, for about six years, Iraq has not improved in the right way.

Colonel Gary W. Montgomery: When we changed tapes, you were discussing the beginning of the resistance.

Abdul Aziz: At one time, the Americans called me to attend a meeting at the presidential office. There were about 60 people sitting there—some ladies, gentlemen, and officers. They asked me many questions, but they were concentrating on just one thing, which was the governing council. And one of the American gentlemen asked me, "What do you think of the governing council?" I told him, "I don't know them."

He was surprised at what I said. He said "This governing council, which we just appointed," precisely concentrating on certain names. He asked me about [Adnan al-] Pachachi. I said, "I don't know him." I wanted to do a comparison. Pachachi was a former minister, this and that. I was a child. I vaguely knew the name. He was a former minister, and you're asking me about him coming back. This gentleman has been out of Iraq for 30, 35 years. How can he control Iraq?

Then he asked me what I thought of Ahmed Chalabi. And I said, "I don't know him, either. But from your information, you said that he has come back from Jordan. He was outside of Iraq since he was 15 years old. What does he know about Iraq?"

And he asked me about another gentleman. He mentioned the name, and he said two divisions of the Iraqi army had been searching for him. It's because he was a gangster between Nasiriyah and Amarah and Kut. How can you make these gentlemen rule Iraq and rule us?

I told him what I think. "We respect some of the gentlemen with the governing council. They have the political background. They were in opposition to the former regime. Like Jalal Talabani and Massoud Barzani, and some of the Islamic Party. They are respectable people. We know about them, and we can't ignore them. But most of the people, we didn't know them at all." This is one of the subjects we discussed. "As we know, the population of Iraq is 28 million. It cannot be acceptable that there are not 28 patriotic nationalist Iraqis who are willing to serve Iraq. When you tell us these 28, I don't know how it happened."

I'll give an example of the secrecy in some matters. I was in the artillery divisions. There was a colonel with me from Tikrit. One day I went to my office, and he wasn't there. I didn't say anything. The next day, he didn't come to the office again. I asked, "Where is this colonel? Why was he taken away?"

They said to keep quiet.

I asked, "Why?

They said, "He has been executed."

"Why has he been executed?"

"Because there was an attempt to overthrow Saddam Hussein."

I tried to take him down myself. I'm an independent Kurdish guy. This officer sat in my office. If he had this thought in his head, he should have talked about that to me because I was always against the regime. I was the closest man to him, and I didn't have this information. This was one of the attempts. Who gave the information to Saddam Hussein? In my mind, it was the American agents.

One of the American officers asked me at one of the meetings, "Why didn't you start a coup against Saddam Hussein?" I gave him this as an example. There have been 28 attempted coups in Iraq so far. Thirty-two hours before, a list of names was handed over to Saddam Hussein, names of the guys who attempted a coup against him. Who used to pass this information to Saddam? This is the secret. It was 50 percent from the Iraqi military to save the regime.

But I think Saddam was backed by you, the Americans. . . .

Major General Ghazi Khudrilyas: On the 10th of April, I joined with the Marines at the Meridian Hotel. I did not join the people who raped my country as a voluntary soldier. No, I joined them to advise them on how to control the looting and to form the new police and army. I met the chief of the Marines at the Meridian Hotel. They had our names in a computer. The things that he asked me were, do I say un-Christian? They had all the information about all the officers then, and he knew that I was an adviser to the former interior minister.

I gave him my opinion on how to integrate the police into the Coalition. And we started to go and form the new police. There was someone from the Marines in charge of the Interior Ministry. His name was Major Mark Stilberg.* He provided me with maps of Baghdad and an operations room inside the office of the Interior Ministry. And we started sending Iraqi police out with the Americans in Baghdad.

The first information we had that the Badr brigade was entering Iraq from Iran, which General Ra'ad mentioned earlier, I immediately informed the Americans that we should close the borders to prevent the Iranians from entering. They did not implement what I wanted.

On 20 April 2003, we had information on the location of the former finance minister, Mr. Hikmat al-Azzawi. Immediately, American and Iraqi police forces went to that location. I told the Americans, "Please, do not enter the minister's house. Let only the Iraqi police enter to arrest him, because he was one of the 55 wanted men whose work we respected." I informed the Americans then that these former ministers are highly-qualified ministers, and they got to their positions by their qualifications. When we brought him with us, I made sure that he brought all his medicine with him because I knew that he had heart problems. . . .

---

* No Marine by this name has been identified.

And precisely on this date—the American Army was taking over from the Marines on the Sadr side of Baghdad—I had an interview with the commander of the Marines at the CNN super channel to thank me in person for the capture of one of the first 55 wanted men, which I assisted in capturing. And the chief of the Marines told me "Now we've liberated you from Saddam Hussein." So I told him, "You didn't come here to liberate us from Saddam Hussein, but to control the other side of the world, and to control the oil in Iraq and the region, and to ensure the safety of Israel for years to come." He said to me, pointing his thumb up, "You are absolutely correct."

After that, I had many of the police joining me to start taking control of the borders. I made a presentation to Colonel King* of the American Army. I presented him with all the names of the Iraqi border police, and I told him where to locate the police officers and set the checkpoints to start controlling the borders. Colonel King went in to the civilian governor, [Jay M.] Garner. I think that was, to be precise, on 2 May 2003. The ambassador wanted to postpone planning for border control and to postpone it indefinitely.

A month later, we had information that the Badr brigade had entered Baghdad, and they were controlling an area called [the Shaab neighborhood], and they were controlling the cars and the people.

During that time, the American forces started forming the new Iraqi police from elements which were sacked by the old regime. These officers had been sacked mainly for managerial or corruption reasons, or for betraying the country.

In late May 2003, Colonel King brought me another Iraqi colonel and asked me to appoint him to a position. And the colonel, I didn't know him, but his name was [Ahmed Kabul]. Later on, I found out that this [Ahmed Kabul?] was a colonel at the Ministry of Defense, and he was sacked from his duty. So I called him, and I said, "Are you a colonel or are you a lieutenant? What are you?" And he said, "Sir, I was only a lieutenant, but the Americans

---

* Probably Col R. Alan King, USA.

promoted me to colonel." It was part of the American administration's mistakes. Can you believe it? This is what's happened to us by bringing unqualified personnel into the police [multiple voices]. And you couldn't believe it. . . .

Ambassador Sa'doon J. al-Zubaydi: He is not our representative. He was actually thrown at our office in New York because they had nowhere to keep him.

Ghazi: Can you believe this [Ahmed Kabul?], who has been promoted by the Americans? They promoted him from the army to become the Iraqi representative at the United Nations office.

Sa'doon: We have a representative, officially. We have a representative by the name of Samir Sumaidaie. He is the ambassador. But [Ahmed Kabul?], they had nowhere to put him. They wanted to put him somewhere out of Iraq to keep him safe and to give him privileges, so he was put at our office in New York. So he's not representing us to the United States, but to the United Nations. . . .

Ghazi: After that, I was appointed to the National Joint Operations Center. That was in July 2004. I worked with the security organizations and with the Coalition forces, and I worked with General [George W.] Casey [Jr., USA], too. Unfortunately, much of the information that we passed to the Americans to implement on the ground was wrong. The American generals did not know the patriotic Iraqis from the false Iraqis who were passing them false information. Many people suffered, especially in certain areas, because false information was passed to the Americans that they were terrorists, which caused them to go and attack them. And I used to tell them, "These are patriotic Iraqis. Do not attack this area."

There was a problem on 6 June 2006. The Americans complained that they had not managed to control the armed militias inside Iraq and outside Iraq. There was a meeting between the Ministry of Interior, the Ministry of Defense, and the Coalition forces. And I attended that meeting as well. The Americans were wondering what step to take next, and the Interior Ministry and Ministry of Defense had no idea how to control the militias. General Casey's deputy, I believe, General [Sir Robert Alan] Fry [British Royal Marines]—he's a British general—was attending that meeting. General [Peter W.] Chiarelli [USA] of the American forces was there, General [James D.] Thurman [USA], the commander of the 4th Division from the American forces, and I was there with the Coalition officers, too.

I suggested something to them to solve this matter, and I told them that this mistake is a mistake of American strategic planning. The mistake was in joining religion with politics. This experience has not happened in any country around the world, and I suggested that you correct your mistake by separating politics from religion so that the country of Iraq is either a religious country or a secular country. I told them, "If you want this country, look at the experience that we had with Iran, our neighbor. Iran is a stable country with no terrorism, and it's developing. In a few years, it will have nuclear weapons. Or bring us a secular system, and the religious people can have their time in their religious places, such as churches, mosques, or husseiniyas, where the Shi'as worship." Most of the American officers whose names I mentioned supported my idea, and the minister of interior and the minister of defense supported me, too. The one who objected to my suggestion was Mr. Mowaffak al-Rubaie, the national security advisor.

The biggest problem we have now is protecting our borders, especially the Iraqi-Iranian border. We have 300 kilometers in the north that is uncontrolled, and Iraqis and Iranians are using this border for smuggling. The border from Khanaqin to the south of Basrah should be protected and secured by independent elements. Because of this mistake of mixing religion into politics, the Iraqi government has integrated 400 militia members into the border police. And these Badr militias are counted as enemies by the Americans.

Mr. Ahmed al-Khafaji, the deputy interior minister for support forces, stated this in front of General [Joseph F.] Peterson [USA], the American general, on 28 May 2006 when Mr. [Jawad] Bulani was becoming the new minister of interior. When General Peterson said at the meeting that the Badr militia is a terrorist militia, Major General Ahmed Janabi answered him, "No, they're not terrorist militias. I personally appointed 400 of these militias to control the borders."

Unfortunately, the Americans know for a fact that the Iraqi-Iranian border is controlled by the Iranian-supported Badr militias. And it surprises me when the Americans are astonished that new weapons or new bombs have entered Iraq, when they know for a fact that the border is controlled by Iranian militias. And with this point, I can say on the record that I think the Americans are joining the Iranians to increase terrorism in Iraq. And I can say that the Americans are supervising the entry of these weapons into Iraq from Iran. I've been to the border. I'm a military officer, and I'm an authority on the border. And the amount of arms that has been entering Iraq, I can tell you, you cannot transport it on animals or by humans—it must be transported on heavy trucks. So these weapons are entering Iraq by road, which is controlled, along with the border, by these militias, as well as supervised by the American checkpoints. This was the main point, which I think General Ra'ad would like to speak about.

Ra'ad: I think there is one more left, gentlemen. The subject is rather important. As former Iraqi officers, whether in service or out of service, our aim is the independence of our country. As for the American administration and the American force, we take it as the responsibility of the Americans, as a historical thing and as a matter of integrity, or there is no hope for Iraq. Now we have taken the American administration as a friend, and we have to keep them as a friend forever and have them consider the Iranian danger that we are facing.

We spoke a lot about the resistance, and the terrorists, and the [inaudible] of the insurgency. Some of these formed the Awakening, and now we call them the Sons of Iraq. We would like to discuss this matter of the Awakening in three main points. How to describe this Awakening? We have Brigadier Muhammad here with us, who has assisted the Marines in fighting the terrorists. And what is the solution for our future?

On the 29 February 2004—as you know, the 29th of the February comes every four years. This date was a great date because my name was crossed off of the black list. I was a professional commander. I have not committed any crimes.

And then I had a meeting at the Republican Palace. I was surprised, because it was a year after I met President Saddam Hussein in this palace, which had been so quiet and pleasant, and only a few people were permitted to enter and see it. Now the whole world was in this palace, I believe. I even saw red Indians. Italians, Fijians—the whole world was in this palace. Some were military. It was a shock to me.

Anyway, I entered the palace, and there were three gentlemen standing over there. One of them was a colonel from the American Army, one from the inspector corps; his name was James. The other, I don't remember his name, but there were three gentlemen. The important thing, we had a meeting in Baghdad with the Americans and the British. And he asked me, "General, explain to us what you see." And I spoke generally about the new strategic situation, but I really spoke about what could have avoided the war. And at that point, we talked about their victory in the war. It was clear to us that you were going to win the war anyway. We assume that you, with the superpower you have, you're going to achieve your objectives. But the question for the wise commander is, "When you achieve your objective, how do you keep it?" And so your biggest mistake was dissolving the former Iraqi army. And the second point that I mentioned to them was, "Why did you leave the border open? And where is the civil-military organization that you have?

So you did the same as us. When we invaded Kuwait, we made mistakes, the same mistakes you made when you invaded us. I used to [shout and scream] in Kuwait, and I was the one who led the invasion of Kuwait, before I lost control of the situation. Where is the military government for civil affairs? This is what we learned. It's impossible for us, for a military, to be changed into police—so it was the case. You can do it in a stage where you couldn't see the Kuwaiti streets anymore.

Then I directed this speech to the military officers in front of me. "We are a Third World army. We are expected to make mistakes. You, the American Army, you're the most powerful army in the world. An army like yours cannot make mistakes. The result is the situation we are living in now, because of the mistakes that have been done by a great army like the United States Army." I told them that "Vietnam will be a red rose compared to the crisis you're going to face here in Iraq. I'm not warning you for your sakes only. I told you—I'm afraid for my country.

"We are a country that is transforming from Bedouin to civilization. We depend on the elite and the notable. And these elite people are the link between us and you, the Americans. Where are the elite people? Where are the notable people? The civilization gap between us, I can say it reaches up to 200 years. Who is responsible for closing this gap between us? So you are the people who came from the future, and the elite people we're talking about understand you and understand Iraqi society. Some of them, like Ambassador Sa'doon, were educated in the United Kingdom."

I could see the concern on their faces. One of them asked me, "Can you assist in forming the new Iraqi army?" And I said to him, "I cannot see that you want to form a new Iraqi army, because any army in the world—whether it's a superpower army like the United States Army or the smallest army in the world, such as the Jordanian Army, for example—it depends on elements and principles to organize or form. And that's what we learned from you—that we should be united on the political aims, and united on the commandership, the authorization for each Iraqi officer, and there are other things that we can speak about. And so the state you are in now, I cannot believe you are ready to form a new Iraqi army. So, for this, I have to decline to assist you. And for other reasons, like people will record in history that you picked a Republican Guard Command officer to assist you in helping destroy the country."

The Iraqi army had great professional officers who were positioned better than me in education, and who retired prior to the war. This means there is a network of officers who could assist you in building this army, but it will not be an army with independent, professional men united to serve the country. What you're going to form is a military force that is different. Each unit will follow its own politico-religious party, and we are in a situation now where all the religious parties are competing for control of the country. And the competition among the religious parties will gradually grow in the military force, and we will have a civil war among these religious parties.

So, see if what you expect will happen. The borders are open and, as you know, we have problems with the six neighboring countries surrounding Iraq. And each of these countries wishes to gain an advantage over Iraq. We have a lot of complications. We have indications, and we have the right to say that Iran has chosen the biggest opportunity to infiltrate into Iraq. And you have identified Iran in all of our regions, and they are entering.

The invasion of Iraq created a huge gap, a gap in leadership, because one man was leading the whole country, and he was overthrown suddenly. With this gap created, anti-American and anti-Coalition forces entered the country. With the gap that was there because of the invasion and the lack of control in governing Iraq, many opportunists entered Iraq, such as the Iranian influence that's infiltrating Iraq. They used the opportunity to locate and choose places where they can gain control and bring their ideology into the country.

Unfortunately, the day the Americans invaded Iraq, they had no knowledge of whom to speak to or whom to approach within the country to get the right advisors. They came in, they took control, and they won the war, but they had no one to advise them at the time regarding whom to speak to and whom to avoid.

The Iranians, as you know—and I've said it many times—the Iranians have a grudge against the Iraqis, not because of the Iran-Iraq War, but because of hereditary enmity going back 2,500 years. Another thing that we, the Iraqis, talk about is that there was an agreement between the Iranians and the Americans for removing Saddam Hussein, and this was an opportunity to take revenge against us.

I come to the other point that I would like to address: resistance and terrorism. I have spoken several times with American generals regarding an appreciation of the difference between resistance and terrorism. They have never agreed to separate the resistance from the terrorists. There is a country that has been invaded by foreign forces. There is bound to be resistance. And there is some resistance—and I said it in several meetings—that a dialogue must be opened between the nationalist resistance and the Americans. The opportunity by the terrorists . . . with the nationalists and patriots seeing the country invaded by foreign forces, with the Coalition forces not understanding the difference between the resistance and the terrorists, the terrorists gained control of many areas. The Americans did not understand at the beginning. Now they realize that we have to distinguish between terrorists and national resistance against foreign countries.

I give the chair now to my brave friend who served with me in the Republican Guards, and who has assisted the Americans. He worked for me, and he was with the Marines, too. When he wanted to join the Marines, he contacted me. He said, "Sir, what do you think? I asked to join the Iraqi forces and assist the Americans. Should I work with the Americans or not?" I advised him, "Please do. Please join the military. Give your advice to the Americans. We need somebody who is a patriot, who is nationalist, to advise the Americans." I supported him in joining and helping the Americans in every way he could to help them understand our culture, our traditions, and the differentiation between us and the Iranians. And I give the chair to him now to speak of his experience.

Brigadier General Muhammed al-Azzawi: I worked at Balad Air Base in September 2003. I worked with the Chinook unit as a deputy of the division. Colonel Arnold was there. He was a great man. I worked with him to implement operations in the [Yudhumariya] district and the [Bamiya] district. These were the most dangerous military areas.

After that, they spoke to me in January 2004 about joining the special forces of the Interior Ministry. I had a friend there, Major General [Jalad?], God bless him, who has passed away. Major General [Salman?], God bless him, and Colonel [Suran Ubaysi?], God bless him, and Colonel Abdul Karim Jubaili, and Major General [Mahi al-Rallawi?]. All the martyrs that I just mentioned, they were all assassinated by government militias. It wasn't in combat against terrorists.

We formed special forces units with our orders in June 2004. I was the commander of the first division, which was linked directly to the Ministry of Interior. General Adnan Thabit was the general supervising.

After we implemented and achieved Fallujah I, we began to see something new. There was a new militia forming in Fallujah, and they were from the Iraqi divisions. They started to have checkpoints from the southern provinces and the Fallujah district. They started to form militias under the cover of the Ministry of Interior. We started kicking them out of Fallujah by order of the Ministry of Interior, and we retook their positions in the Fallujah area.

After that, in November 2004, the same year, Anbar Province fell. The minister of interior, Mr Falah al-Naqib, visited with General [David H.] Petraeus [USA] and General [Renefo?]. There was movement toward Anbar with an extra division, and we began to liberate Anbar the same day. There was combat [inaudible] gangsters [inaudible]. I was in special forces, and most of my friends are from special forces, and there was direct support from the American forces, especially from the 8th Division and the commander at the time, Colonel Patton.

[Conversation with Interpreter.]

Interpreter: The thing what he said about the war—that "we took the province of Anbar." I said, "What do you mean the province of Anbar?" He said, "the headquarters at Ramadi, I mean."

Muhammed: When the headquarters at Ramadi fell, they went there and they looted the headquarters of Ramadi—the government center.*

Chief Warrant Officer-4 Timothy S. McWilliams: When was that, sir?

Muhammed: That was in November 2004, and then we took control of the government offices. Then we started distributing operations, and the [1st division became 4 divisions]. So I was in

---

* He seems to be referring to Fallujah, even though he said Ramadi.

charge of operations on the western side of Iraq. We started moving checkpoints on the highways between Baghdad and Syria. We captured many of the gangsters, of many nationalities.

The Americans expressed appreciation for the work that we had done. General Casey was there, General Petraeus, General [inaudible], by the Ministry of Interior, and the director of the operation, Major General Muthir. The American forces requested from the Minister of Interior at the time, Falah al-Naqib, [that the 3d division would take the 4th division to remain in Anbar Province].

After that, they withdrew me from Anbar to Baghdad to start forming a new division. During this period, power was turned over to Ibrahim al-Jafaari. The first meeting with the new minister of interior, Baqir [Jabr Al-Zubeidi], was held at Adnani palace on 4 May 2005. We all attended the meeting: General Ghazi was there, Mr. Casteel,* Major General Mahmoud al-Wahali, Major General Adnan Thabit, Major General Muther al-Rawi, Major General Rashid Fayed, Hamid Hezejedan, and Major Maqabi. At present, he is in prison in Bucca. He was linked to an operation against the Sunnis using Interior Ministry cars. And this man was highly liked and respected at that time, especially by the new minister of interior.

I want to point out a very important thing. An American delegation visited Iraq headed by a Colonel [McMahon?]. He came to Anbar province on 1 March 2005. We sat with Colonel Patton and the commanders of the units. He asked me, "What's your opinion of the new interior minister, Baqir?" I said, "As an Iraqi, in my opinion, he was the one who was in charge of the operations of the Badr Brigade." And he thanked me for saying so. And the day of the meeting that we're talking about, I realized that the Americans had passed the message to the interior minister that I had told them he was the leader of the militias.

As evidence, in our tradition, the minister, or anyone, whenever you meet, you kiss them on the cheek. He greeted everyone except me.

---

* Although the name on the recording sounds like "Steel," the reference likely is to Mr. Steve Casteel, a career Drug Enforcement Agency employee and the Coalition Provisional Authority's senior advisor to the Ministry of Interior.

These officers that we met in Anbar, they worked in Baghdad. And I am from Anbar. He took my hand just slightly. I am Sunni, and I fought in the Sunni areas. What about me, as a Sunni, fighting in the Shi'a areas? I was kicked out of my position and transferred to operations as a staff officer.

Immediately then, I requested R&R for seven days from Major General Adnan Thabit to visit my family here in Jordan. As you know, my son is disabled. I got to Jordan on 14 May 2005. At dawn on 15 May 2005, I received a call from my mother that the commando brigades that I was commanding were surrounding the area. They took my brother and 11 people from my area . . . [inaudible] under official order [inaudible]. They were wearing the same uniform that I was wearing. There were 40 cars surrounding our residential area at 5:30 in the morning.

Straightaway, I went back to Iraq. I went to see Major General Adnan Thabit. We searched everywhere for my brother and the 11 people that had been taken. The minister of interior was so sorry for me—as a comedian. He was doing comedy. Major General Adnan told me about it. On the 18th, Major General Adnan told me that the minister of interior wanted me to be at his office at 8:00 in the morning. After that, someone called me. He said, "I am your friend. My name is this-this." I won't mention his name, because he is still working in the Interior Ministry. He informed me that "the minister of interior has given an order for your arrest, and he is sending four cars now to arrest you."

So I was careful. I'm a human being, and I'm cautious of people like this. I know for sure that Ahmed and the rest of the guys who were working over there are all from the Badr brigades. They are gangsters, and they are working for him now.

At this time, the 1st division commander was arrested. His name was Major Kana'an al-Gheisi, and he was an officer from the Sadiyah camp. Eleven buses carrying al-Khona militia—and this whole militia is from the south—came into the al-Sadiyah camp. They started destroying the camp, and they told them, "We have an order directly from the minister to destroy this camp." The commander of the division phoned me, and at the time I was concerned because my brother had been kidnapped. I informed Major General Adnan that "12 buses of al-Khona militia have entered your camp, and they are destroying it." They had beards and banners around their heads saying, "The Martyr Hussein." They were supporters of a pro-Iranian group. We have Shi'as in our divisions, but they don't wear banners saying "Hussein." Only the Iranians do it, and they arrested Mahmoud and 11 other officers. And I started to understand my problem then. A few days later, I found my brother and 11 of his friends in the Sadr area. They had been tortured with drills. And after they drilled them and killed them, they burned them.

After that, I submitted my resignation, and attempts to assassinate me started. After that, I moved to Iraqi intelligence in the beginning of 2006. There was a link between the head of Iraqi intelligence and special forces. He had heard that I was special forces, and he had followed the circumstances that I had been through.

During that time, 40 cars with militias were sent by the interior minister to the residential area where I was staying. Two of my brothers were arrested and kidnapped. We found them 40 days later, five kilometers inside Iran. This CD shows the bodies [holding a compact disc in his hand]. It shows you the bodies and the way that the Interior Ministry gave the orders, by the orders of the interior minister and Ibrahim Jafaari, the prime minister.

And intelligence? After the information from so many intelligence reports, and the media, and tens of thousands of files—it's Iran, Iran, Iran, Iran, Iran, Iran. I've read 10,000 reports showing the Iranian penetration and the entering of Iranian intelligence across the border from the north, south, and everywhere into Iraq. The Iranians know how many Iranian militias have been entering Iraq, and I am sure you will see this in the Iraqi intelligence headquarters files, the same as you, the Americans, hold files on how many Iranians have been entering Iraq.

I don't want to make my speech long, because the more I speak, the more I spoil my meaning. But I attended a security meeting in September 2006, and these were the nationalist ministers: Dr. Salam al-Zaubai, the head of the operations from the Interior

Ministry, and the deputy interior minister. We started to speak about the Mahdi militias. And everybody agreed that the Mahdi militias must be arrested, except one man, and that was Mowaffak al-Rubaie, who stood and said, "Now you are saying these militias are not good? They're good, patriotic people." A conflict started between Jawad Bulani, the minister of interior, and the operations commander, Major Aziz Robeidi, regarding the authorizations and responsibilities of the checkpoints. So the minister of interior, Jawad Bulani, emphasized that the Mahdi militia is a traditional army, and they would never fight civilians.

The last position I held was in operations for Iraqi intelligence in 2007, with a liaison officer called Tony—and he's a great liaison officer, because all our talk was about the Iranians.

I'll summarize for our talk. We have been working with the Americans. I fought side by side with the Americans for the sake of my country. But the Americans betrayed me. Americans have assisted by the killing of three of my brothers and my mother. Americans have allowed Bayan Solagh, the interior minister at the time, to kill the whole family. Americans have given the order for the 40 cars to kill the civilians in Baghdad.

I'll tell you, I was a division commander, and when I used to go out on patrol, the Americans allowed me to take only four cars on patrol—only. How can you explain to me now—with the CD that you are going to see—there are 40 trucks going around with flags— with the permission of the Americans. I have made complaints to all the generals. I can't even count the number.

And I gave them evidence regarding al-Islam, and regarding the militias belonging to [Jalal al-Suria?]—the young Jalal. And I gave them evidence on the [Jadriya shelter]. And I was with General [Host?], and I freed all the detainees from the shelter. And I worked as a civilian for the sake of my country, not just for my brothers only. But I worked to release all the innocent detainees who were inside the shelter.

Hadi al-Amri, in charge of the Badr brigade, was going from one side to the other in Iraq. What did the Americans do to him?

Americans fought in Afghanistan to change the white turbans—Osama bin Laden and the Taliban. You go to Iraq, the black Iranian turbans—did they ask the Americans?

The new airport that has been opened in Najaf—did you ask about the military air movement between Mashhad, Qom, Tehran, and Najaf? Or the military weapons being flown into Iraq? Is there one American soldier in that airport? The Iranians are not accountable to the Americans in Najaf and Karbala?

Deputy Iraqi [inaudible] [Muhammed al-Daini?]—his whole family has been assassinated because he objected to the Iranian penetration of Iraq.

What is the difference in your views? The one who fights the Iranians? Iran has invaded Iraq, as the general just said. I myself believe, and all Iraqis believe, that the Americans are working on a plan side by side with the Iranians.

How do you explain this to me? How do you explain to me that Mowaffak al-Rubaie is the advisor for security and intelligence—and he's not an Iraqi. How do you explain to me that Baqir Solagh is the minister of finance now—and he's not Iraqi. He's Iranian. Or explain to me about Ali al-Adeeb, the Iraqi spokesman. His name is Ali Esdid. He changed his name—he is Iranian. Explain to me about Ibrahim Jafaari, the prime minister. He is Iranian. Will you explain to me about the Iranian ambassador in Iraq meeting with Iraqi officers? And what about [Amar Hakim?], who was meeting with the ambassadors and the Interior Ministry officers? Explain all this to me. Who is lying to whom? America is lying to us. When we looked at America, we were looking at this great American rose flower in front of us.

And I can say, as the general said earlier, that the Americans are working to create different militias for one reason—not to build Iraq, but to disintegrate Iraq. I have been asked to go back to Iraq, but I refuse to work in any ministerial or governmental organization controlled by the Iranians.

And [Nouri al-] Maliki and [inaudible], as you know, they are all spies and traitors to Iran. And the Americans have evidence. They have their bank accounts and records of the amount of money they have been transferring to Iran.

One day prior any Muslim feast, just watch Baghdad Airport. Just look and see if any members of the government or the Iraqi members of parliament are in Baghdad. They go back to their shrines.

How do you explain to me [al-Farqay?] in Iraq? Can you believe that we are controlled by Ali [al-Husayni al-] Sistani? That quiet man—Iranian origin, sectarian, traditional—and he is working on changing Iraq into an Iranian territory, with the assistance or friendship of the Americans.

I'll just say something so I can change the atmosphere here. I was in the division on Balad air base. Colonel Ibrahim was taking two jerry cans of gas with him. Colonel Arnold called him. He said, "Look at this colonel. He stole two jerry cans of gas, and he's a ranking officer." The American group was standing together. I said to him, "Colonel, you invaded Iraq and stole all the oil and gas from us, and nobody said anything. So, are you going to arrest him for taking these two jerry cans of gas?" He said, "We are friends now."

Thank you.

Ra'ad: Excuse me. He has been through difficult circumstances. He has a big crisis in his life, a massive crisis in the last few years. This is a reflection. I met him prior to being here. I asked him, "How do you find the work with the American forces?" And that was in the beginning. And he said, "It is a great opportunity for me to work with an army as powerful and principled as the Americans. You always talk to us about civilizations, and now I have the opportunity of living and practicing with another civilization."

This is what I have said. I have said it in front of you, and I have said it in front of many members of Congress, and I said this to Ambassador [Ryan C.] Crocker—that we can understand and separate between a political administration and American civilization. We are thirsty for American civilization, and American civilization is not represented by the big hamburgers or the big Pepsi bottles. And that's what we wish to see—American civilization.

The problem now with the political administration, if you see Iraqis sitting among them—whether there are two Iraqis, four Iraqis, six Iraqis, or 12 Iraqis—at the end of the day, you will see them divided into two groups. Since the invasion, Iraq has been divided. Has it been done on purpose to destroy Iraq, or is it by mistake? Since I have been a major, I never understood American policy.

Ambassador Crocker's answer was so straight. He said, "I am Crocker. I am the American ambassador here in Baghdad. I myself don't understand American policy." So this is an example in front of us of how bad political administration destroys a lot of civilized achievements. So people who are uneducated—simple people—how do they look at the United States with this pressure on them? Especially now, when many of the provinces have been cradling terrorism. These simple men do not differentiate between great gentlemen like yourselves sitting here, and other great American soldiers, and people like President [George W.] Bush, and Richard [N.] Perle, and [Secretary of Defense Donald H.] Rumsfeld. But they devastated our country. These simple people, they do not understand that there are psychological mistakes, like in Samuel Huntington's *The Clash of Civilizations* or Francis Fukuyama's book, *The End of History*. The simple Iraqi does not differentiate between these things. It all reflects on the American soldier who is on the front.

I am a soldier. I sympathize with any soldier standing there. I feel sorry for all the sacrifices that any soldier pays, because in front of you, we are a people who have been victims of bad politicians. I have joined in six wars—and violent wars. I understand the meaning of the decimation of war, and that gives me an understanding of the people.

But we have to learn our lessons. What happened in Iraq were bad American political mistakes. We have met many great American soldiers and technicians, whom we look at as our future. Throughout the education and culture of the Middle East, compared to the American administration and institutions, there is a gap between our civilizations and education. Now we have a saying that "it's stupid to trust the American administration policies." Another is that "it is ignorant to object to the American political decisions." This is a very difficult equation.

We wish that we would benefit from the mistakes that were made. I am sorry that the mistakes occurred, because the civilization occurred over 500 years. We wish that we would benefit from the mistakes that occurred, because the civilization occurred over 500 years, and we don't know how to explain it in our region. I am one of the soldiers and an Iraqi citizen. Somehow I have no understanding of American civilization. And I'm a Muslim. I'm not sectarian. I studied all the religions—Jews, Christianity, and many other religions. There is a great appreciation between Muslims and other religions, but what we have is a gap between the civilizations—this great gap. We wish for more American friends coming in the future to narrow the gap between us. But, unfortunately, what we're finding now is that the gap is getting bigger, not smaller.

The last thing I would like to speak about, the Awakening and the circumstances of the Awakening.

We have a small number of professionals, like Dr. Sa'doon, on all levels. Unfortunately, the American administration did not consider and appreciate people like him who could have assisted in rapidly moving to democracy.

But unfortunately the American policy—I can say the American policy presented by the governor, [L.] Paul Bremer—he wanted to take a shortcut to democracy. Unfortunately, the shortcut was using the religious people.

And 2006 was like 1994 in Rwanda, despite the gap between the civilizations in Rwanda and Iraqi, and the exact people taking power were farmers. We started to be ashamed to call ourselves Iraqis, having these uneducated people leading us.

[Referring to Dr. Sa'doon again] It's very unfortunate for a man with his dignity, with his intelligence, seeking to start over again and seek a new way for his livelihood because thieves were let loose in his own country. The American policy should be to find proud people, to find persons like these people, to prove to the future that America put a seal on helping to develop democracy and a new civilization in Iraq. And we have a saying that "you know a person by his friends." You take a person like Mahmoud Mashhaddani or Adnan al-Dulaimi. Do we count these as friends of America?

Ghazi: Excuse me, General. The last mistake by President Bush's administration, which encourages Iraq to stay at the level it is, is the new Status of Forces Agreement [SOFA]. One of the articles in it says that you have to follow the former regime elements.

Sa'doon: Chase.

Interpreter: Follow or chase?

Sa'doon: Chase. They are criminals.

Ghazi: This article includes all the former regime employees. This is a bad agreement. This article has stopped one thing, and that is Iraqi national reconciliation. The Iraqi government sent a delegation to the regional countries regarding the reconciliation of the former military and other civilian employees, and if you noticed, nobody has signed on to going back to work. The reason is this article in the SOFA agreement, which means that anyone who goes back will be assassinated immediately.

I know that I, myself, can go back to Iraq and have no problem. But if anyone chooses to inform on me to the Americans and say, "This gentleman is a former regime element," according to the SOFA agreement, I could be chased. According to the SOFA agreement, I could be arrested immediately. And I have no problem. I am not a criminal. My job was a former ministry employee.

Sa'doon: This problem has closed the door before a long sought-after amendment of the new Iraqi constitution. The Iraqi constitution was drafted in a spirit of vengeance. I was a member of the drafting committee representing the alienated communities, and I was witness to a constitution that was drafted in a spirit of vengeance, which consequently contained mishaps and mistakes that we have suffered from, and will continue to suffer from.

One of these problems is the reference to former employees, and former Ba'athists, and former members of the old system of government—exactly the subject that is being referred to today, now, by General Khudilyas, who is actually right in seeing that this problem, rather than being an assistant element, to help us amend the constitution, has actually reinstated and strengthened the presence of this concept of vengeance in the constitution.

I, as a reformist, as a member of a community that wants to reform the constitution, now find it more difficult to attend to this problem in the constitution, with the agreement signed with the United States. The significance of this problem is twofold. One is human, and the other is legal, as the general has indicated. It's made it difficult now for us to approach it because it's there in the agreement, and I could not see why—excuse the expression—in the hell would an agreement between two sovereign states refer to former employees of an older regime. I mean, what have you got— you Americans, the United States—got to do with people belonging to a former political system in the country? You're not the police here. You're not the legal system here. This is part of the legal system. This is such a drastic mistake, and I don't know how the American side accepted to see it incorporated in an agreement of that nature. It's impossible to accept. That's how significant this reference is by General Ghazi.

Ghazi: The other point is, regarding the former military, everybody agreed and accepted that dissolving the former Iraqi army was a mistake by President Bush and Bremer. And the Iraqi government itself, from the president to the prime minister to other sectarian groups, agreed and accepted that it was a mistake to dissolve the Iraqi army. The former Iraqi army was an independent army, following orders from the political leaders. And now they're trying to facilitate reconciliation by recognizing that the former Iraqi army only did its duty at the time. Most of the former Iraqi army officers agreed with this reconciliation effort being made. And I say—and many of us say—if they're admitting that the former Iraqi army has not committed a crime, then I ask you why, until this time, the former defense minister has not been released from prison, if he has not committed a crime, and other officers with him, who have been put on death row? What crime have they committed?

General Hussein Rashid was the head of operations, and I worked as the head of the operations 2003. General Hussein Rashid was put on death row for implementing the orders of the political leaders at the time. I implemented the orders of the political leaders after 2003. We planned and supervised operations in Fallujah, in Najaf, in Tal Afar, and north of Babil. If there is regime change again, am I going to be executed, or will the political leaders be executed, too?

I just want to explain to you, to the new American administration, if there is a wish for reconciliation with the former military, we do not wish for you to give us our rights or our pensions—because we do not believe we will ever receive our pensions. If there are good intentions in the government, the first thing they should do is release all the former officers who have been detained by the government.

We hear the Ministry of Defense spokesman, Mohammed al-Askari, saying that the files of the former military officers will be closed, and they will be receiving all their rights back. But I can tell you now, it's all talk in front of the television cameras. The former military officers are not going to the embassy here to check on going back to Iraq, because they know it's a trap for them to go back and be assassinated. If the intention is true, the best way to give our rights back is to publish a statement of amnesty for all the former military officers.

Two weeks ago, Major General (Pilot) Jawad Kathem al-Dulaimi was assassinated, him and his son, in the Adhamiyah district of Baghdad. The checkpoint there took him, and at this checkpoint they are wearing commando uniforms. These are linked to the Ministry of Interior. They assassinated him and his son.

To this minute, about 450 high-ranking officers have been assassinated. The American administration announced that the Iraqi security forces are up and running. So how come 450 high-ranking Iraqi officers have been assassinated and no one has been arrested? These are security forces?

Will you, or I, or the system that is going on now, encourage me to go back to Iraq at this moment? That is because of the American invasion, because it depended on personnel who are not nationalists, and they did not find nationalist and patriotic people to give them advice....

Ra'ad: To speak about the Awakening—it resulted from an environment that had accepted terrorism under the umbrella of resistance against invaders. We mentioned many of the reasons previously. On the ground, it was discovered that these people did not work for the benefit of Iraq. Their objective was to destroy Iraq. Accepting them turned into rejecting them, and for the lack of real security forces, the people who started fighting them were the people who suffered because of them. And that was done by absorbing and using the tribal forces in the areas to fight and hold the main target of the terrorists.

At the beginning of the Awakening, one of them was Sattar Abu Risha. The success of Abdul Sattar Abu Risha broke the fear barrier. The credit does not go only to Abdul Sattar Abu Risha, but we appreciate him for firing the first shot. There are tens and hundreds of thousands of Iraqis better than Sattar Abu Risha who fought the terrorists and al-Qaeda, but they have not come to the surface. As you know, Sattar Abu Risha was not a nationalist, as the Americans understand it. As you know, he was a road gangster, and he committed crimes against Iraqi society previously. For the benefit of the area, and the benefit of the Americans at that time, Sattar Abu Risha was raised above the surface. There are thousands of Iraqi nationalists and patriots who did the same thing he did.

That's why we need actions and reactions. This is a natural thing in Iraqi society, and from the beginning, we knew there was no future for such a thing. It resulted from danger and the mistakes that occurred, as we mentioned earlier. Society was protecting itself. Iraqi society wants to go back to its natural self, which is a peaceful people. But there was no national leadership to take control and resist terrorists coming into the country. Because of the chaos at the time, and Abu Risha, assisted by the Americans, which made it happen and a success, people started to raise Sattar Abu Risha.

And then, suddenly, he started meeting President Bush, meeting the Congress—and these persons, such people do not represent the whole of Iraqi society. And the most surprising thing, these people are now entering the political process.

In 2004, I was called on here in Jordan by the Marine commander, [Colonel] John [C.] Coleman, and he was looking for gangsters to fight the gangsters that we had in Iraq. I told him at that time, "You are a general, and I know that you are intelligent. And there is a principle: when you have gangsters, use another gangster to fight gangsters. You're benefiting from the successful result in the short term, but the results are disastrous in the long term."

I advised him to go back and form new, independent, professional security forces, and let these security forces fight instead of allowing gangsters to take control. And we sat there a while, and his assistant was there. I believe it was Colonel David.* At my next meeting with him, I discovered that there was a political rejection of my opinion.

The problem started to get worse and worse, and the American Army sacrificed heavily in al-Anbar Province. We could have avoided Fallujah I and Fallujah II. I gave my word that we— through me and my officers—we could form a security force for al-Anbar Province to defend it and fight al-Qaeda. We could kill al-Qaeda in a very short time.

This general and his assistant are in the United States, and you can ask him what happened in that meeting. We could have avoided many of the losses to the Americans and to the Iraqis if they had listened to me at that time.

But we get back to the point where there is another political opinion that they cannot explain logically to us. And that occurred in the capital here, Amman, in July 2004, even though I was being followed and chased in Iraq. I was here for advisory reasons only, and I was met by high-ranking Iraqi officers and by the Americans, too. One of them at the meeting was Jerry [H.] Jones, who was the adviser to the officers at the time. Trust me when I tell you, if they had taken my advice then, things would have been different. . . .

---

* Probabl Lieutenant Colonel R. David Harlan.

Then I went to Athens, and I presented a study criticizing the strategic military planning in Iraq. And we gave studies of how to destroy all the terrorism in Iraq. And the well-known professional expert, Anthony [H.] Cordesman, was there at that meeting, too. Raoul [H.] Acala, the American adviser to the Iraqi minister of defense was at the table, and high-ranking professionals of the American Army. I said to Anthony Cordesman, "How do you do listen to advice from the Iraqi ministers and advisers? They're so small-minded. With your personality, how do you accept it? They have no professional advisors. It's surprising." It was a very lengthy and long discussion. But they're all alive, and you can meet with them and discuss what I said in that meeting.

I know the people from the Iraqi army, but we became caught between the hammer and the anvil. Our wish is to serve our country and respect the friendship with the Americans. But the Iraqi government is against us, and the previous Iraqi regime's policies are counted as a traitorous by the Americans. See, we are before you here with big responsibilities and worries. The stupidity of the American administration was in getting the right opportunity and sacrificing so many American soldiers and innocent Iraqi people, too.

I met again with Jerry Jones, and the personal advisor to President Bush. And they told me, "Oh, we are so sorry we didn't take your advice the first time." Every time we used to talk to them or to the American Congress, they wanted to say, "Oh, the American clock is too fast. We have a short time.". . .

Ra'ad: The distance between us in Iraq and the United States is the same distance between us and Mars. This talking is painful, and we are patient, and you are happy when you see our faces here. We smile with intelligence and dignity, so we can tell you about our worries and our concerns.

This is the Awakening, and the other thing—it's nothing to be proud of, taking somebody like Abu Risha to the United States and meeting President Bush. This is a short-term success. It's nothing to be proud of as a superpower, as the president of a great country, to meet with someone like this. This is a leader who is on for a short time and out.

If I were an American general, I would rather pass this stage and not mention it again, because this is an embarrassment. I am sorry to take your time. I'll give the chair to Dr. Sa'doon.

Sa'doon: Colonel Montgomery, gentlemen, I would like to say at the outset that I truly feel we are today, my friends and I, at an opportune moment, especially in view of the kind of thinking that we have indulged in for the past few months. We have given up on a lot of options that we tried during the past few years in order to contribute to the betterment of the Iraqi situation, but we have been faced with such difficulties that we have now opted for the more intellectual approach to the Iraqi problem.

Our intellectual approach is twofold. One has been championed and founded by Lieutenant General Ra'ad al-Hamdani, who pioneered the establishment of the Association of Former Iraqi Officers in order to fight for their civilian rights, for their and their families' rights. That has been a difficult job, but because it's such a just cause, it has met with a limited success, not in terms of the government response as much as in terms of the popular response to such a just cause. General Hamdani, deserves credit and gratitude by both his colleagues and the Iraqi society for this response.

The other page of our practical response to this Iraqi challenge is the establishment of a research center, which we're going to call the National Center for Dialogue and Democracy, in which we address various issues. The National Center for Dialogue and Democracy, which we abbreviated to NatCDD. NatCDD is going to try and address all of our problems, the first of which is going to be the security and military situation. That is why I feel what we are up against today is an opportune moment, because it is this challenge of addressing the military confrontation between Iraq and the United States and its allies that has not yet actually been discussed jointly by Iraqis and the Americans in the same room. That has not been done. We would like to do that. We would like to embark on that kind of job, which I believe is important.

Gentlemen, I belong to this group of people who actually believe that both the Iraqi armed forces and the United States armed forces have been victims to stupid policies by politicians. It is the reputation of the Iraqi armed forces, as well as the reputation of the great forces of the United States, that have been victimized by aberrant, impulsive, and blindly ideological mentalities leading the political situation on both sides, in Iraq and in the United States. I used to be part of the political echelon of Iraq. I was in the hierarchy. I was close to the leadership. I was chief interpreter to the head of state, and I was an ambassador and chief political advisor, and I could see the blindness of the decisions. But I also was extremely sorry to see that political blindness is not a monopoly of Iraq. It extends to other countries and other leaderships.

When the Americans came with their forces to Iraq, they were told, the leadership was told by stupid Iraqis that they would be received with flowers. These stupid Iraqis had forgotten that there were no flowers in Iraq anymore in those days. Iraq had been turned into a barren country. After 13 years of sanctions, Iraq had no flowers, so the people of Iraq would not even have flowers even if they wanted to. They couldn't have flowers to meet the soldiers. But two months after the invasion, you couldn't see roses in Iraq. You couldn't see tulips. You couldn't see carnations. You couldn't see flowers. Iraq became a car nation afterwards, when they opened the borders for cars to be imported to Iraq where you couldn't move, so we became a car nation rather than having carnations in our flower shops.

We could not receive soldiers with flowers, but the general, al-Mufti, told you that he could see—and so could I—American soldiers actually resting two or three meters away from their tanks, with their guns not with them, because they felt secure, because the people of Iraq did not want to fight them. Why the people of Iraq didn't want to fight them is a reflection more on the old regime than on the American invasion. That is my interpretation, which is a fact, I think.

Did the Americans know how to deal with the situation? I don't think they did. I don't think they dealt with it correctly, and I could give you examples. I was invited one day—well, "invited" is a very nice word, but actually it wasn't that—by Ambassador Bremer to his office. He invited me by sending a few Humvees to my humble abode to pick me up and take me. I didn't know where I was going, but it turned out I was going to see him. Apparently, he had invited me to make sure that a photograph, which had me with Saddam Hussein and Dan Rather from a meeting in 1991—you know Dan Rather, the anchorman. . . . Somebody had told him that this was Saddam's office, and that he had this photograph, which was taken with that door behind us, in an interview. And he wanted to make sure that that photograph, which was a photocopy, was stuck on the right door, because there were four doors of the same shape in four corners of the palace. And he said, "Is this the door where you were sitting?"

So I asked, "Have you sent for me to ask me this question?" He said, "Yes." I said, "Thank God for that. I thought you had sent for me for something else." So I said, "No, this is not the door." Actually, I wasn't sure, because things had been changed. But I wanted to behave meanly with him. I was mean. It may have been Saddam's room, but I said, "No, this is not Saddam's room. You're actually working in his secretary's room."

Then he invited me in, and we sat, and he said, "I've heard about you. They tell me you are so-and-so, whatever." He mentioned one or two good things, and he handed me a piece of paper, which was written in Arabic and in English. The Arabic side said, "I, so-and-so, hereby pledge that I will abide by this, and that I will have nothing to do with the bad Ba'ath regime, and that I am not a criminal, and that, and that," and it says the same thing in English. I can't remember exactly, but it was so infuriating at that moment.

As you might gather, this was an application for a job. Actually, at the top, it said "Application for Recruitment." And he had a phone call on his mobile. By then, we had mobiles in Iraq, and he was talking, and he gave me this. But while he was talking, I put it back on his desk. He took it, and he thought I had signed it, but I hadn't. He said, "You haven't signed this. How come?" I said, "Well, ambassador, you're asking me to sign an application for a job." And he said, "Yes." I said, "Ambassador, I have two problems with that. In order to apply for a job, I need to have been sacked from my old job, and I haven't. I simply am lost. Nobody told me I had been dismissed or anything. Neither have I resigned my job."

He said, "No, no, don't worry about that. That is a legal; it's only a small problem. Don't worry about it." I said, "But, ambassador, there's another problem. You are an ambassador, aren't you?" And he said, "Yes." I said, "Do you expect ambassadors to apply for jobs? Aren't they usually invited to do a job? Don't you think it would be more proper for you to write to me a letter and say that you'd like me to do this job? And then I will respond to you in kind and say 'thank you,' whether I accept it or not. Don't you think that this is the kind of civilization that Iraq expects from the United States?" He looked at me, and he accepted it, and he asked his secretary to throw me out of his office. This is the kind of management that we have been given from the outside in Iraq.

Now, leave management, come to the reading of Iraq. Research on Iraq and its problems, and the confrontation with Iraq has been not done by Iraqis. We have not taken part in this effort. You in the United States have your own—the Cordesmans and the Thomas [L.] Friedmans and the rest. They write, we translate their work, and our people read their work. We haven't done any. That's why we would like to embark on a job ourselves of that nature. I believe it is also our responsibility.

One of the problems in which we find ourselves has been referred to by General Hamdani, and this is that we truly find ourselves between the edge and a hard rock. We've been judged negatively by the former regime, because we sit with you, and we talk to you— but not the former regime, I mean, by extremists in the former regime. And we have been rejected by the current system as remnants of the former regime. So we are like the Untouchables of India. We are the political untouchables of Iraq. Nobody would want to talk to us. That is why we believe it is our job to try and express ourselves, through this center.

Unfortunately, the American behavior in Iraq has given the former regime of Iraq a clean bill of health by allowing this kind of system to be in power, to commit such horrific crimes, and to drag the country into the worst lists, international lists of corruption, of poverty, of lack of education, of unproductivity that the former regime has been given a clean bill of health by comparison—a clean bill of health, which in truth the former regime does not fully deserve. But by comparison it does. Can you see the discrepancy in the intention of the whole change of regime? Can you see the irony in the situation that happened? There is a huge irony here.

Gentlemen, history's judgment on the armed conflict which broke out in 2003 can only be guessed at now. But there is plenty of guessing going on. The majority of the guessing is not in favor of the United States. The United States will be lucky to find someone who praises it for what it did in Iraq. The United States will be extremely lucky to find anybody defending what it did in Iraq. But that is not our intention. That is not, because, for many critics of the invasion, the invasion of Iraq will prove to have been irresponsible, a violation of international law, and George Bush and Tony Blair would not really appear to have taken the right decisions at the moment, or adopted the right policies in dealing with Iraq. The results that we deal with are based on misconceptions, allegations, bad reports by the CIA [Central Intelligence Agency], or intelligence reports. This needs to be addressed.

How could you have committed such mistakes? Do you in the U.S. Marines, or you in the U.S. armed forces, in your research, do you actually intend to attend to these questions, because we would like you to attend to these questions. We would like to sit with you on those questions. We would like to show you how wrong you were— I mean, your forces, your leadership—was on Iraq, so that a thing of that nature can never happen again. Western electorates, western legislators have been deceived in order to give the U.S. forces, or the Western forces, the go-ahead. They have been deceived by bad reports. Shouldn't that be looked at in order to be avoided?

What I propose at this moment is that I have seen a lot of good work done, but not in the United States. I have seen some good work done even in Japan on the war policy against Iraq. I have seen some good work done in German institutions, and I certainly have seen some good work done in British institutions. One of them is a friend of mine who has written extensively on the war strategy against Iraq, and especially at the King's College, London, they have an academy, a defense academy, which has produced some good work. Professor Michael Clarke, who is a specialist in war studies, has done a lot of good work. Lord [Timothy] Garden, who won his peerage in 2004—Tim Garden has done some good work on Iraq.

But we have not read true academic analysis, objective analysis, of the war on Iraq from an American source. I have seen a lot of work done by Anthony Cordesman, because he's a strategist, but I have never accepted Anthony Cordesman's objectivity as something that I can trust. Never. He was one who went on urging George Bush to attack Iraq because he jumped on the bandwagon of the WMD [weapons of mass destruction] issue—and he was a strategist, a long-term strategist. And he never bothered to make sure whether Iraq did have WMDs. He just jumped on the bandwagon, and that's the kind of strategist that I wouldn't trust easily today.

Gentlemen, we need to address the military concepts, military planning, that was used in relation to Iraq, and here you have the experts. And we need to also look at Iraq's counter-strategy, which was by my definition anything but symmetrical. It was asymmetrical, it was confused, definitely. But why was it confused? You can learn from our generals. General al-Hamdani did mention aspects of the asymmetrical nature of the Iraqi war counter-strategy, but this needs to be explored. This needs to be elaborated on, as you might. Now, the question of the CBNs [chemical, biological, and nuclear weapons] or the WMDs and their existence and the programs, I mean, are we going to see this repeated against North Korea? Are we going to see it repeated against Iran? Because it was done against Iraq. Should we allow them to commit such mistakes in the future?

This is your job, as historians, to tell the people. We are here to cooperate with you. We extend a hand of intellectual discussion and dialogue, and we can sit with you all the time. We can talk to you. But are we going to have the opportunity to do that? We invite you to look into it and see whether we can work together. You have the generals, and I am sure we can also have the political analysts who can join in to establish a kind of intellectual and research rapport with your institutions so that we can come with something that both our nations can benefit from. I invite you to consider that, because now we have the institutions. We have the officers' associations and we have the research center that is being made now. And the first major activity that we would like to launch, our project, would be a serious study of the war strategy against Iraq.

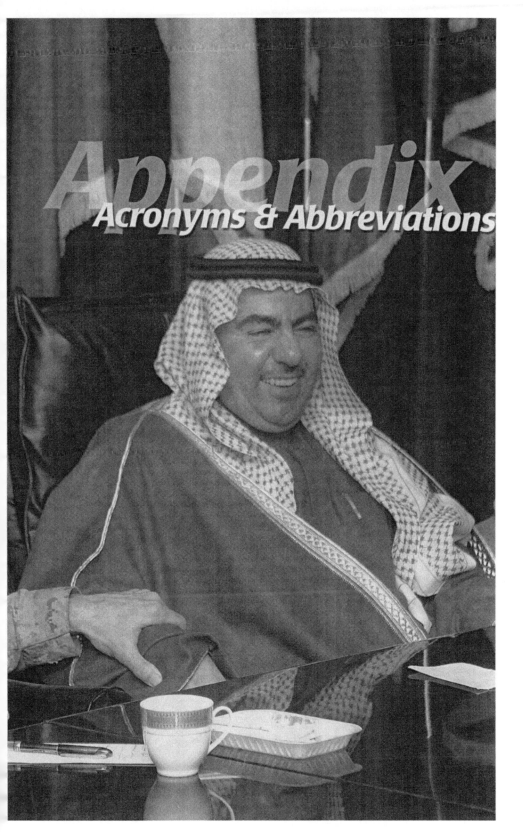

Appendix
Acronyms & Abbreviations

Appendix

Acronyms and Abbreviations

I MEF	I Marine Expeditionary Force
II MEF	II Marine Expeditionary Force
ACE	Air Combat Element
ANGLICO	Air Naval Gunfire Liaison Company
AO	Area of Operation
AOR	Area of Responsibility
APC	Anbar People's Committee
AQI/AQIZ	Al-Qaeda in Iraq
Arty LnO	Artillery Liaison Officer
ASR	Alternative Supply Route
BAT	Biometric Assessment Tool
BBC	British Broadcasting Corporation
BIAP	Baghdad International Airport
BCT	Brigade Combat Team
BTT	Border Transition Team
CA	Civil Affairs
CAG	Civil Affairs Group
CAP	Combined Action Platoon
Casevac	Casualty Evacuation
CBN	Chemical, Biological, and Nuclear Weapons
CentCom	U.S. Central Command, Tampa, FL
CERP	Commander's Emergency Relief Program
CFLCC	Coalition Forces Land Component Command
CG	Commanding General

CHF	Cooperative Housing Foundation
CJTF-7	Combined Joint Task Force 7
CLC	Concerned Local Citizens
CMO	Civil-Military Operations
CMOC	Civil-Military Operations Center
CNN	Cable News Network
CO	Commanding Officer
COA	Course of Action
COC	Combat Operations Center
COIN	Counterinsurgency
COP	Combat Outpost
CPA	Coalition Provisional Authority
CSP	Community Stabilization Program
CSS	Combat Service Support
DCG	Deputy Commanding General
Det	Detachment
DG	Director General
DoD	U.S. Department of Defense
DoS	U.S. Department of State
ECP	Entry Control Points
ECRA	Emergency Council for the Rescue of al-Anbar
EOD	Explosive Ordnance Disposal
ePRT	Embedded Provincial Reconstruction Team
ERU	Emergency Response Unit
EWS	Expeditionary Warfare School, Quantico, VA
FAO	Foreign Area Officer
FLOT	Forward Line of Troops

FLT	Fallujah Liaison Team
FOB	Forward Operating Base
FSSG	Force Service Support Group
GCC	Gulf Cooperation Council
GCE	Ground Combat Element
GDP	Gross Domestic Product
GOI	Government of Iraq
H&S	Headquarters & Support
HUMINT	Human Intelligence
HVI	High Value Individual
IA	Iraqi Army
IC	Intelligence Community
ICDC	Iraqi Civil Defense Corps
ID	Identification
IECI	Independent Election Committee of Iraq
IED	Improvised Explosive Device
IIP	Islamic Iraqi Party
IO	Information Operations
IP	Iraqi Police
IRAP	Iraq Rapid Assistance Program
IRD	International Relief and Development
ISF	Iraqi Security Forces
ISR	Intelligence, Surveillance, Reconnaissance
ITAO	Iraq Transition Assistance Office
IZ	International Zone, Baghdad ["Green Zone"]
JCC	Joint Coordination Center
JMD	Joint Manning Document
JSS	Joint Security Stations
JTAC	Joint Tactical Air Controller

KIA	Killed in Action
LAPD	Los Angeles Police Department
LD	Line of Departure
LNO	Liaison Officer
LOC	Line of Communication
LOO	Line of Operation
LRAD	Long Range Acoustic Device
MAGTF	Marine Air-Ground Task Force
MARCENT	Marine Corps Central Command, Tampa, FL
MARDIV	Marine Division
MarForPac	Marine Forces Pacific
MCIA	Marine Corps Intelligence Activity
MEU	Marine Expeditionary Unit
MLG	Marine Logistics Unit
MML	Mohammed Mahmoud Latif
MNC-I	Multi National Corps-Iraq
MND	Multinational Division
MNF	Multinational Force
MNF-I	Multi National Force-Iraq
MNF-W	Multi National Force-West
MNF-West	Multi National Force-West
MOD	Minister of Defense
MOS	Military Occupational Specialty
MP	Military Police
MSR	Main Supply Route
MSI	Mutamar Sahwa al-Iraq
MTT	Military Transition Team
NCO	Noncommissioned Officer
NGO	Nongovernmental Organization

NPR	National Public Radio
O&M	Operations and Maintenance.
OGA	Other Government Agency
OIF I	Operation Iraqi Freedom I
OIF II	Operation Iraqi Freedom II
OODA	Observe, Orient, Decide, Act
OPA	Office of Provincial Authority
OP	Observation Posts
OpsO	Operations Officer
OVR	Operation Vigilant Resolve
P&R	Programs and Resources
PA	Public Address
PAO	Public Affairs Officer
PDOP	Provincial Director of Police
PFT	Physical Fitness Test
PIC	Provincial Iraqi Control
PGM	Precision Guided Missile
PJCC	Provisional Joint Coordination Center
PM	Prime Minister
PPE	Personal Protective Equipment
PRT	Provincial Reconstruction Team
PSD	Personal Security Detail
PsyOps	Psychological Operations
PTT	Police Transition Team
QRF	Quick Reaction Force or Quick Reaction Funds
R&S	Reconnaissance and Surveillance
RCT	Regimental Combat Team
RFF	Request for Forces
RIP	Relief in Place

RIPTOA	Relief in Place/Transfer of Authority
ROC	Required Operation Capacity
ROE	Rules of Engagement
RPG	Rocket-Propelled Grenade
RTI	Research Triangle Institute
SAA	Sahwa al-Anbar
SAI	Sahwa al-Iraq
SASO	Stability and Support Operations
SeaBees	Construction Battalions (CBs)
SIGINT	Signals Intelligence
SecDef	Secretary of Defense
SOFA	Status of Forces Agreement
SOI	Sons of Iraq
SPTT	Special Police Transition Team
SVBIED	Suicide Vehicle-Borne Improvised Explosive Device
TACON	Tactical Control
TECOM	Training and Education Command
TO	Table of Organization or Task Organization
TOA	Transfer of Authority
TPT	Tactical PsyOps [Psychological Operations] Team
TTP	Tactics, Techniques, and Procedures
UN	United Nations
USAID	United States Agency for International Development
VBIED	Vehicle-Borne Improvised Explosive Device
WMD	Weapons of Mass Destruction
XO	Executive Officer

About the Editors

Colonel Gary W. Montgomery, U.S. Marine Corps Reserve, deployed to Iraq once as field historian for the U.S. Marine Corps History Division and twice as a civil affairs officer. He served as the civil affairs capabilities integration officer for the Marine Corps. In his civilian career, he worked as a policy analyst for the Department of Defense; a military analyst for the U.S. Marine Corps; an artillery trainer for the Bosnian Federation Army under the Military Stabilization Program; and as a United Nations border monitor in Montenegro under the International Conference on the former Yugoslavia. He holds a master's degree in international relations and international commerce from the Patterson School of Diplomacy and International Commerce at the University of Kentucky.

Chief Warrant Officer-4 Timothy S. McWilliams, U.S. Marine Corps Reserve, served in Fallujah in 2004 as a logistics officer. He joined the U.S. Marine Corps History Division in 2007 and has deployed to both Iraq and Afghanistan as a field historian. McWilliams has worked in the marketing and communications field and recently earned a master's degree in history from California State University, Chico.

LaVergne, TN USA
09 September 2010
196544LV00004B/151/P